DRAWING NEAR

A LIFE *of* INTIMACY *with* GOD

JOHN BEVERE

OLIVER
NELSON

THOMAS NELSON PUBLISHERS
Since 1798

For other life-enriching books, visit us at:
www.thomasnelson.com

Published in Nashville, Tennessee, by Thomas Nelson, Inc.

Library of Congress Cataloging-in-Publication Data

Bevere, John.
   Drawing near : a life of intimacy with God / John Bevere.
      p. cm.
   ISBN 0-7852-6116-8 (hardcover)
   ISBN 0-7852-6072-2 (IE)
   1. God—Worship and love. I. Title.
   BV4817.B477 2004
   248.4—dc22   2003027198

Printed in the United States of America
04 05 06 07 BVG 6 5 4 3

CONTENTS

✠

INTRODUCTION

✠

I n 1991 God spoke a very clear word to my heart, "Son, I want
you to write."

The days following were filled with mixed emotions. On the one
hand, fear gripped me and bombarded my mind with thoughts of
certain failure; on the other hand, I felt as if I should laugh. I hated
writing! In school I stared for hours at blank pages of paper when I
was assigned any creative writing. Then I flunked the verbal portion
of the SAT tests. My extreme dislike for anything of a literary nature
drove me to an engineering major in college.

Now God was telling me to write. No way! I could not have heard correctly, I reasoned. So I hedged, but after ten months of doing nothing, God sent two women to me from two different states within two weeks of each other, who repeated identical messages. They both kindly, but firmly warned, "John, if you don't write the books the Lord has given you, He will give them to someone else but you will be judged for it."

When the second woman spoke, the fear of God hit me, and outweighed both my fear and dislike of writing. I began. I remember what happened when I made the decision to obey; thoughts rapidly came together as I typed, which I had never contemplated or heard before. I quickly realized these weren't my messages—they were His. Twelve years have passed since that day; now the messages He gave in book form are in twenty-five languages and number well over a million.

After writing the first, I made a personal promise to God that I would never write a book just to write. I would only write if He told me to do so. This vow was tested; each year from 1992 to 1999 He gave me the message I was to write, but after writing *Under Cover*, I went three years without a word from God to write. Publishers frequently approached me to ask what my next book would be and if they could publish it, but I wouldn't make a move. I didn't have a word from God yet.

Finally after three years, God again gave the word to write—the message you now hold in your hands. I believe one reason for the delay had to do with what the Holy Spirit needed to do in me before this book could be properly brought forth. I have been a believer for twenty-five years, yet I have never been so hungry to be near Him. I have found a deeper intimacy with the Lord in the last year and a half than I have ever known before. I have never wept as much in all my life as I have in the last eighteen months. I've been overwhelmed in hotel rooms, airplanes, my office, car, home, and in the great outdoors as I spend time in focused prayer. The reality of His presence has never been so real and tangible.

I believe this book is a compilation of years of training by the Holy Spirit and contains an invitation from the heart of God to a place of intimacy with you, His child. Before you begin I would like to pray together. Speak these words from your heart and know I have prayed them for you aloud in my study. We have the promise of Jesus that when we "agree on earth concerning anything that they [we] ask, it will be done for them [us] by My Father in heaven" (Matt. 18:19). Let's petition together:

Father, in the name of Jesus, I ask that as I read the message of this book that You will open my eyes to see, my ears to hear, and give me a heart to perceive and understand. I desire to walk in intimacy with You, and to do it on a continual basis. I desire to know Your counsel, will, secrets, and passions, as well as to abide in Your presence. Let this message not only bring understanding, but the power to transform my life into the image of Your dear Son, and my Lord Jesus. For when He walked this earth He perfectly displayed Your glory by how near He was to You. Even so may I display Jesus' glory by how near I become to Him through the person of the Holy Spirit. I commit this to You now, and thank You in advance for the transforming work You will do in me as I hear and heed the words You've inspired in this work. Thank You that my life will never be the same again. I ask this in agreement with Your servant John Bevere. Amen.

Now believe and thank God for fulfilling your earnest prayer. I rejoice in knowing even now the Holy Spirit has begun to position you for greater intimacy by lifting your prayer to the holy throne of the only One who can truly satisfy your every longing. May the Father, Jesus, and the Holy Spirit become more real to you than ever before!

Most sincerely,
John Bevere
November 2003

CHAPTER ONE

THE GREATEST INVITATION OF ALL TIME

✠

"Draw near to God and He will draw near to you."
JAMES 4:8

There is a call—no, a cry—coming from the heart of God and with each passing day its intensity increases: "Why are you satisfied without My presence; why do you remain distant when you could have intimacy with Me?"

All of us have friends or people we admire and want to be closer with. They hold a special place in our hearts, and spending time with them is a treat, especially when it comes at their invitation. Such a request to share their company fills us with anticipation, joy, and excitement. We happily do whatever it takes to clear our calendar and accept their request.

Within the book of James we find the greatest invitation ever issued, "Draw near to God and He will draw near to you" (4:8). Stop a moment and ponder this: the Creator of the universe, the earth, and all its inhabitants, requests your presence. Not only your presence, but He desires to be intimately close, for we are told "he is a God who is passionate about his relationship with you" (Ex. 34:14 NLT).

This is God's unwavering desire. He is the One who has issued the invitation, for He longs to be known by His children. Since the fall of man it has taken thousands of years, intricate preparations, and a huge price to open the way for this kind of close relationship. John, one of Jesus' closest friends, reported,

> No man has ever seen God at any time; the only unique Son, or the only begotten God, Who is in the bosom [in the intimate presence] of the Father, He has declared Him [He has revealed Him and brought Him out where He can be seen; He has interpreted Him and He has made Him known]. (John 1:18 AMP)

Adam knew the Lord openly; but because of sin, or disobedience, was separated from His glorious presence, and his fate extended to all mankind. Men and women could no longer see or know God as Adam once had. However, the Father yearned with great passion and compassion to redeem our fellowship from this terrible separation. In answer He sent Jesus, who'd been with the Father from the beginning, God manifested in the flesh, to pay the price that would liberate us from darkness in order to reconcile us to God, if we receive Him as our Lord.

However, this reunion of God and man has not been preached nor experienced in its fullest extent. We've emphasized the liberation from sin and death, but neglected to declare the intimate fellowship awaiting all who've been made free. This neglect is costly and even disastrous, as so many miss the beauty of knowing God intimately. A parallel of this tragedy was played out in the Old Testament with the descendants of Abraham.

TWO TOTALLY DIFFERENT MOTIVES

I have always been amazed by the contrast of attitudes and behavioral patterns of Moses and his kinsmen, the children of Israel. The book of Exodus opens with Abraham's descendants suffering under harsh captivity. They had been in Egypt for almost four hundred years. In the beginning they enjoyed favor, but it was not long before they were enslaved and cruelly mistreated. In their agony they began to cry out to God for deliverance.

The Lord was moved by their prayers and sent a deliverer by the name of Moses. Though born a Hebrew, he'd escaped slavery and was raised as a grandson to Pharaoh in his household. As a prince of Egypt, he was moved by the plight of his brethren but had to flee for his life to the wilderness only to return years later and deliver Israel from their bondage by God's Word and power.

Israel's deliverance from Egyptian bondage parallels our deliverance from the slavery of sin. Egypt represents the world's system just as Israel is a type of the church. When we're born again, we're set free from the world's system of tyranny and oppression.

It is not hard to imagine how cruelly the children of Israel were used and abused by the citizens of Egypt. Their backs were scarred by the whips of Pharaoh's taskmasters; their homes were the slums, and their food was leftovers. They had no hope of inheritance as they slaved to build the prosperity of their Egyptian masters. They wept as thousands of their infant sons were put to death by the order of Pharaoh.

Though they suffered all this cruelty they were quick to forget. For even after their deliverance from Egypt, whenever things went wrong they would regret their flight from Egypt and mock their prayers for deliverance with comments like "*it was better for us* back in Egypt." They would even be so bold as to suggest, "Let us select a leader and return to Egypt" (Num. 14:4, *author's emphasis*).

But not Moses; he was the only one for whom the conditions had been better in Egypt; in fact, no one in the world had it better. He was raised by the wealthiest man on earth, lived in the best, ate the best, wore the best, and was taught by the best. Servants took care of his every need and desire as his inheritance was great in both wealth and promise. He willingly left all this behind, and, unlike the children of Israel, he never looked back nor longed for what was behind.

What made the difference? The answer is Moses had encountered God. He saw the fire and drew near. He met the living God in a burning bush on Sinai; Israel did not! When the Lord called him aside he drew near. Later when the children of Israel were presented with an even more wonderful invitation, they drew back (see Ex. 20:18–21).

I very frequently ask congregations, "Where was Moses bringing the children of Israel when they left Egypt?" The normal response is "the promised land." Yet that's not true. He was headed for Mount Horeb, or Sinai. Remember God's words to Pharaoh, through Moses, "Let my people go, so that they may worship me in the desert" (Ex. 7:16 NIV). It was not "Let My people go, so they can inherit a land." Why would Moses take them to their promised land before first introducing them to the Promiser—the desire of the ages? If he first brought them to the promised land they would end up loving the promises more than the Promiser, God Himself. Moses couldn't wait to bring them to the very place where he'd met with God.

To a large extent, we have done this in our churches as well; we've preached more of what Jesus will do for us rather than who He really is! As a result we have cultivated many who serve God primarily for benefit rather than in joyful response to who He is. It could be compared to a woman who marries a man for money; her motive is not to know her husband for who he is, but rather for what he can do for her. Oh, she may love him on some level, but for all the wrong reasons.

People who emphasize the blessings of God to the neglect of a relationship with Him create disciples who come to God to get something, rather than those who respond to Him for who He is. He is like no other and none compare to the wonder of Him. Once God is encountered, as Moses experienced, the promises all fall into perspective. He is so much more wonderful than anything—even His blessings.

God's main purpose in delivering Israel was so they could know and love Him. He desired to make Himself known to them. He said, "I bore you on eagles' wings and brought you to Myself" (Ex. 19:4). Yet they missed their destiny.

God's longing for intimacy with His people has never decreased or changed, for this very desire is continually revealed in His Word, and reflected in Paul's passionate prayer,

> [For I always pray to] the God of our Lord Jesus Christ, the Father of glory, that He may grant you a spirit of wisdom and revelation [of insight into mysteries and secrets] in the [deep and intimate] knowledge of Him. (Eph. 1:17 AMP, *author's emphasis*)

He has made His passion known. God desires every born-again child to know Him deeply and intimately! Wow, does this excite you? If not, reflect a moment and allow the wonder of it to overwhelm you.

We serve a living God, the original Father whose heart aches for His children. He is a Communicator, who desires interaction. Paul was quick to point this out to the struggling believers of Corinth: "You will remember that before you became Christians you went around from one idol to another, not one of which *could speak a single word*" (1 Cor. 12:2–3 TLB). From Paul's exhortation we see one of the primary characteristics that differentiates God, our Father, from all false gods and idols—He speaks!

"PULL OFF THE ROAD"

Recently while I was driving, the Holy Spirit spoke to my heart, "I have something to say. Pull off the road."

I've learned when God tells me to do something, I should obey instantly, no matter how trivial or inconvenient it appears at the time. Was not Moses on the back side of the desert tending his father-in-law's flocks when the Lord got his attention (there are different ways

God seeks our attention)? God came to a bush and caused it to burn without being consumed.

We read how Moses said to himself, "I will now turn aside and see" (Ex. 3:3). The words *turn aside* come from the Hebrew word *cuwr*. James Strong, an expert in the original languages of Scripture, defines this word as "to turn off." Moses deliberately departed from his planned course of action to respond to the Holy One who beckoned him.

Once he responded we read, "So when the LORD saw that he turned aside . . . God called to him from the midst of the bush and said, 'Moses, Moses!' "

It wasn't until God saw Moses turn aside that He pursued him by calling him by name. I believe the Lord would have gone no further if Moses had not responded. God did not call him when the flocks were corralled at Jethro's; it wasn't the most convenient time. What if Moses had thought, *If I get distracted from tending these flocks they'll wander all over the place and it will take hours, possibly an entire day, to round them up. I'll check this out later when things are under control and it won't interrupt my day.* Would the outcome have been the same?

Some may reason God would have done something even more dramatic, but is this consistent with His nature? Consider Samuel, when as a young man he served the high priest Eli and his sons (see 1 Sam. 3). One evening he lies down and hears a voice calling, "Samuel! Samuel!"

Samuel runs to Eli and says, "Here I am, for you called me."

Eli responds, "I didn't call you, go back to bed."

Samuel again hears his name called a second time and runs to the priest only to get the same response. This occurs three times and finally the priest catches on and tells the boy how to respond. The fourth time when he hears, "Samuel! Samuel!" he knows how to respond, "Speak, for Your servant hears." Then the Lord speaks and shows him His will and mysteries yet to be revealed.

God could have done something different. Perhaps the second time when He saw Samuel wasn't getting it He could have said, "Samuel, don't run to Eli, it is I the Lord, your God, who is calling for you and I want to speak to you." But is this His way? He desires to be wanted and recognized, as well as to be known. He looks for those who are diligent in spirit, who will seek and pursue, even if it takes tenacious persistence.

Looking at the Gospels we see this similar pattern. Jesus finishes feeding the five thousand with five loaves and two fish. He then tells His disciples to get in a boat and go before Him to the other side of the sea. He departs to the mountain to spend time with His Father. Later that evening the disciples were still toiling against the wind to cross the sea when we read,

> Now about the fourth watch of the night He [Jesus] came to them, walking on the sea, and *would have passed them by.* (Mark 6:48, *author's emphasis*)

Notice the words: "*would have passed them by.*" The NASB version reads, "*and He intended to pass by them.*" However, when they saw Him they cried out, and He responded, "Be of good cheer! It is I; do not be afraid." He got into the boat and the wind ceased. If they hadn't cried out, He would have kept walking. He'd passed nearby, but if they hadn't cried out He would not have forced Himself on their company.

It seems to be God's pattern to make a step toward us, and if we respond, He takes another and draws close. If we don't respond He does not push His way in, or cut in on our dance per se. Who knows, if Moses had not turned aside, would God just have waited as He did in the case of Samuel, and as Jesus did with His disciples? He often waits until we are hungry enough to respond.

To return to my driving experience, what if I hadn't turned off the road when He spoke? Would I have missed His encounter? I am certain there have been times I have, but as it happened then, a half mile down the highway there was a rest stop. The moment I pulled off I heard the Spirit of God whisper to my heart, "Did I not say to you, 'pray without ceasing?'" (1 Thess. 5:17).

I responded, "Yes Lord, you did."

He probed further, "Is prayer a monologue or dialogue?"

I responded, "It's a dialogue Lord, a two-way conversation."

His words came quick, "Well if I said to pray without ceasing then that means I am willing to communicate with you without ceasing!"

Needless to say I was excited. I realized the wonderful opportunity I'd been given and it is not extended to me alone, but to each and every one of His children.

Now you may ask: *Do you mean God will speak nonstop?* That is not what He spoke to my heart. He said He is *willing* to communicate ceaselessly. Words are but one of the many and varied forms of communication. My wife can give me a look and I know what she is saying though no word has been spoken, and can sometimes write up to three pages from what she just said through that one look. Why? I've lived with her more than twenty years and learned the ways and mannerisms by which she communicates. You could be in the room when one of these looks is given and it would mean nothing to you. Why? Because you don't know her like I know her. In fact, the first few years we were married I might not have picked up the message either. Now after twenty-one years with her I've learned a bit more about the way she communicates.

THE CALL TO DRAW NEAR

It is important for you to know this book is not a "how to" manual, but could be more likened to a trail guide or map that gives directions toward our ultimate destination—the heart of God. If I had access to a treasure map showing the way to buried treasure on a deserted island, it would be of no use to me until I traveled to the island destination and familiarized myself with the terrain in order to get my bearings; and then I would need to exert some effort as I walked the paths, climbed cliffs, and traversed valleys to get to the hidden treasure. There would need to be some cost, energy, and effort on my part. The map would only tell me the way and keep me from wasting my time with futile efforts and explorations, as well as protect me from some of the hidden traps. This book is like that map; it is an invitation for you to join me on a wonderful and exciting journey—the journey to the heart of God. The Word of God contained on these pages will guard you from pits, traps, and dangers that would try to sidetrack you. It should keep you from unnecessary trouble and vain expenditure of energy.

So if you're ready, let's begin!

Study Questions

1. What event or experience in your life initiated your desire to read this book?

2. Consider these examples of God's invitation to draw near:

   • Moses saw a burning bush and turned aside to investigate. In doing so, God called out to him.
   • The young boy Samuel heard a voice four times before he responded, "Speak, for Your servant hears."
   • When the disciples saw Jesus walking on the water—walking as if he would pass them by—they cried out.

   Which of these examples best describes God's invitation to you? Have you responded? If so, what was the nature of your response?

3. As you contemplate prayer being a dialogue, a two-way conversation, what has God been communicating to you, both verbally and nonverbally?

CHAPTER TWO

GOD'S PURSUIT

✠

The Lord said, "I esteemed you better than Myself."

The Bible communicates major themes; these truths run throughout the course of Genesis through Revelation. One such theme is God's passionate desire for and pursuit of man. It is a fact, God wants to draw near to us even more than we desire to draw near to Him!

He actually yearns for us (see James 4:5). The word *yearn* means to "long for intensely." This has been His deepest heart cry since the beginning of time. After Adam sinned, God's first words were not a proclamation of judgment; rather, "Adam, where are you?" Can you hear His earnest heart cry, "Why are you hiding from Me?" Let's trace His longing for us through the course of history.

ADAM'S GREAT, GREAT, GREAT, GREAT GRANDSON

Adam's great, great, great, great grandson was named Enoch. I believe the day came when Enoch went to Adam and asked him to tell of his time in the garden. He wanted to know what it was like to actually walk with the living God. You may wonder, how could Enoch speak with his great, great, great, great grandfather? In answer: when you live to be 930 years old, you will see your great, great, great . . . grandchildren. Adam was only 622 years old when Enoch was born.

Mathematically the Bible tells us Adam was 687 years of age when Enoch approached him at the age of 65. This is deduced from the Genesis account of Enoch's walk with God lasting three hundred years though he lived to be 365.

> Enoch walked with God three hundred years, and had sons and daughters. So all the days of Enoch were three hundred and sixty-five years. (Gen. 5:22–23)

It is probable therefore, that at 65 years of age is when it all changed for Enoch, when he drew the blessing and heartache from the lips of the patriarch Adam.

I can only imagine, and I have no writings to back this, that it took Enoch years to muster up the courage to go to his renowned ancestor to inquire of the garden, because Adam was not one to freely talk about it. All of Adam's descendents knew this, and more than likely warned Enoch from a young age not to discuss it with Adam.

Historic Jewish writings tell of the depression Adam suffered after being driven from the garden. The weight of it was almost unbearable. Some writings tell how Adam and Eve sat in darkened caves unable to look at one another for the shame of what had happened.

Adam had lost his splendor. It is one thing to hear of the promise of walking with God, but quite another to have lost the tangible actuality of dwelling in His glory. Adam had suffered an unspeakable loss, but Enoch pressed in and took Adam's ancient account of heartache and mixed it with faith and expectancy. Though generations had muttered among themselves their disappointment at Adam's loss, Enoch perceived a promise, "I will walk with God."

I can just imagine the encounter between the two. Enoch trembled, but his passion finally outweighed his fear. Through the trembling shadows of defeat he pressed in and believed for the light of something more. For him, Adam's story was more than a tale of failure; it was a revelation of the ultimate desire of God to walk with man. I have to wonder if Adam caught a glimpse of Enoch's fire as he transferred the distant blessing found in the memory of his life in the garden of paradise.

Adam wept as he relayed his heart-wrenching account: "Enoch, I walked with Him . . . in His glory. The Creator of the universe, the Maker of all you see, walked beside me! He shared the intimate wisdom of His master plan; how He placed and arranged the stars of the universe with His fingers. Those very fingers created me as well as held my hand. He called each star by name and set them as signs for navigation and seasons. He showed me how He balanced the earth with gravitational and electromagnetic fields, and created a perfect climate. He shared the secret of the seed and how it brings forth life after its kind; how it is watered by the springs of the deep, strategically placed throughout the earth. Enoch, He trusted me with the privilege of naming all the animals—over five billion species of them! We discussed them together, but He left the final choice to me!"

The more Adam spoke the hungrier Enoch became, until the passion overwhelmed him. He must walk with God as Adam had; he would not be denied.

Enoch even inherited something Adam did not; the dust of Adam returned to the earth, but Genesis tells us, "And Enoch walked with

God; and he was not, for God took him" (Gen. 5:24). He left this earth without seeing death.

In his life Enoch was a great prophet. He spoke to his day as well as prophesied to our own. He prophesied of the impostors who would arise in the church in the last days, acting as if, and even believing, they were saved by grace, and the judgment that would follow (see Jude 1–15). He saw the visions of God's judgment, declaring the Lord's second coming thousands of years before His virgin birth.

Why did God take him when he was only 365 years old? Was it because of this great prophetic ministry? No, it was because he "walked with God," and the book of Hebrews tells us this "pleased God" (Heb. 11:5).

Don't get me wrong, His walk with God produced a powerful and effective ministry, but it was His burning desire to know God intimately that pleased the Lord. He had touched the longing in God's heart, an intimate relationship with Him, the way He longs for us.

GOD'S HEART CRY THROUGHOUT THE AGES

This has been God's heart cry throughout the ages! A people who would desire to know Him in response to His desire for us! After Enoch there is Noah, another great grandson who touched God's heart. Genesis tells us, "Noah walked with God" (Gen. 6:9). Noah responded to God's desire for fellowship and drew near. As he drew near, God drew near to him and warned of things to come. The judgment that took a world unaware was first a secret between Noah and God. Noah's close relationship with God was born out of a confidence that God would respond to those who pursue Him, to those who dare to believe and draw close to experience intimacy with Him.

We witness this again with Abraham when God invites him to "walk before Me" (Gen. 17:1). This invitation is extended again and again with Isaac and Jacob; even before Jacob was born God said, "Jacob I have loved" (Rom. 9:13). The Lord pursued him, as He does with us all, even when Jacob was not pursuing God. As Jacob ran from his brother he found God waiting to capture him. When Jacob slept on a pillow of stone, God awoke him to a dream, a ladder with angels coming up and down. A divine connection revealed between God and man.

After four hundred years of bondage the children of Israel, the descendants of Jacob, were confused by His primary purpose for delivering them from bondage. They thought it was all about inheriting a promised land, but it was about something so much more. God's ultimate desire was for intimacy, and He clearly stated His intentions when He addressed the entire nation with passionate and poetic words:

> You have seen what I did to the Egyptians, and how I bore you on eagles' wings and *brought you to Myself.* (Ex. 19:4, *author's emphasis*)

However, His desires were not mirrored in the words of the children of Israel; their dialogue betrays a very different motive: "You have not brought us into a land flowing with milk and honey, nor given us inheritance of fields and vineyards" (Num. 16:14). Their hearts were set on the *what*, rather than the *Who* they were to inherit.

Moses repeatedly clarified God's desire to the descendents of Abraham; one such comment was recorded:

> For He is a God who is passionate about His relationship with you. (Ex. 34:14 NLT)

God declared to all of Israel, "I have loved you." Yet in ignorance and hardness of heart they answered back, "In what way have You loved us?" (Mal. 1:2). Blind to the fact His heart was yearning for them, they mistook His attempts to reach out as acts of judgment.

Even through repeated disobedience His desire remained steadfast. In the days of Jeremiah He cried out, "I spoke to you, rising up early and speaking, but you did not hear, and I called you, but you did not answer" (Jer. 7:13). He made it known He'd pursued them in this manner from the day He'd brought them out of Egypt until this very moment (see Jer. 7:25).

In all this His love never wavered, but the greatest evidence of His ultimate desire for us is found in Jesus. Jesus Himself explains with, "I, the Son of Man, have come to *seek* and save those . . . who are lost." (Luke 19:10 NLT, *author's emphasis*). He didn't just come to save; He came to *seek* as well, even when we were His enemies!

HIS THOUGHTS TOWARD US INDIVIDUALLY

When we long for another we think of them frequently. We find our thoughts turning toward them throughout the day and often reaching out to them even as we sleep at night. We may even make ourselves vulnerable and share with others how frequently we desire their company and visit them in our thoughts. God is no different. God told David about His thoughts toward us. David relates the awesome reflection God has for each of us:

> How precious are your thoughts about me, O God!
> They are innumerable!
> I can't even count them; they outnumber the grains of sand!
> (Ps. 139:17–18 NLT)

It is almost impossible to grasp, but His thoughts about each one of us are more than all the grains of sand on the earth! Think on it a moment, imagine every granule of sand collected from the entire planet; every beach, desert, lake, sea, and ocean floor, and of course every golf course. When I look at just one sand trap on the golf course I can't imagine the number of grains of sand in that one small pit. Yet, God speaks of every grain on the earth! The number is unfathomable! Over the past twenty-one years, I've thought many lovely thoughts about my wife, but even in all my musings I doubt if my most impressive day would have even filled a small jar, let alone the entire earth!

YOU PURSUE WHAT YOU VALUE

These types of thoughts are reserved for those you love, long for, and desire intimacy with! Are you beginning to glimpse how much He loves you? Have you ever stopped and meditated on how much you mean to Him? When we shop we wander through stores filled with items bearing price tags. Some items are discounted, others expensive; each assigned a price in accordance with the value they bear. But if we are wise shoppers we will always purchase items that are worth as much, or more, to us than what we give for them.

Everything in life has a value assigned to it. That value is determined by the perception of the purchaser. A few years ago a baseball was up for sale. But it was not just any old ball; it was the one struck by Mark McGuire when he hit his seventieth home run. At that time he set the major league record for the most home runs hit in a single season. The ball sold for 2.7 million dollars! Even if I had the money I certainly would not have paid that much for the ball. Why? Because it was not that valuable to me. Yet I remember reading at that time there were some who would have paid even more for it if they'd been given the opportunity. But now that this home run record has been broken, I doubt anyone would pay a fraction of that price for this once highly coveted ball. Its value has dropped.

So the question is not: What is our value to society? That would vary. Even the value of human life differs among men, for there are millions of parents who kill their unborn children. The baby's life is not worth the inconvenience to them. There are husbands who leave their wives and children because they don't see the relationship as worthy of their time and energy. Their own comfort and pleasure is worth much more to them than the lives of their mate or children. There are those who sell themselves in prostitution. The list extends endlessly and results in millions of wounded in our society. There are those who feel unloved or unwanted because of the fact they've seen their worth through the eyes of others.

OUR VALUE TO GOD THE FATHER

What is our value to God? It is there we find our true value. God is the One who sets the standard for worth in this universe, not men. For "what is highly valued among men is detestable in God's sight" (Luke 16:15 NIV).

Jesus said, "What profit is it to a man if he gains the whole world, and loses his own soul? Or what will a man give in exchange for his soul?" (Matt. 16:26). Consider for a moment all the wealth in this world. Think of all the multimillion dollar mansions; all the gemstones and precious metals; all the fine cars, yachts, and planes; all the state-of-the-art electronics, and these are but a few of the "nice" things. There are so many more treasures in this world it is almost unimaginable. Recent studies estimate the gross world product to be 35.8 trillion U.S. dollars. That is $35,800,000,000,000.00. That is a lot of wealth, and that's even before we include the real estate. Yet Jesus tells us a man who exchanges his life for all this wealth makes a bad deal!

If our true worth, the value God places on us, is more than all the wealth in and of this whole world, what is our value to Him? We're told, "For God so loved the world that He gave His only begotten Son" (John 3:16). We were under the reign of the wicked prince, Lucifer, after we were turned over by Adam (see Luke 4:6). Adam's disobedience spread to all and we were slaves to sin, a domain over which Lucifer reigns as lord. He laid claim to us and would not release us. Our destination was eternal darkness with no hope of liberation. The only way we could be freed was if we were purchased back—but the price was too high for any man to pay.

God gave Jesus as the ransom for us. No one and nothing else could have purchased us, for God says, "The ransom for a life is costly, no payment is ever enough" (Ps. 49:8 NIV). God values our souls so highly He purchased us with Jesus Himself. Paul says, "God bought you with a high price" (1 Cor. 6:20 NLT). Again he says the Father "is so rich in kindness that he purchased our freedom through the blood of his Son" (Eph. 1:7 NLT).

There is no one or nothing more valuable to Father God in this universe than His Son, Jesus. Yet with this purchase God declared our value as compared to His greatest treasure. Here is something amazing: if we would have been worth one cent less to God than the value of Jesus Himself, the Father would never have given Him, for God never makes unprofitable deals! A bad purchase or exchange happens when you give something of more value for something of less. Wow! Do you see how important you are to the Father? Jesus confirms this by saying, "I have given them the glory You gave me, so that they may be one, as we are— I in them and You in Me, all being perfected into one. Then the world will know that You sent Me and will understand that You love them *as much* as You love Me" (John 17:22–24 NLT, *author's emphasis*). Jesus plainly declares the Father loves us as much as He loves Jesus! Did you hear that? Do you see your true worth? Do you see why He pursues you?

"Yes, but I'm Just One of Many"

Some may argue, "Yes, God did that for all mankind cumulatively, but who am I among so many?" The answer to this is if you had been the only one, He still would have pursued and ransomed you at this great price. This is clearly seen in Jesus' ministry. He had spent the entire day teaching multitudes about the kingdom of God. He was tired, yet there was something that could not wait. By the leading of the Holy Spirit, Jesus tells His disciples to get into a boat and cross the Sea of Galilee. In the midst of the sea a storm arises and threatens their lives, but Jesus is so exhausted He is asleep. In fear the disciples awake Him and tell of the pending danger; Jesus responds by commanding the waves and wind to be still.

They'd spent a good part of the night crossing this troubled sea. Now that they have come to the other side, maybe they can finally get some rest. But just as they disembark they are met by a demon-possessed madman. He lives among the tombs and cannot be restrained even with chains. All day long and throughout the night, he wanders among the tombs screaming and cutting himself with stones (see Mark 5:3–5 NLT).

If alive today he would have been placed in a mental institution, most likely in solitary confinement. He would have been given drugs and left to himself. Most would consider him an outcast, only to be kept alive because the laws do not permit him to be killed. He would be viewed as a worthless drain on society. His value would be almost nothing. Very few would pursue his acquaintance.

Yet this madman had great value to the Father, Jesus, and the Spirit of God. Jesus ministered to him in a powerful way. So mighty was his deliverance, before day's end he was seated next to Jesus, clothed and in his right mind. Now here is the amazing part: after Jesus had ministered to him, He got back into the boat and "crossed over again by boat to the other side" (Mark 5:21). I will never forget the day God showed me this. I came unglued. I was so in awe that Jesus, exhausted from a hard day, would cross a sea and fight through a storm, just to minister to a possessed outcast that society considered worthless, only to get back into the boat and travel all the way back again. He did it all for just one man!

When I saw this I fully realized that if I had been the only one He still would have sought me out and paid my ransom, so I could have fellowship with Him. No wonder the angels of heaven sang the evening He was born—celebrating peace on earth, and goodwill toward men! God's pursuit of us was unfolding before the world!

THE WAY JESUS VIEWS EACH OF US

One of the greatest revelations the Lord ever gave me came shortly after I received salvation. I was fellowshipping with Him while driving my car and seemingly out of nowhere He began speaking something that revolutionized my thinking. I heard Him whisper to my heart, "John, do you know I esteem you more important than Myself?"

I remember that when I heard this statement I briefly considered it to be blasphemous and inspired by hell. I reasoned it to be utterly presumptuous and irreverent. I almost blurted out, "Get behind me, Satan!" Yet deep in my heart I sensed it was the Lord's voice. So I did what I knew was the safe thing to do. I responded, "Lord, this is too extreme for me to believe. It seems blasphemous that You, Lord Jesus, who created the heavens and earth, would consider me, the puny person I am, more important than You. The only way I will be able to accept such a thought is if You give me three New Testament Scriptures to prove it."

After saying this, I sensed His pleasure and immediately heard in my heart, "What does Philippians 2:3 say?"

Being familiar with this verse I quoted it aloud, "Let nothing be done through selfish ambition or conceit, but in lowliness of mind let each esteem others better than himself."

The Lord said, "You have your first Scripture."

I countered, "Lord, that is Paul speaking to the Philippian believers telling each to esteem the others better than themselves. That is not talking about Your relationship with me."

Immediately I heard, "Son, I never tell My children to do anything I don't do Myself!" He then showed me this as the problem in many homes. Parents expect behavior of their children they themselves do not observe. The Lord never expects anything from us that He does not model Himself.

I could see this point, but it still did not convince me He esteemed me better than Himself. I said, "Lord that is only one Scripture, I need two more." I was not irreverent, but rather cautious.

He then spoke words in the form of a question that riveted my heart: "John, who hung on the cross, you or Me?"

Startled by what I already knew, but now became much more real, my response was sober, "You did, Jesus."

He continued, "It should have been you hanging on that cross, but I bore your sins, judgment, sickness, disease, pain, and poverty. I did it because I esteemed you better than Myself."

I trembled as I heard His words. All doubt was eradicated by what He spoke. I soberly thought how He did not deserve a bit of what He got. He was righteous and innocent. 1 Peter 2:24 came to me, "Who Himself bore our sins in His own body on the tree, that we, having died to sins, might live for righteousness—by whose stripes you were healed."

I knew then that He truly considered me more important than Himself. I began to tear up and worship. I already knew there would be a third verse, and sure enough He spoke it to my heart: "What does Romans 12:10 say?"

It was another familiar Scripture and again I quoted it, "Be kindly affectionate to one another with *brotherly* love, in honor giving *preference to one another*."

I heard Him say, "Am I not the first born of many *brethren* (Rom. 8:29)? I prefer my brothers and sisters and esteem them better than Myself."

I had heard often how Jesus loved us. But when He spoke these words to my heart it became so real just how special we are as individuals to Him. In fact, He calls those in His family His treasures. He tells us we are special. He tells us we're the apple of His eye. Try to grasp this: He rejoices over us! Oh yes, listen to these true and beautiful words, "The LORD your God in your midst, the Mighty One, will save; He will rejoice over you with gladness, He will quiet you with His love, He will rejoice over you with singing" (Zeph. 3:17).

WHAT IS MAN?

The angels look curiously on as they see the majestic and holy God give such attention to mere men. We read, "When I consider Thy heavens, the work of Thy fingers, The moon and the stars, which Thou hast ordained; What is man, that Thou dost take thought of him? And the son of man, that Thou dost care for him?" (Ps. 8:3–4 NASB). Even though these words were penned by David, I feel certain God allowed him to hear the thoughts of the mighty angelic beings that surround His throne. These angels watched this mighty God form the universe. They are so in awe of Him they continuously cry out "Holy, Holy, Holy" to each other, for every moment that passes reveals another facet of His glory so that all they can do is shout "Holy!" for all eternity. They cry so loud they shake the doorposts of the throne room (an auditorium that seats at least ten million people!). Yet, they wonder why this most magnificent God is so mindful of us. They perceive His thoughts of love and goodness toward us cannot be numbered for they are greater than all the granules of sand found on earth. They are amazed by this!

We are His prized possessions; His sought-out jewels—the living stones—who make up the tabernacle He desires to dwell in. Why would God feel this way toward us? What have we done to deserve such love? This is the greatest truth of all. We have done nothing to merit His love and pursuit. For when we were still decrepit, lost sinners—enemies—He sought us out. He saw in us what only His love could see. He saw treasures in the midst of corruption, sin, and depravity. He purchased as precious what many considered worth little or even worthless. He saw beyond our state and saw what only His grace could produce.

Now we can more readily understand the words of Scripture, "God purchased you at a high price. Don't be enslaved by the world" (1 Cor. 7:2 NLT). Why would any person who has been so loved and valued want to return to the system where they were once enslaved and viewed as so insignificant in relationship to our true value?

When we really understand that He is the most prominent being in the entire universe, yet the most personal, and is in hot pursuit of us, how can we ignore such a wonderful invitation to draw near? We can no longer refuse Him, for only ignorance would permit such a tragic lack of action.

(Important note: Scripture states that even though God pursues us, we must respond in order to come into a relationship with Him. If you have never before received Jesus Christ as your personal Lord and Savior, then at this point it is most important that you immediately go to Appendix A in the back of this book.)

STUDY QUESTIONS

1. When the children of Israel were released from four hundred years of Egyptian bondage, they were confused about God's primary purpose for setting them free. The Lord declared, "I . . . brought you to myself," yet they whined and complained, thinking it was all about inheriting a promised land. As the author states, their hearts were on the what and not the Who they were to inherit.

   God has set you free from the bondage of sin, desiring to bring you to Himself. Have you ever been whiny or complaining? How have you confused the what with the Who?

2. In this chapter, the question was asked, "Why would any person who has been so loved and valued want to return to the system where they were once enslaved?" How would you answer that question?

3. The author shared a dialogue he had with God, shortly after having received salvation, regarding how highly esteemed he was in the Lord's sight. How does, or should, the knowledge that you are a highly-valued "sought-out jewel" modify your life and relationships?

CHAPTER THREE

PROTECT YOUR HUNGER

✠

We will hunger for what we feed on.

Before an unsaved person can approach the living God, the Lord Himself must first draw him. A.W. Tozer writes, "Before a sinful man can think a right thought of God, there must have been a work of enlightenment done within him" *(The Pursuit of God,* p. 11). Jesus Himself tells us, "No one can come to Me unless the Father who sent Me draws him" (John 6:44). This is why intercession for others who don't have a relationship with God through Jesus is so critical. Even though God "desires all men to be saved and to come to the knowledge of the truth" (1 Tim. 2:4), and has pursued this end consistently throughout history, He still wants His children to catch His passion for the lost and cry out to Him on their behalf. For this reason Jesus said, "The harvest truly is plentiful, but the laborers are few. Therefore pray the Lord of the harvest to send out laborers into His harvest" (Matt. 9:37–38).

Once we've been saved through the revelation of Jesus, we have an open invitation to God. He says to His own, "Draw near to Me." God has already taken the first step through this timeless invitation. The bush is burning . . . He calls our name . . . He's just outside the boat! Waiting for our response!

Recently another believer shared, "John, the more I've lived and served God the more I've come to realize our approaching Him depends on His drawing us."

I countered, "No, that is not accurate."

He then quoted Jesus' words that no one can come to Him unless the Father first draw them.

I replied, "Yes, this is true for unbelievers. But God says you are His own, and asks you to 'Draw near to Me, and I will draw near to you.' He states clearly we can initiate this step at any moment in time."

Yes, there are times when He wants to meet with us and He initiates it. However, that doesn't mean we cannot first initiate a move toward Him. We are in relationship with Him, and just as with any normal relationship between father and child, there are times the child initiates contact and there are times the father does the same.

WHY DON'T MORE RESPOND TO HIS INVITATION?

The baffling question is: Why do so many believers have a shallow relationship with God? Why don't they delve into a deeper, more consistent relationship with Him? What holds them back? What would ignite and cause them to respond to His call to draw near? The answer is not complex: it's our hunger and thirst to know Him. David cried out,

> My soul thirsts for God, for the living God.
> When shall I come and appear before God?

My tears have been my food day and night,
While they continually say to me,
"Where is your God?"
When I remember these things,
I pour out my soul within me.
(Ps. 42:2–4)

Before continuing, reread these verses slowly and digest each word. Notice David said, "When I *remember* these things, I pour out my soul within me." The Hebrew word for *remember* is *zakar*. W.E. Vines tells us this Greek word, just as its English counterpart, means: "more than 'to recall'; it means 'to retain in thought.' " This certainly applies here. David is actually saying, "When *I retain desire for God in my thoughts* it causes me to pour out my soul within me." This creates an insatiable hunger for Him! This hunger calls out to us to draw near no matter what obstacles we face—spiritually, mentally, or physically. So it is important we protect, as well as increase, our hunger for Him!

LORD, INCREASE MY HUNGER!

Many pray, "Lord, increase my hunger for You." Yet this is not accurate. We are the ones who determine our hunger, not Him. In America we have an abundance of material possessions, entertainment, pleasure, and wealth. The only way we can create and maintain a hunger for God is to protect our soul by choosing what we fill it with. Proverbs 27:7 states that, "A satisfied soul loathes the honeycomb." Simply put, if your soul is filled with cares, pleasures, the love of riches, or the desires of this world, you'll be full and actually despise the sweet honeycomb of God's fellowship.

Think of Thanksgiving Day. Most Americans gather together with family and friends to feast on this holiday. Many skip breakfast to increase their capacity for food later. The feast begins; out comes a huge turkey, stuffing, sweet potatoes, vegetables, cranberry sauce, pies, and so forth. We consume huge quantities because our appetite has been enlarged. After it is over we groan because we ate too much.

We're full! Then a couple of hours later we go to another family member's home. The food comes out again in all its glory! This time the recipes are even more gourmet, but instead of longing for this excellent food we are repulsed and turn away. We are still so full from the previous meal we take one look at the feast and know it is just not going to happen. It no longer matters that this meal might be far superior; we actually despise it. This is what Proverbs is conveying.

To take this truth a step further, we must realize it is proportional. If your soul is weighed down by the desires of this life, you might not despise the feast, but you might take it lightly. If you are not stuffed, but just had a normal meal two hours earlier, and you're presented with a feast, you won't despise it; you might just nibble, or ignore it. Often I'm offered meals at nice restaurants when I arrive in a city, but I'm not hungry because I ate a few hours earlier so I politely turn down the invitation. The thought of eating doesn't repulse me as described with the Thanksgiving scenario above, it just doesn't appeal to me. But the same offer made to someone who has gone hungry for a day or two will garner a totally different response. This man will intensely crave the food you view with indifference. So the truth is, to the degree you're filled with the things of life determines your response to His call.

Too often people in churches are indifferent in their desire for the things of God. Most do not despise His presence, but compared with the hungry man they are casual towards the feast before them. After all, they ate from the table of the world a few hours ago and are satisfied. I've watched as they say they want Him, but their actions betray their words. You have this book because I believe you want more of Him, but does your soul pant for Him? Are you like the man who hasn't eaten in days, or the alcoholic who hasn't had a drink, or the addict who needs his fix? This is the type of hunger we need to develop in order to press in.

AN INDIFFERENT CHURCH

Upon careful examination of Jesus' words to the final church in the book of Revelation, you discover an amazing fact. First, understand that Jesus sent letters to seven Asian churches, but these messages were not intended only for those historic churches, but for all of us, or we would not have them in Scripture. The very fact they appear in Scripture means they have prophetic application or they still speak to us today.

Prophetic messages can, and often do, have many applications, meanings, or fulfillment. Not only does each church's letter carry a message to us today, but it could be this message appears last because it deals with the church prior to His return. This would make sense, for upon completing this letter John said, "After these things I looked and behold, a door standing open in heaven. And the first voice which I heard was like a *trumpet* speaking with me, saying, 'Come up here'" (Rev. 4:1, *author's emphasis*). Notice the word *trumpet*. We know in the final days the Lord Himself will come for His own by descending "from heaven with a shout, with the voice of an archangel, and with the *trumpet* of God" (1 Thess. 4:16–17, *author's emphasis*). I believe there is a special emphasis on this church's message for the day in which we live.

Jesus declared this church to be in a lukewarm state; to put it in more modern terms, they lacked passion and casually treated what is important to Him. They rarely went out of their way to please Him. What caused this behavior? Remember this is not some self-proclaimed church that God doesn't acknowledge—Jesus Himself identifies them. The answer is found in their outlook on life. Jesus says, "Because you say, 'I am rich, have become wealthy, and have need of nothing'" (Rev. 3:17). These words betray their lack of passion—for their souls are satisfied; sadly not in Him—but in things.

A SHALLOW DIAGNOSIS

Some would say their problem was the issue of too much money or material things. This would be at best a shallow assessment of what Jesus said. If you look at David, he was a man with multitudes of servants and wealth. In fact he turned over to Solomon "four thousand tons of gold, nearly forty thousand tons of silver, and so much iron and bronze" that it could not be weighed (1 Chron. 22:14 NLT). Yet when he describes himself, "Bow down Your ear, O Lord, hear me; for I am *poor and needy*" (Ps. 86:1, *author's emphasis*). He calls himself poor and needy! Now we know he wasn't merely being politically correct for you cannot deceive when you are divinely inspired. He really saw himself as poor and needy, even with stockpiles of silver! His need was for God Himself; and it was cultivated by divine hunger. Hear again his cry, "Bow down Your ear, O Lord, hear me . . ." He's desperate for God's response. He's hungry and thirsty for intimacy! This is why there is such passion: "My tears have been my food day and night, while they continually say to me, 'Where is your God?' " (Ps. 42:3).

The Laodecian church's issue was not material things, but rather that they'd allowed the material things to satisfy their souls. David never let this happen. He never allowed his great wealth to fill his soul's appetite. More than likely the members of this church body had far less than David, but fed themselves with what they possessed and were satisfied. This hindered the passion within them for God's presence and fellowship.

A STARK CONTRAST

I have seen this so often in the past twenty years. I recall traveling once to the Cree Indians in northern Canada. They were the last North American Indian tribe to settle on a reservation. In fact, only twenty years earlier these noble people lived in tepees as they moved along the moose trails. They were a simple people who possessed little. Only in the previous ten years had they acquired televisions for their modest homes.

Approximately a thousand gathered for the meetings. I was there a few days and noticed something strange. Almost without exception, all those over twenty years of age were extremely hungry for the things of God. They were passionate far beyond most in North America. They were desperate to know God. However, those under twenty were indifferent and seemed to lack any form of hunger.

In one meeting the anointing was so strong to teach and preach. The people in the large tent were really receiving. At one point I noticed outside the tent and in the back the young people looked extremely bored and indifferent. I know when preaching is boring, but this was not the case; there was an amazing empowerment of the Holy Spirit to proclaim His Word. Suddenly before I realized what I was doing, I found myself running through the aisles, passing the hungry to make my way to the youth on the fringe of the tent. I pleaded with them to come in and listen. They just looked at me as if I were nuts and didn't have a clue about life.

It was then that I noticed their shirts and baseball caps; it was as if what was written on them became illuminated and stood out. They had on various professional basketball and football team insignias. The Holy Spirit showed me they'd become intoxicated and full from what was on television. Sadly they had given the hunger of their souls over to that which would not profit them! I realized the older people had not been brought up on a diet of television. This answered my perplexity concerning the discrepancy between the under- and over-twenty.

Please understand what I'm communicating. Television is not always detrimental to our growth and hunger, but rather how we handle it is. Our family has a television now, although when we were first married we didn't have one for years. I've been inspired and educated by various programs. I can keep a pulse on world affairs through the use of television. However, it is not what feeds or satisfies me. It is not my passion. I can watch it and still long for the things of God and stay in communion with the Holy Spirit. Though poor, these young people had given their appetites to what did not profit.

Shortly after this trip I went to the northwest part of the United States. I was asked to preach on a Friday evening. The meeting was open to the entire church, but to my amazement I noticed that over five hundred of the seven hundred people in attendance were teenagers. When the meeting was over I found myself surrounded by dozens of teenagers all asking questions about spiritual things. I looked at my watch and the hour was approaching midnight. We had been talking about the things of God for a very long while after the service was over. Finally I blurted out, "I love this! You all are so hungry for God!"

They asked me if they could all take me out to lunch the next day before I left. I couldn't refuse their offer so they secured a large upstairs room in a restaurant and the discussion continued. It was amazing and fresh! There was an ironic contrast between the two sets of young people, the young and well off in the Northwest were hungry even though they possessed far more than the Indian youth.

In the church of the Northwest, the over-twenty-year-olds were not as hungry as the youth. Why weren't they the ones who surrounded me? Why did the teenagers far outnumber all the other age groups combined in the service? I believe the adults' souls were weighed down with the cares and pleasures of life. The things of God were a part of their life, but not their passion, even though they confessed the lordship of Jesus.

After meeting both the senior and youth pastor of this church it became evident that the senior pastor reproduced himself in the people, and the youth pastor had done the same. Hosea 4:9 became evident to me, " 'Like priests, like people'—since the priests are wicked, the people are wicked, too" (NLT). It could just as easily have read, " 'Like pastor, like people'—if the pastor lacks passion, the people are indifferent, as well." God moved this youth pastor, who was so full of vision and zeal, and today he is touching a different city in powerful ways.

REMEDY FOR AN INDIFFERENT CHURCH

This apathy, which is so prevalent in the church, was exactly what Jesus dealt with in His message to this Asian church. Hear His words:

> "Here I am! I stand at the door and knock. If anyone hears my
> voice and opens the door, I will come in and eat with him, and
> he with me." (Rev. 3:20 NIV)

It amazes me how often ministers use this Scripture as a call to the unsaved, yet it is not at all what Jesus was talking about. He is speaking to this church; He is speaking to believers who lack passion. Notice He said, "If anyone hears . . ." What keeps us from hearing?

The soul that is already satisfied is what keeps us from hearing His voice. God sent Moses to the back side of the desert, away from the distractions of Egypt to get his attention. In one encounter God secured Moses' interest and he was never distracted again, no matter where he was—even when he returned to Egypt!

Jesus said if anyone hears His voice and opens the door of their soul He will come in and break bread with them. He will serve the "Bread of Life" to our soul—He is the Bread of Life. One translation reads, " 'If you hear me calling and open the door, I will come in, and we will share a meal as friends' " (NLT). I love that because back then, even more so than today, a shared meal denoted a higher level of social intimacy. As I travel I always love to have at least one meal with the conference leader or pastor before I leave, for in this time of fellowship we have the opportunity to really know each other. An exchange takes place over meals that is greater than in any other setting. This is why Paul tells us not to eat with someone who claims to be a believer yet lives in habitual sin (see 1 Cor. 5:11). We open our heart and become intimate over a meal, and if it is with one who lives in blatant rebellion the exchange is not spiritually healthy.

WE WILL HUNGER FOR WHAT WE FEED ON

Hunger is the key element to whether or not we pursue intimacy with God. Therefore we need to keep in mind we are in control of our appetite, not God. The question is: What appetites and cravings are we going to develop? There is a spiritual principle that never changes:

We will hunger for what we feed on.

I was born-again in 1979 while in a college fraternity. I was in our frat kitchen one night looking for something to eat when I heard the Lord say, "Your body is My temple, take care of it!"

At the time I was a "junk food junkie." I think the term *junkie* is appropriate as it describes someone hooked on something. I'd eat unhealthy food just because it appealed to my appetite. I loved sodas, candy, fast food, donuts, fatty foods of all sorts, bleached flour products—you know the list. I craved most anything that was unhealthy and appealed to my taste. My idea of a fine meal was a Big Mac, Coke, and fries.

When God spoke this to me I realized my body was a complex housing unit for His Spirit, as well as mine. The thought came to me that if I owned an expensive new car I would never put dirty gas or recycled oil in it. I would only put in the finest gas and oil so it would run better and last longer. I reasoned I'd been given only one physical body that could not be replaced, but an expensive car could be replaced. I immediately changed my eating habits. I began to read and ask questions to learn what my body needed to function at its maximum potential and to last for the long haul. It was a process, but after a few years my entire eating and drinking patterns changed.

This all was great, but there was an added benefit I hadn't realized would take place. When I first began to eat healthy food, I didn't like the taste, but I ate it because it was good for me. Then after awhile my appetites changed. It used to be that if you gave me a choice between a fast-food meal and a wild-mix field green salad with fish and whole grain bread, I'd grab the burger without a second thought while turning my nose up at the fish and salad. But today, if the same two choices were presented, I'd grab the healthy one and not think twice about the junk food. In fact, often while traveling I've gone without eating if only fast food was available. I would rather go hungry than to eat what I used to crave. I have absolutely no appetite or taste for it any longer! I don't even like it!

The same principle is true for our souls. Our souls desire what we feed them. If we have a steady diet of sports, we will crave ESPN. If we have a steady diet of movies and Hollywood gossip we will crave movie channels, magazines, and conversation that appeals to this appetite. If we constantly feed on the business world and current events, that is what we'll long for. If our satisfaction is in our homes, cars, clothes, and so forth, then we will light up with passion when we discuss shopping, or a new car, or decorating ideas, and we'll find spiritual conversations mundane. We'll have a hard time reading the Scriptures or tarrying in the prayer closet. However, if we feed on a steady diet of the Word of God, it is easy to set aside time for prayer, and conversations on spiritual things will come easily and flow naturally. We will crave the presence of God and desire intimacy with Him.

AN UNHEALTHY EXTREME

This can be taken to an unhealthy extreme. We live in a physical body. Periodically we need recreation and healthy entertainment. Back when I was in Bible school, I worked a forty-hour-week job and took a full load of classes. One weekend my roommate invited me to go and play touch football with a group of friends. I declined the offer so I could study the Scriptures. The moment he left I pulled out my Bible to read and pray, but everything was shut down. I couldn't hear from God. It was as though I was just reading words that didn't make sense. My roommate had been gone for almost an hour and I cried out, "Lord, why is it I'm having so much trouble getting anything from the Scriptures or hearing Your voice? What's wrong? Have I done something displeasing or committed a sin?"

In reply I heard Him say, "Go out and play touch football."

I recoiled; then questioned, "What! Play football? That's not faith building, nor will it bring me closer to You! How can You tell me to do this?"

The Lord brought me to a verse that suddenly became alive: "Of making many books there is no end, and *much study is wearisome to the flesh*" (Eccl. 12:12, *author's emphasis*). He said, "Son, you live in a physical body (part of that is a brain) and it needs various forms of rest. If you don't give it the rest it requires you will actually block your ability to hear from Me and grow." Then He showed me how after the disciples had ministered to many He invited them to "Come aside by yourselves to a deserted place and rest a while" (Mark 6:31). To put it simply, Jesus was saying, "Come apart lest you come apart."

I left and went to play football. Later that afternoon when I sat down again with my Bible the Scriptures opened up, and once again

I sensed the life of God flowing into my being as I fellowshipped with the Holy Spirit around God's Word.

TOO BUSY

This error of spending excessive time in study, while neglecting rest that the soul and body needs, is not one many fall into in this day and age. Rather the greatest thief that steals our hunger for God is our busy lifestyle. Many well-meaning believers have fallen into this trap and replace time with God with busy Christian lifestyles. This can also include the deceptive and continuous labor of ministry.

Let's ask a simple question to enlighten us: Why do we feed ourselves physically? Your answer will hopefully be: to bring nourishment and strength to our bodies. Can you imagine not eating but continuing to carry on your life at full speed? If as an experiment we skipped food for a few days, but continued the pace of long hours of physical labor and no additional sleep—what would happen? Just think about it for a moment. We'd collapse!

Yet how easily we do this spiritually; there is a reason we will tolerate it spiritually but not physically. If we go without food too long our stomachs complain, and not just once. They will continue getting louder and scream with more pain as time progresses. Our whole body cries out, "I'm hungry, feed me!" Yet our spirit does not scream like this. The opposite seems true; the voice of our inner man becomes quieter as time goes on. Yet the reason is that we don't hear it. Our spirit is weakened and our flesh becomes more dominant.

We lose our appetite when we don't eat over an extended period of time. If you go without food for longer than five days, the physical scream of hunger quiets. Food loses its attraction and a piece of steak looks about as appealing as eating a shoe. Your appetite is gone and will not return until all your inward reserves are gone and starvation settles in.

I've noticed if I've allowed a busy lifestyle to replace my time with the Lord the same thing happens. First my interest in the Scriptures dwindles and then my desire to pray wanes. If I do sporadically pray or read I don't sense life flowing into my being. The Bible will not speak to me like it did when I consistently fed on the Scriptures.

I have gone without physical food to the point where my appetite left and found the only way to get it back was to make myself eat. The same is true spiritually. If I have lost my spiritual appetite, I open my Bible, repent of laziness, and then with anticipation seek to hear God's voice. I continue to read until something speaks to me! Usually it doesn't take long; as I continue He is always faithful to speak. Another way I reconnect is to get away for a day or two and just read and pray until I am saturated.

YOUR SPIRITUAL THERMOMETER

This is a discipline we all must have. Backsliding does not begin when a person finds himself in bed with a strange woman, or discovers he again craves alcohol or pornography. It does not begin when he despises the ones he loves and neglects his children, and the list goes on. No, backsliding begins when we find ourselves indifferent to the Scriptures and things of God. It happens when we find ourselves more excited about natural things than the things of God.

Hunger is your spiritual thermometer. Think of it naturally. What is the first thing that leaves when a person gets sick? The answer is their appetite. If you've ever had the flu you'll remember . . . you just don't want to eat. Look at patients who are in the end stages of a terminal disease; they waste away to seventy or eighty pounds, and have to be fed intravenously. The sick have little or no desire to eat. You have heard it said, "He has a healthy appetite." It is no different spiritually; a sign of spiritual health is an appetite for God's Word. A sign of spiritual sickness is a loss of appetite for the things of God.

I have been around ministers who find it more exciting to talk about their building program, new car, sports teams, and so forth, rather than the things of God. They act as if you were talking shop when you mention the things of the Lord or what He has been speaking to your heart. They light up when they talk about the new home they just built. I watch them in worship; they are looking around, talking to others, or reviewing their notes they are about to preach, rather than lifting up their hands and focusing on the One who should be so dear to them. This is but a symptom of a deeper issue.

In these churches I've noticed a lack of the presence of God. When I present a call to repentance and invite them to draw near to God, the Holy Spirit comes and they are amazed. They either remember where they've fallen from, or they brush it aside as just a special gift of our ministry. Some even resist what happens. In any case, if there is any remote desire in them, the presence of God awakens their hunger again.

Isaiah tells us, "Smoking flax He will not quench" (Isa. 42:3). The phrase refers literally to the expiring wick of a lamp, when the oil is almost completely consumed, and the flame yields to a feeble dying vapor of smoke. He is identifying what is weak, small, thin, feeble, and fragile. He will not quench the dying ember, but would rather fan it back into a flame. Remember, He continues to pursue us even when we are but a smoking ember. How much better it is if we cooperate and respond, as He will not force Himself upon us!

I see it so often. I've watched as the Lord fanned back into a flame the fire that was on the verge of dying in so many. In churches and conferences I am repeatedly told they didn't even realize how far they'd fallen, until the flame was rekindled and their desire to seek Him was ignited. They realized they had not guarded their heart and lost the appetite that accompanies a healthy heart.

GUARD WHAT IS MOST PRECIOUS

We're told "Above all else, guard your heart" (Prov. 4:23 NIV). There is nothing more important to guard, watch over, or protect! When I consider these words I think of how men protect items of value. We have all seen precious stones on display in the shelter of unbreakable glass. They sit in a controlled environment, sensitive to any changes in weight or temperature where the slightest infraction will set off alarms and doors will lock. There are electric-eye beams that if broken instantly summon armed men to the invasion. They pay security men to watch over these items 24/7. Multiple thousands of dollars are spent to guard and protect—a *rock!*

God tells us the most valuable possession on earth is our hearts—not rocks. Yet believers give their hearts over to things that not only do not profit, but even harm us. We'll watch and read just about anything as long as it does not contain excessive nudity or swearing. We fail to recognize the spirit of the world that is at enmity with the Spirit of God. Yet in this, the men of this world are so much wiser, for they guard diligently what they value most; while believers are careless as they walk through life failing to guard their hearts from the lusts and desires that steal their hunger from the only One who can truly satisfy.

The Lord "satisfies the longing soul, and fills the hungry soul with goodness" (Ps. 107:9). He's waiting to satisfy us, yet His goodness will not satisfy us if we are already full of other things. Let's keep our hearts hungry and not take lightly His call to us. For when we draw near He has promised to draw near to us!

STUDY QUESTIONS

1. Proverbs 27:7 says, "A satisfied soul loathes the honeycomb." As you reflect on this verse, what cares, desires, and pleasures are you most vulnerable to? How can they dull your hunger for the "sweet honeycomb" of God's fellowship?

2. In this chapter, the author shares his observations of over-twenty-year-olds and under-twenty-year-olds in two different church settings in regard to their passion—their hunger—for God. As you look at the life of your church, how would you characterize the appetite of your spiritual family—satisfied, hungry, indifferent?

3. In light of the admonition in Proverbs 4:23 to "above all else, guard your heart," what steps can you take today to protect your heart? Is there some spiritual "junk food" in your diet which needs to be eliminated or replaced?

CHAPTER FOUR

PASSION FOR HIS PRESENCE

✠

The spoken Word is heard when we are in His presence.

Over the past twenty years of ministry I've traveled to every continent, except Antarctica, teaching God's Word in both churches and conferences. I've had the privilege of working on two church staffs for a combined seven years before traveling full time. Over this time I've discovered two major groups within the church, and the gap of their differing thoughts seems to be widening as the Lord's coming draws closer. The first are those who seek God for what He can do; while the second seek Him for who He is.

ISRAEL'S CORE MOTIVATION

This contrast is seen with Moses and the children of Israel. Let's explore this in more depth. Israel passionately desired to be free from oppression and cried out to God, acknowledging Him as their deliverer. These descendants of Abraham could be compared to the group who seeks Him for what He can do. There are those who are in the church who don't want the bondage that accompanies the world's system; however they unknowingly are still captive. They profess and acknowledge Jesus as Lord and look to Him for deliverance and provision. Yet, just as with the children of Israel, their heart is revealed by their desires, actions, words, and worldliness.

For hundreds of years Israel wept for God's deliverance. Then God appeared to Moses and told him it was time and gave His word to carry it out. Before approaching Pharaoh, Moses met with the elders of Israel and proclaimed God's promise of liberation. Upon hearing the good news they "were soon convinced that the Lord had sent Moses and Aaron. And when they realized that the Lord had seen their misery and was deeply concerned for them, they all bowed their heads and worshiped" (Ex. 4:31 NLT).

Imagine the emotion of this gathering! For their entire life these leaders had heard of God's coming deliverer. The promised hope of a land of freedom and milk and honey had been handed down from fathers and grandfathers. They watched as their elders lived and died and never saw it. These leaders had wrestled with the same question: Will we see it in our lifetime or die before the promise's fulfillment? Now, they are in the presence of a former prince of Egypt, a trained leader, who possesses the miracle confirmation of God's hand upon him. The very one who should have ruled over them will now be their deliverer. Only God could do such a wonder! Their hearts overflow with awe and joy. They can do nothing but praise God in worship and thanksgiving.

Moses leaves them and meets with Pharaoh. But Egypt's leader is not at all impressed with God's delivering word. He scorns Moses and the descendants of Abraham and increases their hardship with brutal workloads that are almost impossible to bear. Now, how quickly everything begins to change. The very same leaders lash out and rail harshly against Moses. Forgotten is their worship; they become so disheartened and frustrated with Moses that they call judgment upon him! (See Ex. 5:21.)

Yet over time God in His mercy still delivers them with many signs and wonders. When Pharaoh finally gives the command, there is again a dramatic change in attitude. They are filled with joy and go out with great glory and blessing. Imagine the atmosphere of release as they danced their way out of Egypt basking in God's goodness and faithfulness. Not only are they free, but there are abundant treasures of gold and silver lavished upon them, as well as health and strength imparted as they ate the Passover lamb. These former slaves were not only grateful to God, but their confidence in Moses was at an all-time high.

Once out of Egypt, God directs Moses to lead them to the shores of the Red Sea; they look back and realize Pharaoh is marching out against them. There is another huge attitude change. They bitterly complain again and lash out at Moses, "Because there were no graves in Egypt, have you taken us away to die in the wilderness? Why have you so dealt with us, to bring us up out of Egypt? Is this not the word that we told you in Egypt, saying, 'Let us alone that we may serve the Egyptians'? For it would have been *better for us* to serve the Egyptians than that we should die in the wilderness." (Ex. 14:11–12, *author's emphasis*). In Egypt when things didn't go well, they told Moses to leave them alone; now again they are unhappy with their incompetent leader and repeat the complaint. They thought they murmured against Moses and Aaron, but Moses told them, "Your complaints are not against us but against the LORD" (Ex. 16:8). Their desire for whatever was in their best interest overrode their desire to fulfill God's will. Notice the words *it would have been better for us*. They lacked a burning desire for God's heart, but were consumed with a love for their own lives.

Once again God is merciful as He splits the Red Sea and brings them across on dry ground. Then in one sweep God buries the most powerful military on earth and the Israelites' oppressors for over four hundred years. Now they are exuberant! They rejoice and dance before the Lord. We read, "Then Miriam the prophetess, Aaron's sister, took a tambourine in her hand, and all the women followed her, with tambourines and dancing" (Ex. 15:20 NIV). Can you imagine between eight hundred thousand to a million women dancing and playing tambourines? Wow, what a praise service! They'd never known such joy. But it was short-lived when water was scarce a mere three days later. Again they bitterly complain and again God provides.

A few more days pass, and now food is the issue. They whine, "Oh, that we had died by the hand of the LORD in the land of Egypt, when we sat by the pots of meat and when we ate bread to the full! For you have brought us out into this wilderness to kill this whole assembly with hunger" (Ex. 16:3).

Can you see their pattern? They are happy and thankful as long as God is doing what they want when they want it and unhappy whenever God isn't doing what they want when they want it. Their core motivation is evidenced by their behavior and words under pressure; it's all about them. They elevate their desires over His heart or presence.

MOSES' CORE MOTIVATION

This cycle repeats itself over and over until even God is fed up with it. He tells Moses:

> Now that you have brought these people out of Egypt, lead them
> to the land I solemnly promised Abraham, Isaac, and Jacob. I told
> them long ago that I would give this land to their descendants.
> And I will send an angel before you to drive out the Canaanites,
> Amorites, Hittites, Perizzites, Hivites, and Jebusites. Theirs is a
> land flowing with milk and honey. But I will not travel along with
> you, for you are a stubborn, unruly people. If I did, I would be
> tempted to destroy you along the way. (Ex. 33:1–3 NLT)

God told Moses he could lead this people into the promised land, which they'd waited for so long, and He'd even send a choice angel with them to drive out their enemies so the land could be secured; however, He (His presence) was not going!

It's a good thing God said this to Moses, for if He had made this offer to the children of Israel they would have gladly accepted it, had a party, packed, and gone! Why do I think this? Think of it—if they were willing to return to Egypt without an angel or God, just to escape the desert discomforts, I'm sure they'd have taken the promised land with an angel. Yet hear the reply of Moses to God's offer:

> If Your Presence does not go with us, do not bring us up from here. (Ex. 33:15)

We must remind ourselves where "here" was. It was the desert; the place of hardship; a land void of comfort or pleasure! There was no abundance, only daily needs met, and even that was often done supernaturally. There were no gardens, natural resources, or security in this land. No homes, rivers, vineyards, fields, or fruit trees to eat from. No shopping, recreation, or entertainment. (Unless you enjoyed watching your loved ones picked off by snakes.) You are surrounded by the arid and mundane. There was nothing of beauty in this place, yet Moses declares, "I would rather have Your presence in the unwanted and uncomfortable than a land of abundance and beauty void of Your presence!"

What was his heart cry? God's presence! He desired the Lord Himself more than His promised blessings. He prized intimacy with God above any treasures God could provide. This set Moses apart from the children of Israel. They sought God for what He did while Moses sought God for who He is! This driving motivation separates believers into two groups even today. The division goes beyond denominational lines. There are those who do not know they can seek God for more than merely His protection, provision, and promotion; they can embrace Him for who He is and know Him intimately. How different is this from a woman who marries for money? She does not marry her husband for who he is, but rather for what he can do for her. In this arrangement both miss out, because intimacy can not flourish in the soil of such motivation.

THE REWARD

I have visited some of the most beautiful places in the world and seen homes and buildings beyond compare in luxury that mean nothing to me because they are void of the presence of God. I have been in unpleasant places as well, such as prisons, third world nations, and in homes filled with little to be desired, yet full of God's presence. I can honestly say I'd rather be in those hard uncomfortable places where God's Spirit dwells than in mansions filled with treasures, yet void of His presence.

I was privileged to play NCAA tennis, the USTA circuit, junior Davis Cup matches, and win our state title. I achieved scholastic awards and social status and the respect of my peers, leaders, and business executives. I dated beautiful and popular girls. These all represent what most people not only desire, but pursue wholeheartedly. In truth, the glory and pleasure of all these combined could never remotely touch just thirty seconds in God's presence. The comparison is impossible! Hear how Scripture describes Moses:

> By faith Moses, when he became of age, refused to be called the
> son of Pharaoh's daughter, choosing rather to suffer affliction
> with the people of God than to enjoy the passing pleasures of sin,
> esteeming the reproach of Christ greater riches than the treasures
> in Egypt; for he looked to the reward. (Heb. 11:24–27)

Notice he chose to suffer affliction. His was in a different position from the children of Israel's; they had no choice. Yet they complained and he did not. Of his own free will he left behind the finest the world could offer, as well as the highest status a person could achieve. Why? He sought another reward. His reward wasn't the promised land, but the promise of His presence. After just one encounter at the bush, all he wanted from that point on was to know God intimately.

I've preached to thousands in conferences and churches; ministered to millions by television and books. God has blessed us in ways that have blown my mind. Yet if I had to choose, without hesitation I'd trade the apparent success He's given for His manifest presence. There is nothing like it. To sense His nearness and hear His voice whisper things I've never known to my heart is far greater than preaching to multitudes and book sales in the millions. The glory of His presence is much greater than anything!

My heart breaks when I watch ministers pursue success, believing that is where they will find satisfaction. To be esteemed and recognized by others is their unspoken goal. I've watched those who seek their significance and fulfillment through ministerial accomplishments fall into despair, and eventually the snares of darkness. They build huge ministries and then end up in immorality or ensnared in covetousness before they realize how empty it all is.

I've witnessed even greater numbers who never experienced the success of others yet met their same tragic end. They were discouraged because they could never build a church above two hundred, five hundred, a thousand, five thousand, or some other targeted goal their hearts were set on. Their book sales never reached their expected goals and they were not invited to the "big" conferences where they wanted to speak. They sought fulfillment where it was not to be found. This is no different than those who pursue status and accomplishments in the secular market. These believers miss out on what they were truly created for.

In contrast, I've met men and women with large ministries who have experienced success, yet their hearts yearn for more of God. They've shared how they would gladly give it all up and serve another ministry or do something else if that was God's desire. Most never sought the position they now hold so loosely. They confess they know God placed them there and all they want to do is please Him. I've heard their heart cry in our conversations and observed it in their actions; they are not unlike David who experienced great success yet called himself a poor and needy man.

I've also met those with small ministries in comparison, yet they walk in peace and blessing because they know they've done what they were called to do. Their passion is not in numbers or outward success, but rather to know God more intimately and to walk in His manifest presence. This should be true for every human. We were all created for God, and none of us will ever find true fulfillment outside of knowing Him and walking in His presence. This is where all true peace and satisfaction lie.

TWO PRESENCES OF GOD

At this point we must define the two presences of God presented in Scriptures; first, there is His *omnipresence*. David speaks of it when he writes, "Where can I go from Your Spirit? Or where can I flee from Your presence?" (Ps. 139:7). Omnipresence describes His being in all places. David went on to say, "If I go up to heaven, you are there; if I go down to the place of the dead, you are there. I could ask the darkness to hide me and the light around me to become night—but even in darkness I cannot hide from you. To you the night shines as bright as day. Darkness and light are both alike to you" (vv. 8, 11–12 NLT). This speaks of the Lord's promise to never leave us nor forsake us (Heb. 13:5). Though we cannot sense this presence, it doesn't negate His being there. We are just unaware of it.

The second presence Scripture defines as His *manifest presence*. The word *manifest* means to bring from the unseen, unheard, or unknown into the seen, heard, or known. The manifest presence of the Lord was what Moses passionately desired. This is when God reveals Himself not just to our spirits, but it is when our mind and senses become aware of His nearness as well. It is when His knowledge is revealed to our minds. This is the presence Jesus spoke of when He said,

"I will love him and manifest Myself to him." (John 14:21)

The psalmist refers to it by declaring, "Blessed are those who have learned to acclaim you, who walk in the light of your presence, O LORD" (Ps. 89:15 NIV). Peter exhorted hungry inquirers on the day of

Pentecost, "Repent therefore and be converted, that your sins may be blotted out, so that times of refreshing may come from the *presence* of the Lord" (Acts 3:19, *author's emphasis*).

God can manifest His presence in various ways. In Scriptures some saw Him, others heard His voice without seeing Him, while others sensed His nearness and immediately knew things they'd never known before because of His revelation. But one thing is certain, when He comes, you know it, you'll sense Him within your innermost being, and know He is there.

SEEKING THE LORD OR MANIFESTATIONS?

I've seen people, desperate for the experience of His presence, misled. They look for a manifestation rather than the person of the Lord. God passed by Elijah and there were several great manifestations. First there was a great and mighty wind, but the Lord was not in the wind; then an earthquake, but Scriptures make it clear that He was not in the earthquake; then there was a fire, but again He was not in the fire. After the fire there was the still, small voice; it was then Elijah knew he'd personally encountered the presence of God.

I have watched people seek manifestations, thinking they will find God through the manifestation, rather than seek the Lord in their heart and in turn experience His manifest presence. Often after preaching a God-breathed, heart-convicting message I'll call people to the front to meet with God. There are times when some will pray in such a way it is disturbing or distracting and rubs against the flow of what is going on. Others will laugh, or shake, or display some other type of outward gesture. The reason is that at one time they sought God and shook, cried, or laughed in His presence so now they subconsciously do these very things in the hope God will be found in those manifestations, but He is not. Many times I still the people and tell them not to do anything, just to be still and turn to Him in their hearts to seek the person of Jesus. If there is a manifestation, great! But we are not to seek Him by way of manifestations. We are to seek the Lord Himself!

I recall a meeting in Asia where many responded to the call for repentance. There was no room to bring them to the front, as so many in the auditorium responded, so I instructed them to pray and seek Him right where they were. After prayer I encouraged them to turn to the Lord where they stood. God's presence swept into the auditorium in a wonderful way. It is amazing to watch as He takes over and manifests Himself. I've experienced it many times but it never becomes common or ordinary. Often you can sense Him more clearly than the people around you. Once His presence came, a number of people started laughing, but I sensed a grieving, and it was confirmed; far quicker than He had come into the building, He left, even as people continued to laugh and raise their voices as though He was yet present.

I stopped them and brought rebuke realizing they were just mimicking what had happened in His presence a few months earlier when an evangelist had been to their nation. The evangelist's ministry carries a very strong manifestation of what many call "holy laughter." I do believe that there are times when God comes that people will laugh. In fact I've experienced it personally as well as seen in it in our own meetings. Once while in Indonesia, the Spirit of God fell on the meeting one day and for two hours my interpreter and I watched people laugh so hard that they were rolling on their backs. It started with five women who were weeping and it turned into hilarious laughter which spread throughout the congregation. They had never experienced anything like this. They were seeking God!

However, this was different. Their eyes were set on the manifestation rather than the Lord Himself. They'd come to the conclusion that if there was no manifestation of laughter then there had not been a manifestation of God's presence. I have often been in God's presence and sensed Him strongly, yet experienced no outward demonstration of it. I've been in His presence and wept uncontrollably, yet I realize it is only a result of seeking Him and coming into His presence.

To make this clear, consider this simple example of putting on a pair of pants. What if after putting them on I stick my hands in my front pockets to straighten them and discover a hundred dollar bill? I didn't put on the pants to get money, but discovered it there in the process of putting on the pants. I sought to clothe myself and in doing so got the benefit and surprise of money. We don't seek the manifestation, but rather the person of the Lord; and anything else is a benefit.

After bringing correction to the Asian congregation, I told them I understood their hunger for His presence and warned them not to replace God Himself with an experience. After this exhortation the presence of the Lord returned in a holy awe. This time many were weeping, not laughing, but bottom line, all of us who were seeking were profoundly touched by His wonderful presence, whether we wept or not.

MANIFESTATIONS DON'T SATISFY

Never forget, manna never satisfied the children of Israel. God gave them manna in the wilderness to practically show their desperate need for something more—His presence. Moses said,

> You shall remember that the LORD your God led you all the way these forty years in the wilderness, to humble you and test you, to know what was in your heart . . . So He humbled you, allowed you to hunger, and fed you with manna . . . that He might make you know that man shall not live by bread alone; but man lives by every word that *proceeds* from the mouth of the LORD. (Deut. 8:2–3, *author's emphasis*)

Examine carefully the word *proceeds*. He did not say *proceeded*, but *proceeds;* this is present tense not past. The spoken Word is heard when we are in His presence! Elijah did not get caught up in the manifestations of God passing by; but rather waited for the still small voice of His presence before responding. In Asia they had gotten caught up in the manifestation of when God previously passed by, but God had moved on. He was no longer there. He had gone on to something new, while they remained behind to try to find Him where He had been.

Just as manna never satisfied the children of Israel, so manifestations (manna-festations) were never given to satisfy our deeper longings; they are not an end in themselves. To pursue them will lead us down a road of dissatisfaction, until we turn from what cannot fulfill us and seek the intimacy that comes from Him.

SETTLING FOR A MENTAL RELATIONSHIP

Another sad thing occurs when believers exalt manifestations above seeking the Lord for Himself. It turns many others off from the true presence of God. Disillusioned by the out-of-sync and offbeat behavior of the manifestation seekers, they will be guarded and settle for a mental relationship with God. This is tragic when we were created for so much more. A.W. Tozer wrote that in these last days the doctrine of justification by faith has been:

> . . . interpreted by many in such a manner as actually to bar men
> from the knowledge of God. The whole transaction of religious
> conversion has been made mechanical and spiritless . . . The man
> is 'saved,' but he is not hungry nor thirsty after God. In fact, he
> is specifically taught to be satisfied and is encouraged to be con-
> tent with little. (*The Pursuit of God*, pp. 12–13)

A mental relationship with God is mechanical and spiritless. We were created to dwell with Him in reality, not theory alone. Until we experience the fullness of this we should never be satisfied. Jesus died to remove the veil that separated us from the very presence of God. For this reason we hear the psalmist cry out:

> How lovely are Your tabernacles (dwelling places), O Lord of
> hosts! My soul yearns, yes, even pines and is homesick for the
> courts of the Lord; my heart and my flesh cry out and sing for
> joy to the living God. Yes, the sparrow has found a house, and
> the swallow a nest for herself, where she may lay her young—
> even Your altars O Lord of hosts, my King and my God.

Blessed (happy, fortunate, to be envied) are those who dwell in Your house and Your presence; they will be singing your praises all the day long. Selah! (Ps. 84: 1–4 AMP)

The New King James Version records the second verse, "My heart and my flesh cry out for the living God." The writer then goes on to say that the sparrow and swallow have found homes, yet he confesses himself homeless, because he yearned for the dwelling place of God. He declared it his longed-for home—where the presence of God is. Notice he says, "Happy, fortunate, [and] to be envied are those who dwell in Your presence." This is the goal of those who love God! They hunger for His manifest presence. The closer we are to Him the stronger it becomes, and the more we are affected.

STUDY QUESTIONS

1. In the beginning of this chapter, the author writes, "Over this time I've discovered two major groups within the church . . . The first are those who seek God for what He can do; while the second seek Him for who He is." Be honest—in which group do you see yourself?

2. Following their release from captivity in Egypt, the Israelites were frequently praising and worshiping God for His provision on one day, only to be grumble and complain on another day because He had not provided what they wanted. As you remember "desert experiences" in your own life, what similarities do you see in your attitude as compared to the children of Israel?

3. You may be reading this book because you are currently having a "desert experience." If so, what can you learn from Elijah's experience with the manifestations of wind, earthquake, and fire?

CHAPTER FIVE

BEHIND
THE VEIL

✠

*"God's presence separates us from all others
on the face of the earth."*

T he presence of the Lord always brings greater revelation of
who He is, and with each encounter we are forever changed.
Scanning the Bible we find that those who walked in a greater understanding of God's ways, were those who pursued and experienced
His presence.

THE SEPARATING FACTOR

In the last chapter we saw Moses given an offer by God that he
turned down. The Lord made available His promises, but void of His

presence. Moses quickly responded, "If Your Presence does not go with us, do not bring us up from here" (Ex. 33:15). Moses set the precedent that closeness with God outweighed the promises apart from His presence. Listen now to Moses' reasoning for rejecting the angelic escort:

> If Your Presence does not go with us, do not bring us up from here. For how then will it be known that Your people and I have found grace in Your sight, except You go with us? *So we shall be separate, Your people and I, from all the people who are upon the face of the earth.* (Ex. 33:15–16, *author's emphasis*)

A powerful truth is brought out in his response; it is God's presence that separates us from all the others on the face of the earth. It is not that we confess Christianity; attend Bible-believing churches; or are nice people who once prayed the sinner's prayer with a friend, or in response to an altar call. It is His very presence that distinguishes us and makes us holy (separated to Him). His presence is what makes this evident to those who dwell on earth.

Why then have so many resigned themselves to an intellectual relationship with God? Why have we settled for Christianity void of the presence of Christ? How did we learn to be content without intimacy? Why have we taught Christianity in a way that does not build passion in people to draw near and abide in His presence? In answer, A.W. Tozer writes:

> God wills that we should push on into His presence and live our whole life there. This is to be known to us in conscious experience. It is more than a doctrine to be held; it is a life to be enjoyed every moment of every day. (*The Pursuit of God*, p. 34)

Many have settled for the intellectual knowledge of belonging, without ever pursuing the reality of interaction with Him in the moment. So deeply embedded is the concept of salvation that few go any further. They've said their prayers and will one day die and go to be with Him. Yet, the reality of Christ is missed, and the powerful revelation of God's desire to walk with us is lost. It is not a one time or far away experience, but His very real desire for abiding communion. Let's travel the Scriptures together to investigate.

WHO EXPERIENCED HIS PRESENCE?

We see His manifest presence woven throughout the entire Bible. In the garden, Adam and Eve walked with God until disobedience caused them to hide "themselves from the presence of the LORD God" (Gen. 3:8). At this point man separated himself from God's presence. Their son Cain further distanced himself from God's presence as a result of a hardened heart.

Yet God did not give up, and was still desirous of intimacy with man whom He loved. Eventually men like Enoch and Noah responded and in turn touched God's heart by their relentless pursuit. As a result they walked closer to Him than anyone else in their millennium since Adam left the Garden of Eden.

Abraham often experienced His manifest presence during the course of his life. One such encounter happened when God came to discuss the future of Sodom and Gomorrah. After the judgment of the cities we read, "The next morning Abraham was up early and hurried out to the place where he had stood in the LORD's presence" (Gen. 19:27 NLT). This was only one of numerous times Abraham enjoyed fellowship with God in His very presence. In fact, in his old age Abraham addressed his servant with, "For the LORD, in whose presence I have walked, will send his angel with you and will make your mission successful (Gen. 24:40 NLT).

We read Samuel "grew, and the LORD was with him and let none of his words fall to the ground" (1 Sam. 3:19). How could it be that not one of these man's words could fail? The answer is found in the following verse, "And the LORD gave Hannah three sons and two daughters. Meanwhile, Samuel grew up in the presence of the LORD"

(1 Sam. 2:21 NLT). Again we see it is in the presence of the Lord that He is revealed. When we know Him we'll speak what He speaks and our words will not fail.

David, who loved and experienced God's presence as much as any in the Old Testament, with the possible exception of Moses, cried, "May the dynasty of your servant David be established in Your presence" (2 Sam. 7:26 NLT). Like Moses, he wanted nothing to do with success at the expense of God's presence. In fact later when he committed his grievous sin of adultery and murder, his passionate repentant cry was, "Do not banish me from your presence, and don't take your Holy Spirit from me" (Ps. 51:11 NLT). He knew life would be indeed empty and meaningless outside God's presence! He penned the words, "You will show me the way of life, granting me the joy of your presence and the pleasures of living with you forever" (Ps. 16:11 NLT).

Psychology tells us the relationships we've had over the last five years will shape our personality. I cannot help but agree with this as Scripture tells us, "Do not be deceived: 'Evil company corrupts good habits' " (1 Cor. 15:33); and again, "He who walks with wise men will be wise" (Prov. 13:20). What about David? He was alone in the wilderness when, "Everyone who was in distress, everyone who was in debt, and everyone who was discontented gathered to him. So he became captain over them. And there were about four hundred men with him" (1 Sam. 22:2). Wow, what a crowd to spend more than ten years with! The discontented, distressed, and in debt! They're angry, uptight, and more than likely rude and insensitive. Do they mold David's personality? No! Why? Because David spent so much time in God's presence that he maintained a princely bearing, and consequently forged them into great leaders of renown for many generations!

One of my favorite Scriptures is David's response to God's great invitation. He wrote,

> My heart has heard you say, "Come and talk with me." And my heart responds, "Lord, I am coming." (Ps. 27:8 NLT)

This was his life; he spent so much time with the Lord he not only influenced four hundred grumpy men, but impacted an entire nation. He was an influencer, because he spent time with the Source of all wisdom, knowledge, and understanding. Yet David didn't do it to "get" God's wisdom; he pressed in because he longed for His heart. He loved Him more than anyone or anything else, and the reason is that he had spent so much time with Him.

If only David's son Solomon had inherited this burning desire. He saw the God of Israel twice, and commanded greater wisdom than all those before or after him, yet he failed to realize the importance of abiding in His presence. At the close of his life when his years were spent he writes the sad book of Ecclesiastes. Though he possessed wisdom, riches untold, the earth's most beautiful women, as well as fame and influence far and wide, all he can do is cry out "futility and vanity!" If he had had the heart of his father David, Israel's history would have been much different.

In fact, much of Bible history would be different if various individuals had known the importance of pursuing the presence of God. Tragically, quite a number experienced a degree of His presence, but somehow failed to realize what they'd tasted. They remained ignorant of the fact that in God's presence is an enduring satisfaction, and longevity is only found in continual pursuit of Him. One of these men was a distant descendant of David named King Uzziah. He sought God in his early years, and as a result experienced great success, only to later forget where his success had come from. In his pride he no longer pursued the Lord, and as a result died in isolation as a leper (see 2 Chron. 26).

THE GREATEST TRAGEDY

We could continue throughout the Old Testament, but one of the greatest tragedies is seen years before David when his ancestors, the descendants of Abraham, came out of Egypt. In an earlier chapter we learned God's desire was to deliver them in order to bring them to

Himself. He wanted to draw near so He could manifest His presence, but as He did we sadly read, "So the people stood *afar off*, but Moses *drew near* the thick darkness where God was" (Ex. 20:21, *author's emphasis*). How tragic. God reveals Himself and they draw back! Only Moses had the passion to press in and draw near. Because of their response God had to form a priesthood who would stand before Him for the sake of the people. A tabernacle would be erected in order for God's veiled presence to dwell among them. After carefully constructing it according to God's specifications it was finally erected and we read:

> Then the cloud covered the Tabernacle, and the *glorious presence* of the Lord filled it. Moses was no longer able to enter the Tabernacle because the cloud had settled down over it, and the Tabernacle was filled with the awesome glory of the Lord. (Ex. 40:34–35 NLT, *author's emphasis*)

VARIOUS DEGREES OF GOD'S PRESENCE

At this juncture, I must take a side step, and discuss the various degrees of God's presence. Notice the words, *glorious presence* in the above verses. When the tabernacle was first erected His presence was so glorious that Moses, the man who spoke to God face to face as a friend, couldn't enter in. Can you imagine the intensity of His awesomeness—a presence both wonderful and terrible in that moment?

Years later under the leadership of Eli, a judge, priest, and distant descendant of Aaron, the presence of the Lord was almost negligible in the tabernacle. In fact they could not only enter it, they committed blatant sin near the very place Moses couldn't enter. We read, "The word of the LORD was rare in those days; there was no widespread revelation" (1 Sam. 3:1). Why was the word of the Lord rare? Again, the revelation of God including His word is found in His presence. Where there is no presence there is no revelation, where there is but a small measure of His presence there is rarity of revelation, and where there is a strong presence there is great revelation! In this chapter we are told the lamp of God (His presence) had grown dimmer and was on the verge of going out (no presence). This happened at the end of Eli's rule, when the ark was captured by the Philistines. On the last day of his life, the name *Ichabod* was announced, which means "the glory has departed."

Unlike the days of Eli, when the presence of God was rare and almost undetectable due to sin, there are settings where, though His presence is not glorious, like when the tabernacle was erected, His presence remains very real and revelation is rich. In these times God will draw near in a more subtle way, choosing not to manifest His glory. We see this with Jacob. He wrestled with God and saw Him face to face, but obviously not in His glory. Yet Jacob was transformed and grew in the revelation of God as a result of this encounter (Gen. 32:24–30). Joshua saw the Lord and didn't even recognize it was the Commander of the armies of heaven whom he spoke with. Yet on the other hand, Moses cried out to see the Lord's face and was answered, "You cannot see My face; for no man shall see Me, and live" (Ex. 33:20). We see Moses' desire to see God in all His glory, but couldn't; but Joshua and others saw the face of the Lord and still lived. Why? They didn't see the Lord in the fullness of His glory.

THE LIGHT OF HIS COUNTENANCE

First, let's briefly discuss the glory of the Lord. Some think of it as a mist, cloud, or some such manifestation. This gives rise to statements like, "Oh, the glory of God fell in the service the other night." But this limits and darkens His counsel with words without knowledge (see Job 38:2).

First, the glory of God is not a cloud. You may ask, "Then why is a cloud mentioned almost every time God's glory is manifested in Scripture?" The reason: God hides Himself in the cloud. He is too magnificent to behold so the cloud screens His countenance, or all flesh around Him would be consumed and instantly die. Remember, God told Moses no man could see His face and live. This then brings up the question: How could Isaiah, Ezekiel, and the apostle John see the glory of the Lord and survive to write about it? The answer is simple: they were in the spirit and out of the body. Mortal flesh cannot stand in the presence of the Holy Lord in all His glory. He is the consuming fire in whom there is no darkness (Heb. 12:29, 1 John 1:5). Paul writes of Jesus:

> He who is the blessed and only Potentate, the King of kings and Lord of lords, who alone has immortality, dwelling in unapproachable light, whom no man has seen or can see. (1 Tim. 6:15–16)

Jesus dwells in unapproachable light, whom no man has or can see. In fact, the psalmist declares the Lord wears light as a garment (see Ps. 104:2). Paul could easily write this because he'd experienced a measure of this unapproachable light of His glorious presence on the road to Damascus. He related it to King Agrippa this way:

> At midday, O king, along the road I saw a light from heaven, brighter than the sun, shining around me. (Acts 26:13)

Paul did not see Jesus' face; he only saw light emanating from Him that overwhelmed and overshadowed the bright Middle Eastern sun! He was in the presence of His glory. It was not morning or late afternoon sun, but rather noonday sun. I lived in "the sunshine state," Florida, for twelve years, and I never *had* to wear my sunglasses. However, several years ago I traveled with Lisa to the Middle East; there I *had* to wear sunglasses! The sun was so much brighter in the dry desert climate, and its proximity to the equator magnified its brightness many times. The sun was tolerable in the early morning and late afternoon, but from eleven to two o'clock it was very bright. Yet Paul said the light of Jesus was brighter than the very noon sun of the Middle East! Take a moment and remember the last time you tried to look directly at the midday sun. It is difficult, unless it is veiled or under the cover of a cloud. The Lord's glory exceeded this brilliance manyfold.

This explains why both Joel and Isaiah said in the last days, when the Lord's glory is revealed, the sun will be turned to darkness. "Behold, the day of the LORD comes . . . the stars of heaven and their constellations will not give their light; the sun will be darkened in its going forth, and the moon will not cause its light to shine" (Isa. 13:9–10).

Allow me to explain further. In a clear night sky what do we see? Stars! They are everywhere in the night sky. But when the sun rises in the morning what happens? Where do they go? Do the stars run away until sundown and then hurry back to their places from hiding under the horizon? The answer is obviously, no. What happens then? The glory of the stars is one level, but the glory of the sun is so much greater that when the sun appears they are darkened in contrast. They are still there, but can't be seen. Likewise when Jesus returns His glory will be so much greater than the sun, He'll darken it. It will be unseen though still present! Wow! Do you understand why Paul writes, "Whom no man has seen or can see"?

The glory of the Lord overcomes all other light. He is perfect and all-consuming light. This is why with His second coming the men of this earth will "go into the holes of the rocks, and into the caves of the earth, from the terror of the LORD and the *glory of His majesty*" (Isa. 2:19, *author's emphasis*). John depicts it:

> And the kings of the earth, the great men, the rich men, the commanders, the mighty men, every slave and every free man, hid themselves in the caves and in the rocks of the mountains, and said to the mountains and rocks, "Fall on us and hide us from *the face* of Him who sits on the throne and from the wrath of the Lamb! (Rev. 6:15–16, *author's emphasis*).

WHAT IS THE GLORY OF GOD?

Let's answer the question: What is the glory of the Lord? To answer we return to Moses' interlude with God. Moses not only requested God's presence, but went on to ask to see His glory.

And he [Moses] said, "Please, show me Your *glory*." (Ex. 33:18, *author's emphasis*)

The Hebrew word for *glory* is *kabowd*. It is defined by Strong's Bible Dictionary as "the weight of something, but only figuratively in a good sense." Its definition also speaks of splendor, abundance, and honor. Moses was requesting God to "Show Yourself in *all* Your splendor." Look carefully at God's response:

I will make all My *goodness* pass before you, and I will proclaim the name of the LORD before you. (Ex. 33:19, *author's emphasis*)

Moses requested all His glory and God answers back with "all My *goodness*." The Hebrew word for *goodness* is *tuwb*. It means "good in the widest sense." In other words, nothing withheld.

God then says, "I will proclaim the name of the Lord before you." Before an earthly king enters the throne room, his name is announced by the herald. The proclamation is accompanied by trumpet blasts as he enters the throne room in his splendor. The king's greatness is revealed, and in his court there is no mistaking who is king. His majestic presence fills the people with awe. But what if this same monarch was to walk the street of his city dressed in ordinary clothes, without any attendants? The truth is, what was obvious in the court setting would be lost outside as many who pass by him wouldn't realize his true identity. His presence would not be as breathtaking and noticeable as in the glory of his throne room. In essence, this is exactly what God did for Moses, by saying, "I will proclaim My own name and pass by you in all My splendor."

In the New Testament, we're told the glory of the Lord is revealed in the face of Jesus Christ (2 Cor. 4:6). Many who have been in the presence of the Lord have testified of seeing a vision of Jesus and looking upon His face. This is very possible, but I will tell you this, they did not see His full glory.

Others may question that the disciples looked at the face of Jesus after He rose from the dead. This too is correct, but it was not an open display of His glory. As I mentioned there were those who saw and experienced the Lord's presence in the Old Testament, but not in the revelation of His glory. The Lord appeared to Abraham by the terebinth trees of Mamre, but not in His glory (Gen. 18:1–2). Jacob wrestled with God, and Joshua (Josh. 5:13–15) didn't even recognize Him, and there were others.

When Joshua looked at His face before the invasion of Jericho, the Lord appeared as a Man of war. Not realizing who He was Joshua questioned, "Are You for us or for our adversaries?" The Lord then *revealed* himself as the Commander of the army of the Lord and ordered Joshua to take off his sandals, for the ground was holy! Jacob wrestled with the Lord all night and toward daylight finally cried out, "Please tell me your name" (Gen. 32:29 NASB). Return to our example of the king in ordinary clothes walking the streets of his kingdom—passing unrecognized by many. This portrays what happened to Joshua and Jacob, yet they still received great revelation of Him.

The same is true after the Resurrection. The first person Jesus spoke with was Mary Magdalene and she thought He was the gardener (John 20:15–16). The disciples ate a fish breakfast with Jesus on the seashore (John 21:9–10) and at first did not recognize Him or the sound of His voice. It wasn't until He did something familiar that they recognized Him. Again after His resurrection, He walked with two disciples, who had been told before His death what would happen, but they didn't perceive Him because "their eyes were restrained" (Luke 24:16), and they too did not recognize His face, form, or voice. They all beheld His face and experienced His presence, but not in an open display of His glory, yet they all received revelation from His presence.

In contrast, John the apostle saw Him in the Spirit while on the island of Patmos, but had a totally different encounter from the breakfast by the sea, for there John saw Him in His glory. He described Jesus: "His countenance was like the sun shining in its strength. And when I saw Him, I fell at His feet as dead" (Rev. 1:16–17). The Lord's glorious presence was so strong John fell down as though dead.

The glory of the Lord is everything that makes God, God. All His characteristics, authority, power, wisdom—literally the immeasurable weight and magnitude of Him; with nothing hidden or held back! This glorious presence may be experienced whether God's form is partially seen like with Moses when only His feet and backside are seen, or as was the case with Saul on the road to Damascus—no form, just unapproachable light and a voice.

HIS DWELLING PLACE

Let's return to Abraham's descendants. When God first manifested His presence on Mt. Sinai, they recoiled and cried out, "Surely the LORD our God has shown us *His glory* and His greatness, and we have heard His voice from the midst of the fire . . . Now therefore, why should we die? For this great fire will consume us; if we hear the voice of the LORD our God anymore, then we shall die" (Deut. 5:24–25, *author's emphasis*). They could not endure His glorious presence, because their consciences were stained with their self-seeking ways.

Then the tabernacle is erected and God dwelt in the inner section called the "Most Holy Place." It was here the high priest would enter once a year. On this occasion the priest entered first by way of the outer court where a blood sacrifice was offered on the brazen altar to make amends with God for his sin and those of the people. After this was done the priest would wash himself at the laver adjacent to the altar. Then he entered the Holy Place through a veil. In this place no natural light entered. The only light came from the golden candlestick, which represented Jesus, our Light (John 9:5). Also in this place was the showbread that spoke of Jesus as our Bread of Life (John 6:48). The third article in that place was the altar of incense, which represented a life of continuous prayer and worship.

Even there he still had not entered the place where God's presence dwelled. There remained yet another veil separating the Holy Place from the Most Holy Place or the Holy of Holies. In this place above the mercy seat dwelt the actual manifest presence of God. This is the veil that was torn when Jesus gave up His spirit: "the veil of the temple was torn in two from top to bottom" (Matt. 27:51). Notice it was torn from top to bottom, not bottom to top. God, not man, rent this veil because He was moving out! He was readying a new place of residence, the dwelling place He'd longed for all along—the heart of His regenerated children. When did this happen? Fifty-three days later, on the day of Pentecost, God inhabited His longed-for tabernacle. We read:

> And suddenly there came a sound from heaven, as of a rushing mighty wind, and it filled the whole house where they were sitting. Then there appeared to them divided tongues, as of fire, and one sat upon each of them. And they were all filled with the Holy Spirit. (Acts 2:2–4)

Just as God's presence did not enter until Moses *finished* the work of the tabernacle, when Jesus said, " 'It is *finished!*' bowed His head and gave up His spirit" (see John 19:30) again, the Lord moved to His new dwelling made ready by the blood of the eternal Lamb.

> Therefore, brethren, having boldness to enter the Holiest by the blood of Jesus, by a new and living way which He consecrated for us . . . let us *draw near* with a true heart in full assurance of faith, having our hearts sprinkled from an evil conscience and our bodies washed with pure water. Let us hold fast the confession of our hope without wavering, for He who promised is faithful. (Heb. 10:19–23, *author's emphasis*)

We have boldness to *draw near* to the One who dwells in the "Most Holy Place!" This place is not in a tent or a temple, it is now our bodies! Yes, God moved into the hearts of human beings who were consecrated by the sacrifice of Jesus. Often when we call on Him, we imagine ourselves entering a distant throne room millions of miles away. No, His dwelling is our hearts! We have not yet learned to turn within; we are still looking without! New Testament Scripture plainly tells us, "You don't need to go to heaven (to find Christ and bring him down to help you)" (Rom. 10:6 NLT).

Yes, God has a physical throne room located in the third heaven. Yet, He so longed for nearness to His people that in the Old Testament He set up a dwelling place in a tent on earth where His very manifest presence resided. Now He's set up another dwelling for Himself in the hearts of those who've given their lives to Jesus and asked to be filled with His Spirit. He's made a place for Himself that is nearest to the object of His love and affection. When we draw near to Him who is in our hearts, we enter the throne room millions of miles away as well. How is that? There is no distance in the Spirit of God. To be in His presence is to be in the throne room with Jesus and the Father, because He is the Spirit of Christ and of God! (See Rom. 8:9.)

Notice the writer says, "Let us hold fast the confession of our *hope* without wavering, for He who promised is faithful." The writer also says:

> This hope we have as an anchor of the soul, both sure and stead-
> fast, and which enters the *Presence* behind the veil. (Heb. 6:19,
> *author's emphasis*)

The rending of the old veil made way for every worshiper in this world to come into the presence of God by a new and living way. The veil now becomes our flesh. If we can get beyond the outer court of our flesh by crucifying or denying it (see Gal. 5:24), we enter into the new "Most Holy Place" of the heart where continuous communion is available. His presence becomes a constant reality. He guaranteed if we draw near with true hearts He will manifest His presence! He never said it was for a limited or set time! Just as in the tabernacle His presence was a constant when they were true to Him, likewise His presence is constant within His tabernacle of our hearts.

Hear James's words again, "Draw near to God, and He will draw near to you." What hope, what pure assurance, God promises and swears by Himself, for "it is impossible for God to lie, [that] we might have this strong consolation that we might run to the refuge and lay hold of the hope set before us" (Heb. 6:18). What is this hope? If we draw near; He will draw near to us! He has guaranteed it!

So why don't many more enjoy His manifest presence? As A.W. Tozer cried out:

> With the veil removed by the rending of Jesus' flesh, with nothing on God's side to prevent us from entering, why do we tarry without? Why do we consent to abide all our days just outside the Holy of Holies and never enter at all to look upon God? We hear the Bridegroom say, "Let me see thy countenance, let me hear thy voice; for sweet is thy voice, and thy countenance is comely" (Song of Solomon 2:14). We sense that the call is for us, but still we fail to draw near, and the years pass and we grow old and tired in the outer courts of the tabernacle. What hinders us? (*The Pursuit of God,* p. 41)

The question is still: What hinders us? Why are we struggling in our own strength, missing the mark due to our blindness? Why are so many dissatisfied and bored when we have such a wonderful hope backed by His promise which can't be broken? As we continue we'll discover what hinders this wonderful relationship of fellowship God makes available to every believer.

STUDY QUESTIONS

1. In the beginning of this chapter, these questions are asked: "Why . . . have so many resigned themselves to an intellectual relationship with God? Why have we settled for Christianity void of the presence of Christ? How did we learn to be content without intimacy?"

    How would you answer these questions?

2. The author mentions that psychology tells us that relationships we've had over the last five years will shape our personality. He also states that this is affirmed in Scripture: "Evil company corrupts good habits" (1 Cor. 15:33), and "He who walks with wise men will be wise" (Proverbs 13:20). Have you had periods in your life which exemplified either or both extremes? What were the results?

CHAPTER SIX

THE FRIENDS
OF GOD

✠

He offered them intimacy,
but they by their own choice couldn't have it.

As I write these opening chapters, such a hunger stirs within my
own heart. Speaking of these things fans the flame and increases
my desire to pursue the One who loves us so wonderfully. He has consistently pursued us as individuals in this romance of all ages. However, this
One so worthy of our pursuit is not an "easy catch" *per se*. He is the holy
and great King and as such is to be revered. Therefore you certainly cannot speak of "drawing near" without addressing the issue of "holy fear."

THE PARTING OF WAYS

At this juncture "seeker friendly messages" and truth often part ways.
These messages can be found in any denomination or circles; they

speak of a God who desires men and longs to bless them, yet the messages err because they omit His holiness. Often this is done out of well-meaning intentions; some have seen or experienced the tragedy of legalism; while others simply desire to see people loved and nurtured. Then tragically some messages are preached intentionally incomplete to generate a greater following.

Those who've fled the grip of legalism and only preach a loving, understanding God who compensates for our lawlessness and worldliness, are reactionary in their motives and tactics. This counsel is not drawn by getting into the presence of God to hear for themselves His Word. If they did they would realize there is no other way to approach Him but by the path bordered by both holy love and fear.

These messages preach an "easy Lord," at the expense of the very goal it tries to accomplish. By leaving out the fear of the Lord, it in essence "shuts out His presence" from men.

HELD IN REVERENCE

There is an ever-existing, never-changing truth concerning an audience in His presence. It is summed up in this one Scripture:

> God is greatly to be feared in the assembly of the saints,
> And to be held in reverence by all those around Him. (Ps. 89:7)

Let's read the second part of the verse again. "God is . . . to be held in reverence by all those around Him." This is always true and ever remains: you'll never find God manifesting His presence in an atmosphere where He is not revered. He will not come near or dwell in an environment where He is not held in the utmost honor, esteem, and respect. It doesn't matter how good the singing or "worship" is, or how good the preaching or teaching is, nor how scriptural the prayer is; if He is not feared, He will not come near to reveal Himself. It is no different than with Eli and his sons.

Over the years as I've entered auditoriums where hundreds or thousands of believers were gathered, there have been countless times when sadly there was not a hint of God's presence. The reason: there was a lack of holy fear among the people and sometimes even the leadership. The praise and worship teams can be excellent, with banners waving and dancers, and skilled musicians and singers. The services can be innovative and high tech with media announcements. The event can be creative and entertaining where the people are greeted with humor and topics of interest, but there is something missing. The atmosphere is void of God's presence. The heartbreaking fact is the majority in attendance are unaware of how truly empty the atmosphere is. (At this point let me interject that innovative ways to communicate are fresh and in no way by themselves hinder the manifest presence of God. I've been in such cutting-edge places and enjoyed the richness of God's presence. The presence of God has nothing to do with technology or the lack thereof, but it reflects the condition of the heart.)

In these situations, the Lord leads me to share on obedience and the fear of the Lord, and each time the call to repentance is given I've witnessed a majority respond, often including the leaders themselves. Almost without fail before a prayer is uttered, the presence of God manifests, and people begin to weep. Why does this happen? Because God is drawn to those who love, honor, and fear Him. For this reason James says,

> Draw near to God and He will draw near to you. Cleanse your hands, you sinners; and purify your hearts, you double-minded. (James 4:8–9)

In an initial look at this verse you might think James is speaking to the unsaved, as we usually refer to the unregenerate as "sinners." Yet fifteen times in his discourse James refers to his audience as *brethren*. He is talking to those who are born-again.

So let's look at the word for sinner; it's the Greek word *hamarto-los*. Vine defines the word to mean literally, "one who misses the mark." It is proper that this word can refer to an unsaved person, but it also is used in reference to a Christian. In this context it would refer to a believer who is off target in his thinking, which in turn creates repeated wrong actions or behavior. He continues, "Purify your hearts, you double-minded"; with this statement he goes to the root issue of why the believer is missing the target.

It is most important we understand that the fear of the Lord begins in the heart and manifests itself in our outward actions. God at one point said of His own—and note the words "draw near":

> These people *draw near* with their mouths and honor Me with their lips, but have removed their hearts far from Me, and their fear toward Me is taught by the commandment of men. (Isa. 29:13, *author's emphasis*)

Drawing near to God always begins in a heart that fears and loves God more than anyone or anything else. It is not just outward actions, but the heart's motive. Therefore, in initially defining the fear of the Lord we must first address the heart's attitude.

Let's begin: to fear God is to esteem, honor, and hold Him in highest regard; as well as to venerate, stand in awe, and reverence Him. It is to tremble with the greatest respect for Him, His presence, and His commands, as well as wishes. This is only the beginning.

COMING TO GOD WITH IRREVERENCE

Sometimes in order to understand what something is it helps to know what it is not. An excellent example of approaching God's presence without holy fear is seen in the lives of Aaron's two sons.

Prior to the completion of the tabernacle the Lord instructed Moses, "Now take Aaron your brother, and his sons with him, from among the children of Israel, that he may minister to Me as priest, Aaron and Aaron's sons: Nadab, Abihu, Eleazar, and Ithamar" (Ex. 28:1).

These men were set apart and trained to minister to the Lord and stand in the gap for the people. They were authorized to come near His presence. Their duties and parameters for worship were outlined by specific instructions passed on from God to Moses. Following their training they were consecrated, then God's presence filled the tabernacle, and their ministry began.

But for the two it was short-lived; even after the glory of the Lord had been revealed in the tabernacle. A little while later:

> Nadab and Abihu, the sons of Aaron, each took his censer and put fire in it, put incense on it, and offered *profane* fire before the LORD, which He had not commanded them. (Lev. 10:1, *author's emphasis*)

Notice Nadab and Abihu offered *profane* fire in the presence of the Lord. One definition of *profane* in *Webster's Dictionary* is: "Showing disrespect or contempt for sacred things; irreverent." It means to treat what God calls holy or sacred as if it were common. These two men grabbed the censers, set apart for the Lord's worship, and filled them with the fire and incense of their own choosing, not the offering prescribed by God. They were careless with what was holy and it led to their disobedience.

They approached the presence of the Lord bearing an irreverent, unacceptable offering by treating what was holy as common. Look what happens:

> So fire went out from the LORD and devoured them, and they died before the LORD. (Lev. 10:2)

These two men were instantly judged for their irreverence and met with immediate death. This irreverence took place in the very presence of God and though they were priests, they were not exempt from rendering God honor. They sinned by approaching a holy God as though He were common! They had become too familiar with His presence! Hear the words of Moses immediately following their judgment and note the words *near Me:*

And Moses said to Aaron, "This is what the LORD spoke, saying: 'By those who come *near Me* I must be regarded as holy; and before all the people I must be glorified.' " So Aaron held his peace. (Lev. 10:3, *author's emphasis*)

This is an eternal as well as universal decree. God says no one can *draw near* by holding Him in light esteem or regarding Him as common. He must be deemed holy and held in reverence by all in His presence.

The Lord had made it clear that irreverence could not survive in His presence, but Nadab and Abihu did not take heed. Today is no different; He is the same holy God. We cannot expect to be admitted into His presence with disrespectful attitudes!

There are no special exceptions because of family connections. These two priests were Moses' nephews as well as Aaron's sons. But both knew better than to question God's judgment, for He alone is just. In fact, Moses warned Aaron and the two surviving sons not to even mourn their judgment lest they die as well. This would have further dishonored the Lord, so the bodies of Nadab and Abihu were carried outside the camp and buried.

These two young men took lightly God's specific instructions. They came with irreverence and lacked the fear of God and these heart conditions produced disobedient actions. We see the root of sin is the lack of the fear of the Lord.

SCARED OF GOD VERSUS THE FEAR OF GOD

When God appeared to the children of Israel at Mount Sinai they could not stand in His presence. The reason: they lacked the fear of the Lord; for once they withdrew from His presence Moses addressed them:

Do not fear; for God has come to test you, and that His fear may be before you, so that you may not sin. (Ex. 20:20)

Moses said, "Do not fear" because God has come to see if His "fear is before you." It sounds like a contradiction, but it's not. Moses was differentiating between being afraid of God and the fear of the Lord. The difference is huge. The person who is scared or afraid of God has something to hide; he doesn't want to come near because the pure light of God's presence will expose what he hides. Paul tells us, "All things that are exposed are made manifest by the light" (Eph. 5:13).

God does not want us to be scared of Him, but to fear Him. Paul writes, "God has not given us a spirit of fear" (2 Tim. 1:7), and John writes, "There is no fear in love; but perfect love casts out fear, because fear involves torment. But he who fears has not been made perfect in love" (1 John 4:18). These men are addressing the spirit of fear, not the fear of God with these statements; for the New Testament writers also tell us to "work out your own salvation with fear and trembling" (Phil. 2:12); and again Paul tells us we are to "serve God acceptably with reverence and godly fear. For our God is a consuming fire" (Heb. 12:28–29). Peter is even more blunt as he writes, "It is written, 'Be holy, for I am holy.' And if you call on the Father, who without partiality judges according to each one's work, conduct yourselves throughout the time of your stay here in fear" (1 Peter 1:16–17). In reading these statements you certainly cannot rule out holy fear as being a vital part of New Testament Christianity.

Notice Moses says to the people when God's presence came: "that His fear may be before you, so that you may not sin." It is not the love of God, but the fear of the Lord that keeps us from sin. Paul says, "Work out your own salvation with fear and trembling" not "love and kindness." In another epistle he exhorts that since we have the promise of God's presence dwelling among us: "Let us cleanse ourselves from all filthiness of the flesh and spirit, perfecting holiness in the fear of God" (2 Cor. 7:1). Notice he didn't say "in the love of God."

I will never forget visiting a well-known minister who was in prison for fraud. I questioned, "When did you fall out of love with Jesus?"

He looked at me and said without hesitation, "I didn't!"

Puzzled I replied, "But what about the fraud and adultery?"

He said, "John, I loved God all the way through it, but I didn't fear Him." And then he said something that riveted me: "John, there are millions of American Christians just like me. They call Jesus their Savior and love Him, but they don't fear Him as their supreme Lord."

A light went on inside of me at that point. I realized we can love an image of "Jesus" we have created from our own imagination and under-standing, but it not be the real Jesus; for Scriptures tell us the fear of the Lord is the beginning or starting point for knowing God intimately (see Prov. 1:7; 2:5). I realized this man had loved a distorted image of Jesus.

"Oh, That They Would Fear Me"

Moses makes it very clear: it is the fear of the Lord that keeps us from sin, and sin separates us from intimacy with God. The Lord told His covenant people: "Your iniquities have separated you from your God; and your sins have hidden His face from you" (Isa. 59:2). Notice He said our sins have separated us from Him, not Him from us. He is talking to His own when He makes this statement, not the heathen. We are the ones who separate ourselves from intimacy with God, and the root is a lack of holy fear.

Unlike the man who is *scared* of God, the man who *fears* God has nothing to hide. He knows his life is an open book before the Lord. He puts God's desires above all else. It's weighed heavier than what friends, family, or even his soul wishes. He realizes there is nothing more fulfilling than to obey God. He denied himself, took up his cross, and is following Jesus. He lives for God.

This describes Moses' life. He feared God. Israel didn't; they esteemed their desires, needs, and comfort above what God desired. They didn't trust Him, though they repeatedly vocalized that they did. They constantly doubted though they confessed otherwise. They did not esteem His Word, desires, or commands above all else and because they did not fear Him, they could never truly love Him. Why? They never experienced a real revelation of Him. This is why they withdrew from His presence. There were issues to hide from the light of His presence. They knew at some level this light would force them to deal with these issues and choose who they would serve.

As Israel drew back, Moses drew near. He must now tell the Lord the very people He'd so powerfully and wonderfully delivered from bondage and brought to Himself didn't want to come any closer. Moses dreaded the moment, but God already knew, and surprised Moses by replying:

> I have heard the voice of the words of this people which they
> have spoken to you. They are right in all that they have spoken.
> (Deut. 5:28)

I can just picture the shock on Moses' face. Not only was he caught unaware of God's knowledge of their words (isn't it amazing how we forget He knows everything) but what a shocker to find out the children of Israel were finally right in what they said! Moses then blurted out something like, "Why can't they come near You?"

You can hear the sorrow in God's voice as He explains why the people cannot *draw near:*

> Oh, that they had such a heart in them that they would fear Me
> and always keep all My commandments. (Deut. 5:29)

With His response God made two things crystal clear. First, it is impossible to draw near to God if there is a lack of holy fear; and second, the evidence of this fear is obedience to His commandments. The children of Israel knew how to talk the talk and look the part, but their hearts were void of the fear of God. It always begins in our heart and manifests in our obedience!

The Lord then makes one of the most tragic statements in the Old Testament. He passes this message through Moses to His people:

> Go and say to them, "Return to your tents." (Deut. 5:30)

How God's heart must have broke, and how heavy was Moses' heart as he returned. Even now my heart feels the weight of it. God brought them out of Egypt for one reason—to bring them to Himself—and they missed it (see Ex. 19:4). This was His divine purpose in His great deliverance. Yet, when the opportunity arose to reveal Himself, they drew back; they could not stand in His presence, because they did not fear Him. They would return to their tents and remain apart from His presence and voice. He offered them intimacy, but they by their own choice couldn't have it.

Friendship with the Lord

On the other hand, hear the words God speaks to Moses after telling the people to return to their tents:

> But as for you, stand here by Me, and I will speak to you. (Deut. 5:31)

Wow! "Stand here by Me, and I will speak to you." What ecstasy! What absolute joy! What an unfathomable privilege! Moses is invited to remain and hear God's heart! There is nothing better in the entire universe! To be invited to remain in the presence of the One who is infinite in love, wisdom, knowledge, and power. To stand near the One all of heaven adores and longs for. Moses was given this invitation!

Moses had embraced the fear of the Lord and therefore could have intimate fellowship with Him. We see the evidence of this in the psalmist's words, "He made known His ways to Moses, His acts to the children of Israel" (Ps. 103:7). Moses often knew what God would do even before He did it, because the Lord would share His heart with Moses as he remained near in the very place the people could not come.

Israel knew God by His answers to their prayers. They did not know His motivation, wishes, plans, or any other deep thing of His heart. They knew what He did, but never why He did it. Moses knew Him by what was spoken in the secret place. One of my favorite Scriptures is:

The secret of the Lord is with those who fear Him,
And He will show them His covenant.
(Ps. 25:14)

Without changing the context we could say it like this: "The secrets of the Lord's heart are with those who fear Him, and He will show them His covenant ways." We all have secrets (not all are bad), but we don't share them with acquaintances, rather we entrust them to close friends, those we are intimate with and trust. There is good reason for this: we know they'll never use the precious things of our heart to hurt or take advantage of us. We know they will handle what is precious to us with care. We know they'll not misconstrue what we share, nor twist it for their gain. They know our heart and have our best interests in mind.

God is no different; He doesn't share His secrets with those who are overly concerned with their own pleasure and welfare. He shares His secrets with those who have His heart and have laid down their lives—those He calls friends. One translation confirms this by announcing, "Friendship with the Lord is reserved for those who fear him, with them he shares the secrets of his covenant" (Ps. 25:14 NLT).

ABRAHAM, THE FRIEND OF GOD

There is a man called the friend of God in the Old Testament—his name is Abraham. Why was he the friend of God? The answer is found in the greatest test he ever faced. He had waited twenty-five years for the promise of God: the son born to him and Sarah, his barren wife. Long after the season of normal childbearing had passed, God gave this son, and they named him Isaac, which means *laughter*. This young man brought to their home joy beyond what they imagined.

God watched this family closely as a tender love grew strong between Abraham and his dearly loved Isaac. The time came for a test and God asked Abraham to "Take now your son, your only son Isaac, *whom you love*, and go to the land of Moriah, and offer him there as a burnt offering" (Gen. 22:2, *author's emphasis*).

Can you imagine Abraham's shock at this request? This was the promised child; the very one he'd patiently waited twenty-five years for. Ishmael had already been driven out—he would be left with nothing! Why now when the bond of love was so strong? Why did God wait so long? Why didn't He ask for this when he was an infant? Many Bible scholars believe Isaac was thirty-three years old at the time.

Can you imagine that night? A fight must have raged in Abraham's soul. How could God ask this of him? Everything was going as planned. Isaac would one day marry, and his descendants would produce the nations and kings God had promised. How could God ask for his life so early? Can you hear the questions that warred against his soul: *Why did He ever give me Isaac in the first place? Why would He give him only to take him away? Does He love Isaac as I do? Why not take my life instead?*

Yet something in Abraham overrode all these questions and council: his fear of the Lord. God had spoken and he would obey. We read, "*Early the next morning* Abraham got up and saddled his donkey. He took with him two of his servants and his son Isaac. When he had cut enough wood for the burnt offering, he set out for the place God had told him about" (Gen. 22:3 NIV, *author's emphasis*). Notice the words, *Early the next morning.* Have you ever heard someone say, "God has been dealing with me about this for the past several months—I just haven't done it yet"? They just revealed a lack of the fear of the Lord.

To fear God is to tremble at His word. This means we obey even if we don't see the reason or benefit of it. It means we obey even when we don't understand. It is obedience even when it hurts! As messengers of the gospel we've done a great disservice to the body of Christ. Far too often we develop an approach to obedience only when benefit is realized. We say things like, "If you give, then God will . . . ," or "If you pray, then God will . . . ," or "If you obey, then God will . . . ." It is almost a "Come to Jesus in order to get" message. Do I believe He blesses? Absolutely! However, blessings should never be our motive for serving Him. We should serve based on who He is, not because of what He can do for us.

Abraham's obedience was immediate as he traveled three days to the mountain God showed him. Why didn't God choose a closer place? Why a three-day journey? I believe He gave Abraham time to think it over, even to turn back. It is one thing to initially move when you hear the voice of God, but what about the follow-through? How about three days later when you haven't heard anything from Him, and you are now staring at the mountain where you are to put to death the most important person and thing in your life?

Nevertheless, Abraham went to the top of the mountain, built an altar, bound Isaac, and lifted the knife. Then suddenly the Angel of the Lord calls out to Abraham:

> Do not lay your hand on the lad, or do anything to him; for now I know that you fear God, *since* you have not withheld your son, your only son, from Me. (Gen. 22:12, *author's emphasis*)

How did God know Abraham feared Him? Because he obeyed even when he didn't understand; even when it hurt; and even when it wasn't to his own benefit. God watched as Abraham placed the Lord's desires above everything else. God then knew, "This is a man I can reveal Myself to, and share My heart with."

A REVEALED FACET OF GOD

Immediately following this, Abraham lifted his eyes and saw a ram caught in the thicket, and out of his heart came the cry, "Jehovah Jireh!" (Which means, "the Lord who provides.") He was the first to ever know God as Jehovah Jireh. God revealed this facet of Himself that no man had ever known before in response to Abraham's reverence and obedience.

You may know me as "John Bevere the author." Some of you may know me as "John Bevere the speaker." But there is another, her name is Lisa, and she knows me as "John the husband." She is my intimate friend as well as wife and I share secrets with her no one else knows. There are sons who know me as "John the daddy." I interact with them in ways only a father and sons share. You have such people in your life as well. God is no different.

God shared with Abraham things no one else knew. The Lord even shared His plans with Abraham and allowed him to interject his opinions. They discussed it together. One such situation was Sodom and Gomorrah. God said, "Should I hide my plan from Abraham?" (Gen. 18:17 NLT). The Lord approached Abraham to discuss this situation and God valued and heeded his input. Sodom would now be spared if there were ten righteous men residing in it. Yet, there weren't even ten!

CLUELESS TO GOD'S PLAN

It is amazing that Abraham's nephew, Lot, whom the Bible calls "righteous" (see 2 Peter 2:7) was so different. Lot was fleshly and did not fear God. His story is completely different. He started with Abraham but whenever flesh dwells with spirit there will eventually be a conflict. Abraham being more interested in the things of God than what this world had to offer, presents Lot a choice. Abraham would take the leftovers, which unknown to both men would eventually be the most fruitful, for it would be the land flowing with milk and honey.

We read, "Lot took a long look at the fertile plains of the Jordan Valley" (Gen. 13:10 NLT). At the time it was the most desirable and fruitful land. Why a long look? He knew the cities of Sodom and Gomorrah were full of wickedness. This long look probably entailed trying to figure a way to enjoy their abundance without being caught up in their influence. He decided to pitch his tent on the plains of Sodom, rather than dwell within the city. This way he could maintain a distance from the epicenter of its wickedness, but still enjoy the abundance of the area. We read, "Lot moved his tents to a place near Sodom" (Gen. 13:12 NLT). However, no matter how well you plan to stay away from sin, if you don't fear God you'll eventually gravitate toward it. This was true of Lot; he started out in a tent on the plains, but six chapters later he had a house inside the gates of Sodom (see Gen. 19:2).

Sodom was thriving and prosperous. They had no idea they were only hours away from being wiped off the face of the earth. This should not surprise us. What is alarming though is that Lot was unaware as well. God sends angels to warn him, messengers of mercy. In contrast is Abraham, who fears God and knows His intimate council before it is even finalized, while Lot is just as clueless as the sinners of Sodom. Abraham is God's friend, because he feared Him!

THE REAL JESUS?

While examining the lives of Moses and Abraham in the light of the fear of the Lord we further expand the definition. The fear of the Lord encompasses the love of what God loves as well as to hate what He hates. What's important to Him becomes important to us, and what is not so important to Him is not so important to us. We make His priorities and desires, our own. The manifestation of the fear of the Lord is unwavering obedience to the desires and will of God.

According to Scripture, as we embrace the fear of the Lord, God draws closer. Once He is encountered intimately, the intensity of our love for Him grows. We love the revealed true and living God, not just a perception of Him. Without a deep and abiding fear of the Lord we merely profess a love without a true intimate knowledge of Him. We know about Him but do not know Him; therefore our affection is directed toward an image of "Jesus" formed within our imagination, rather than the actual One seated at the right hand of the Father.

It could be compared to the way fans look at Hollywood stars or great athletes. They love the image the media portrays of these superstars by way of interviews and newspaper articles. Their names become common in American households. I have heard fans speak as though these celebrities were close friends. I've seen their emotions caught up in celebrities' personal affairs as though they were family. But if they were to meet them in person they might find the real person very different from the marketed image. The relationship between celebrities and fans is one-way. If they met there would be little common ground, and even less to talk about, because they don't truly know each other.

I have seen this dynamic in the church as well. Many talk about the Lord as if He is very close, yet as you listen to their conversation you have the sense they speak of One they only know about—not know. They know the talk, but not the voice; the acts, but not His ways; what He said, but not what He is saying.

An extreme example of this happened last year. My family and I were vacationing in Hawaii. I was up early because of the time zone difference. On this morning I was praying on the beach, when a man approached me and started talking. He was so excited about the island, and almost immediately he blurted out, "The girls here are wonderful. They're so friendly and outgoing." He continued to chat about a party he had recently attended and other carnal topics; all along his conversation was punctuated with profanity.

He asked me what I did for a living and I told him. When he heard I was a minister, he got so excited and began to talk to me about the Lord. He shared his involvement in an outreach ministry his church had to bikers and then talked about his pastor. He shared how he'd come to know Jesus and even gave me a tract he had in his possession. Then he talked about his wife and children asleep in the hotel (my thoughts immediately returned to his excitement about the island girls). My heart broke as it was evident this man believed he knew the Lord, but his life showed otherwise. This is why Jesus says we will know believers by their fruit or lifestyles, not by their words or ministries (see Matt. 7:20–23).

This is only one of several examples I could cite. I am certain you have encountered ones just as dramatic. In all these cases the professing "Christians" knowledge of God is like the fan with the superstar. My heart breaks over this. Here are people who want salvation, yet love the world, and elevate their pleasures, schedules, and agendas above God's desires.

Then there are those who are really saved, but like Lot they are fleshly and entangled in the world's affairs. They want to serve God but they are enslaved by their appetites. They have not allowed the cross to slay their self-life as they resist God's purifying work. They do not passionately seek His will and the kingdom's advancement. Though saved, they lack intimacy with Him. They still live in the outer court; restricted by the veil of their own flesh they cannot draw near into the new and living way. They are close to His very presence, yet so far.

Those who live in the outer court have failed to realize why He delivered them from the world's oppression. They miss the high call of knowing God intimately. They love the messages that speak of God's love, blessings, protection, provision, and abundance—and all of these are true, but they shun what deals with issues of the heart. They have chosen things that cannot fulfill them, while passing by the fountain of Living Water abiding in their own heart.

We must make it known that God wants an intimate relationship with us and that He is holy and will not be mocked. He paid so great a price to bring us to Himself, how can we remain a friend of this world? James warns before his exhortation to draw near: "Do you not know that friendship with the world is enmity with God?" (James 4:4). He continues by saying if we seek worldly passions we make ourselves an enemy of God! Remember, he is speaking to believers. Paul also uses no uncertain terms: "For the grace of God that brings salvation has appeared to all men, teaching us that, denying ungodliness and worldly lusts, we should live soberly, righteously, and godly in the present age" (Titus 2:11–13). Again, this is why Paul tells us to work out our salvation with fear and trembling.

FRIENDS OF JESUS

Often we hear messages that proclaim all who receive Jesus are now His friends. Hopefully you now realize God is not a cheap, group friend. Once while in prayer He cried out, "Ask my people, if they want Me to be as faithful to them as they have been to Me?" Jesus did not come as Savior so everyone could join His "born-again club." He is looking for relationship with those who love Him as He has loved them; here we find His friendship. This is confirmed by His own words,

You are My friends if you do whatever I command you. (John 15:14)

There are parameters placed on friendship with Jesus. He did not say, "You are all My friends if you believe I am the Christ." Rather He said, "You are My friends if you do whatever I command you." We have discussed in this chapter that the power "to do whatever He commands" is found in the fear of the Lord.

Jesus made this statement after Judas left to betray Him. If we continue to the following verse we find Jesus addressing the eleven: "No longer do I call you servants" (John 15:15). The fact He said, "No longer" implies there was a time when He looked upon them as servants, but now there was a new level. After this statement, He continues,

For a servant does not know what his master is doing; but I have called you friends, for all things that I heard from My Father I have made known to you. (John 15:15)

Notice friends of the Master know what He is doing. They know His ways! Why are they now called friends and not at the beginning of their relationship? The answer is they proved their loyalty and obedience as they followed Him both through trials and difficult times as well as rejoiced with Him in the miraculous and the good. Their faithfulness was evidenced by their obedience.

His statement extends to all who call upon His name: "You are my friends if you do whatever I command you." Notice He made it plain: friendship is reserved for those who obey Him. This reflects what we saw in the book of Psalms: "Friendship with the Lord is reserved for those who fear him."

Why would God hold back friendship? I believe it is to protect us from the dangers of familiarity. Remember the sons of Aaron and the exhortation given to their father Aaron: "By those who come *near Me* I must be regarded as holy."

This happened again in the New Testament when a man and his wife entered the presence of a holy God with unhealthy familiarity. They died in His presence (see Acts 5:1–11). "Great fear" came upon the church as the body of believers came into the understanding of the seriousness of the lack of reverence. Again, "God is to be held in reverence by all those around Him."

Last year I discovered a wonderful secret. As I entered my times of prayer I'd refrain from words and just meditate on my Father's wonderful splendor and greatness. I would think of Jesus' magnificence and the glorious battle He won for me to be His own. I pondered on His awesome Spirit and the fact He chose to live with me. How overwhelming is all that!

I discovered by doing this, before even uttering a word of my own, the Lord's presence would meet me. Puzzled by how easy it was becoming to enter His presence I inquired of the Holy Spirit. He spoke to my heart, "Son, what did Jesus tell His disciples to do when He taught them to pray?" I recited the Lord's Prayer, "Our Father which art in Heaven, hallowed be Thy name." I was stunned; I cried out for joy, "That's it, that's it!" There it is, right from the onset, He is to be regarded as Holy: "Hallowed be Thy name." We are to come into His presence by way of holy reverence! How many years I recited this prayer, without realizing what Jesus was really saying!

THE KEY TO THE TREASURES OF LIFE

The fear of the Lord is the key to intimacy with God, and the foundation for life. Isaiah tells us:

> The LORD is exalted, for he dwells on high; he will fill Zion [the church] with justice and righteousness. He will be the sure foundation for your times, a rich store of salvation and wisdom and knowledge; the fear of the LORD is the key to this treasure. (Isa. 33:5–6 NIV)

Holy fear unlocks the treasury of salvation, wisdom, and knowledge. Why? Because it is the foundation for intimacy with God and in that place of intimacy His treasures are revealed. Alongside the love of God, it composes the very foundation of life. We cannot truly love God and enjoy intimacy with Him until we first fear Him.

STUDY QUESTIONS

1. In your own words, how would you describe what it means to fear God, versus being scared of God?

2. This chapter contrasts Abraham, "a friend of God," with his nephew Lot, who was called "righteous." As Lot surveyed the desirable lands toward the wicked cities of Sodom and Gomorrah, he obviously was trying to figure out a way to enjoy the cities' abundance without being caught up in their influence. Are you ever inclined to reason in the same way?

   How would proper fear of the Lord prevent such faulty reasoning?

3. Thinking back on the author's Hawaiian encounter with the man on the beach, have you ever had similar encounters? How did you deal with them?

   Whether they were as extreme as that incident or not, have there been times where you were the man on the beach—where your conversation or actions betrayed where your heart really was at the time? What have you learned, or are you currently learning, from those instances?

4. In light of Psalm 25:14 ("Friendship with the Lord is reserved for those who fear him"), the author points out that God holds back his friendship to protect us from the dangers of familiarity.

   What are the "dangers of familiarity"?

CHAPTER SEVEN

WHAT HINDERS TRUE INTIMACY?

✠

The deceived take comfort in a knowledge of a
God they simply do not possess.

The fear of the Lord is the foundation of intimacy with God. This is made clear in the beginning of the book of Proverbs. We read, "The fear of the LORD is the beginning [foundation] of knowledge" (Prov. 1:7). What kind of knowledge? The writer tells us a few verses later:

If you receive my words,
And treasure my commands within you,
So that you incline your ear to wisdom,
And apply your heart to understanding;

Yes, if you cry out for discernment,
And lift up your voice for understanding,
If you seek her as silver,
And search for her as for hidden treasures;
Then you will understand the fear of the LORD,
And find *the knowledge of God.*
(Prov. 2:1–5, *author's emphasis*)

The word *knowledge* is defined by the *Dictionary of Biblical Languages* as "information of a person, with a strong implication of relationship to that person." *Vines Expository Dictionary* tells us this word for *knowledge* implies, "to have an intimate experiential knowledge of Him (God)." He then goes on to say, "Positively 'to know' God is paralleled to fear Him."

You can see in the preceding Scripture that the fear of the Lord is to treasure His commands. To treasure His commands is to incline your ear to His word with all readiness to obey no matter what the circumstances. The converse of intimacy awaits those who lack this holy fear for James tells us we "deceive ourselves" (James 1:22) when we know His will, yet refrain from obeying it. Deception is a scary thing, for the deceived believe they are accurate, when in reality they are not. The deceived take comfort in a knowledge of God they simply do not possess.

A DISTORTED IMAGE OF THE LORD

Without the fear of the Lord we really don't know God. An incorrect image is developed, shaped, and molded within our own soul or imagination. Even though we profess a relationship with Him and honor Him with our lips, our heart is not near His and our life is out of sync with His desires. This is evident in the children of Israel.

As stated in earlier chapters, Moses brought them to meet with God at Sinai and yet, "the people stood afar off, but Moses drew near" (Ex. 20:21). How heartbreaking that they could not draw near to this awaiting glorious interlude. Who knows what would have happened? They had an opportunity to hear His words spoken by His very own voice! Yet, as already discussed they could not handle His presence because they did not have hearts that feared Him and therefore could not keep His commandments (Deut. 5:29).

Disappointed, God establishes a mediator between Himself and the people. He addresses Moses: "Come up, *you and Aaron* with you" (Ex. 19:24, *author's emphasis*). God called Moses and Aaron to Himself as mediators. They would hear His words for the people, and bring theirs to Him. It was a far cry from the original intimacy He'd planned.

Yet, as we continue to read through Exodus we discover Moses up on the mountain and Aaron back at the camp. It seems he began the ascent but eventually ended up back among the people. Why? He felt more comfortable in the presence of people than in the presence of God. He lacked the fear of the Lord. Aaron feared man more than God, and therefore, served them; he would eventually give the people what they wanted, and, as we are about to see, it wouldn't take long.

Moses is now on the mountain for almost forty days and we read:

> Now when the people saw that Moses delayed coming down from the mountain, the people gathered together to Aaron, and said to him, "Come, make us gods that shall go before us; for as for this Moses, the man who brought us up out of the land of Egypt, we do not know what has become of him." (Ex. 32:1–2)

Aaron had the gift of leadership that carries with it certain qualities, one of which is to draw people like a magnet. It will draw others whether the gifted leader has been with God or not. This explains how you can have a church of thousands void of God's presence where His desires are misrepresented. Too often the leader who lacks the fear of the Lord uses his God-given gifts to carry out the people's wishes, not the Lord's.

The people urged Aaron, "Come make us gods that shall go before us; for as for this Moses . . . we do not know what has become of Him." Notice they did not say, "As for God we do not know what has become of Him." They don't deny God, they merely disqualify Moses.

GOD OR GOD?

In my study of the original texts, I have to wonder if the translators drew back from what was really said here. They used the English word *gods*. However, the Hebrew word for *gods* is *elohiym*. This word is found 2,606 times in the Old Testament; roughly 2,350 of its occurrences (over 90 percent) refer to almighty God, whom we serve. It occurs 32 times in the first chapter of Genesis alone, and each one refers to the Lord. For example, the first verse of the Bible reads: "In the beginning God [*elohiym*] created the heavens and the earth" (Gen. 1:1). Here *elohiym* is translated "God."

Approximately 250 times in the Old Testament, this word is used to describe a false god. So we always have to read it in context to discern the correct reading.

Aaron said to the people, "Break off the golden earrings which are in the ears of your wives, your sons, and your daughters, and bring them to me" (Ex. 32:2). The people did, "And he received the gold from their hand, and he fashioned it with an engraving tool, and made a molded calf" (32:4).

Once he formed this gold into a mold of a calf with his tool, all the people said: "This is your god, O Israel, that brougth you out of the land of Egypt!: (Ex. 32:4)

The Hebrew word for *god* is again *elohiym*. The people are saying, "This is your *elohiym*, O Israel, who brought you out of the land of Egypt!" Are you beginning to see what's happening? Let's continue to read to know for sure what these people are saying.

> So when Aaron saw it, he built an altar before it. And Aaron
> made a proclamation and said, "Tomorrow is a feast to the
> LORD." (Ex. 32:5, *author's emphasis*)

The Hebrew word *Lord* in this verse is the word *Jehovah* or *Yahweh*. *Yahweh* is the most sacred word in the Old Testament. It is the proper name of the one true God. It is never used in the Old Testament to describe or to name a false god. The word was so sacred the Hebrew scribes wouldn't even write it all out. They would take out the vowels and just write YHWY. The Jewish scribes referred to it as the sacred tetragrammaton, the unspeakable four letters. This was the unmentionable name, the holy name guarded from profanity in the life of Israel.

So in essence what Aaron and the children of Israel did was mold a calf, point to it and say, "Behold Yahweh, the one true God, who brought us out of the land of Egypt!" They did not say, "Behold Baal, the one who brought us out of Egypt." Nor did they ascribe their deliverance to another false god. They called this calf the name of the Lord.

Worship Followed by Indulgence

They were not blatantly denying God, rather they reduced His glory to the level of the image of this formed calf. They were deceived in their knowledge of Him. They still acknowledged Yahweh as savior and deliverer from Egypt. They did not deny His healing power; they just changed the image of His person! Continuing on we discover:

> Then they rose early on the next day, offered burnt offerings, and brought peace offerings; and the people sat down to eat and drink, and rose up to play. (Ex. 32:6)

Notice they brought their offerings. Why bring offerings? To honor the One they professed to serve, Yahweh! After a presentation of offerings or worship, they played and indulged in their fleshly appetites. The NIV says they "got up to indulge in revelry."

Could this be happening today? Are there those who have been delivered from the world by His saving grace, who lack holy fear and call on the Jesus they've formed in their imagination? All the while they hold fast to their new-birth experience and receive and confess Him as Lord while they come to church, sing songs of deliverance and freedom, hear messages, give money, but go out and lie to get a sale, all the while testifying how God is blessing their business. Perhaps they gossip about their pastors and others, justifying it with, "Well it is the truth, and others know it"; commit fornication or other lewd acts, and then excuse it all by the fact that even though Jesus has saved them, they still live in a body and have needs! The list is almost endless.

Do they know Jesus? Ask them; they'll emphatically answer, Yes! Are they deceived? Do they confess the One who is now seated at the right hand of Majesty on High, or a Jesus they have created in their own image who will give them what they want? More important than all this: Do we see ourselves in any of this?

You'll discover when people lack the fear of the Lord, they may call on Him but they gravitate towards fleshly appetites and the flesh is enmity with God, for it is not subject to the will of God (see Rom. 8:5–7). They are disobedient to His desires even though they call on His name, profess knowing Him, and believe He approves of their behavior. Their lack of obedience stems from a heart that lacks holy fear; the root of all disobedience, and the misconnect is clothed in the deception of "knowing Jesus."

NOTHING HIDDEN

This is seen throughout the Bible. It didn't take long to show up after the fall and began with Adam's own son Cain. When Cain's parents sinned in the garden, out of ignorance they covered themselves with fig leaves—the fruit of the ground. God showed them His will which was the offering of an animal. He clothed them in tunics of the animal's skin, which I believe was a lamb.

Cain, however was not ignorant; he knew from his parents that God desired the sacrifice of an animal, not the fruit of the ground. Yet we read: "in the process of time it came to pass that Cain brought an offering of the fruit of the ground *to the LORD"* (Gen. 4:3, *author's emphasis*). He was obviously attempting to serve God, for it does not say that he brought an offering to a false god. He diligently worked to bring God his offering; yet was in obvious disobedience.

What is the root of his disobedience? Nothing other than a lack of the fear of the Lord. This is clearly seen when God questions him about the whereabouts of his slain brother; his reply is a defiant, "I do not know. Am I my brother's keeper?" (Gen. 4:9). You see again, just as with Israel and the calf, that in this lack of the fear of the Lord, God's image is reduced, and acceptable ways of serving Him are changed. Deceived, Cain now even thinks he can hide something from God, as he could with another human being. God's image has been reduced in Cain's eyes to the level of man. Paul gravely warns us that in the latter days we will see this pattern as well: "Although they knew God, they did not glorify Him as God . . . and changed the glory of the incorruptible God into an image made like corruptible man" (Rom. 1:21–23). Just as with Cain, the lack of godly fear gives them over to deception and they believe God does not notice their contrary ways.

Cain's response shows he has forgotten that nothing is hidden from God. God is not a man; He sees and knows all. When we lose the fear of the Lord we lessen our spiritual common sense, for even a blatant sinner knows God is aware of his rebellion. Those with a knowledge of God apart from His holy fear comfort themselves with, "The Lord doesn't see it!" (Ez. 9:9 NLT), or if He does see surely He understands. Even leaders are not exempt from this. God says, "Son of man, have you seen what the leaders of Israel are doing . . . they are saying, 'The LORD doesn't see us' " (Ez. 8:12).

Have we forgotten Jesus' urgent words to us to fear God? For He tells us, "There is nothing covered that will not be revealed, nor hidden that will not be known" (Luke 12:2). Yet when we lose the fear of God we reduce Him down to our level, and subconsciously think we can hide things from Him. If questioned about God's omnipresence and His omniscience, they without hesitation strongly agree. But deep within their person they've lost the awareness of His awesomeness; for if they still possessed it they would not seek to keep things secret. They hide things from godly people and are often successful, yet they forget, "The eyes of the LORD are in every place, keeping watch on the evil and the good" (Prov. 15:3).

BELIEVING YOU'RE IN OBEDIENCE
WHEN YOU'RE NOT

Yet this is not where it ends. The next step of deception leads to the belief you are in obedience when in reality you are not. This is portrayed with one of David's descendants, a king named Uzziah. When he was sixteen years old his father Amaziah died and Uzziah was made king of Judah in his place. When you're sixteen and made king, if you're smart you'll seek God, and Uzziah did. As a result he prospered greatly. For years he enjoyed abundance and success. Then we read, "So his fame spread far and wide, for he was marvelously helped till he became strong" (2 Chron. 26:15).

But when Uzziah was strong his heart was lifted up with pride. Pride and the fear of the Lord oppose each other. When a heart lacks holy fear, it cultivates pride. Read carefully what happened:

> But when he was strong his heart was lifted up, to his destruction, for he transgressed against the Lord his God by entering the temple of the Lord to burn incense on the altar of incense. So Azariah the priest went in after him, and with him were eighty priests of the Lord—valiant men. And they withstood King Uzziah, and said to him, "It is not for you, Uzziah, to burn incense to the Lord, but for the priests, the sons of Aaron, who are consecrated to burn incense. Get out of the sanctuary, for you have trespassed! You shall have no honor from the Lord God." Then Uzziah became furious; and he had a censer in his hand to burn incense. And while he was angry with the priests, leprosy broke out on his forehead, before the priests in the house of the Lord, beside the incense altar. (2 Chron. 26:16–19)

Now the question we must ask is: When Uzziah's heart was lifted up with pride, did he become more or less spiritual? When asking this question of audiences, most answer that he became less spiritual. Yet this is not true for he entered the temple to *worship*. He actually became more spiritual (religious) in his actions. Very often you will find hyper-spiritual behavior and pride running hand-in-hand together; the one covers the other. Pride keeps a person from admitting they are religious, and religion covers up the pride with its spiritual mannerisms. Both are a lack of the fear of the Lord and true humility!

Notice Uzziah became furious when confronted with truth. This is exactly what happened with Cain, when confronted with truth. The Scriptures tell us, "Cain was very angry, and his countenance fell" (Gen. 4:5). Cain was angry with God! Whenever you use truth to confront a person who is living in disobedience, due to a lack of holy fear, they'll become angry. Why? They really believe they're right! They're deceived, and to be deceived is to believe you're right when you're wrong.

Why else would Uzziah become furious with the priests if he didn't believe he was right? He entered the temple to worship, but like the sons of Aaron, had neglected to honor the Lord's statutes and reduced His image. He was totally out of sync in his disobedience; in seeking intimacy with God, and he certainly appeared to be doing so, he was in reality further distanced from the One he sought to worship.

Does this answer why there are so many in the church who profess intimacy with God yet are out of sync with His desires? Without an understanding of these principles we've discussed, you could be baffled when you observe people sharing what God has revealed to them that contradicts the truth of Scripture. How could they come out of a time of prayer criticizing leaders, whom God told them to honor? If you venture to repeat what the Scriptures say, they become angry. They think you're out of tune and unspiritual, when in reality, they're the ones opposing His ways.

As a leader, numerous times I've had the opportunity to speak with people who've shared what they believe God has revealed and my spirit is troubled. Even though they are convinced they've heard from God they shun any words I might share from the Scriptures. They don't do this with me alone—they do this with all who try to help them. They use other Scriptures out of context to justify what they say and are not open to further discussion. Afterward they avoid me and isolate themselves from all who try to help them, as we are no longer spiritual in their eyes. As time progresses the fruit of their ways prove contrary to God's will, or what they anticipated does not happen. Could it be they heard the voice of their own imaginings and not Jesus at all? Did they seek intimacy only to find deception?

APPROACHING GOD WITH AN IDOLATROUS HEART

There is a way to keep from this terrible deception, and it is again found in the fear of the Lord. When we fear God we should come to Him with a neutral heart, ready to hear His words of instruction or correction. We don't lean to our own understanding or selfish desires, but passionately desire His will.

Approaching the Lord with strong desires that are not in line with His will, when He has made it known to us, can prove to be a most unwise and dangerous thing; for this can lead us to the next level of deception, one that is most sobering. This level of deception is when God Himself will actually give, or allow us to have, what we want:

> And the word of the LORD came to me, saying, "Son of man, these men have set up their idols in their hearts, and put before them that which causes them to stumble into iniquity. Should I let Myself be inquired of at all by them? (Ezek. 14:2–3)

The Lord was grieved that His people came before Him to ask for direction, counsel, or wisdom, with idols hidden in their hearts. It is not clear whether they were fully aware of this; however, it appears the truth was shielded from their eyes. These idols caused them to stumble into iniquity. This Hebrew word for *iniquity* is *awon* and it signifies an offense, whether intentional or not, against God's will.

Notice God did not say they'd set up idols in their yards, living rooms, or bedrooms. This idolatry was in their hearts. Remember, idolatry is not limited to calling on a foreign god's name. As previously stated, a form of idolatry is the reduction of God to a lower image; one who will give us what we passionately desire. You'll find the root of all idolatry is covetousness. The New Testament affirms this:

> Therefore put to death your members which are on the earth: fornication, uncleanness, passion, evil desire, and *covetousness, which is idolatry.* (Col. 3:5–6, *author's emphasis*)

In Ephesians 5:5, Paul again says a covetous man is an idolater. It is clear that idolatry is defined as covetousness; so let's define *covetousness. Webster's* defines it as a "strong desire of obtaining and possessing some supposed good." In prayer I asked the Lord for His definition. His response was, "Covetousness is the desire for gain."

This does not limit covetousness to the desire for money. This encompasses possessions, position, comfort, acceptance, pleasure, power, sexual lust, and so on. Covetousness is the state we find ourselves in when we're not content. We strive because we lack peace or rest with what God has given us. We knowingly or unknowingly resist His plan or process in our own life. For this reason we are told, "Let your conduct be without covetousness; be content with such things as you have. For He Himself has said, 'I will never leave you nor forsake you' " (Heb. 13:5). When we live in the assurance, "In Your [the Lord's] presence is fullness of joy; at Your right hand are pleasures forevermore" (Ps. 16:11), we will not seek fulfillment outside of His presence or plan for us.

Covetousness dwells amid unrest and is fueled by ceaseless desire. This perfectly describes the children of Israel as they came out of Egypt. They continually grasped for what they thought was best for them, even when God made His will known. They did not like the process God had chosen to prepare them to take the promised land, and complained about the conditions, water, food, and so forth. They lacked holy fear, and their hearts were ripe for the cultivation of covetousness. When God manifested Himself they ran for cover longing to hide the truth that their secret desires for pleasure and gain overrode their desire for God Himself.

Once the Lord and Moses withdrew together, the people were able to form God into an image of one that would give them their covetous desires. Interestingly enough it all revolved around the gold. This love for money was evidenced by their lack of godly contentment in His will. They were now operating in the thick fog of deception.

(As a side note, covetousness is the root of other forms of idolatry as well. All mankind is created with an innate desire to worship God. Yet many do not want to submit to the true Creator. So they set up a false god, but who is at the root of this false god? The answer is the one who created it—man. Now man worships this false god who ultimately gives him what he desires. Again, the root is covetousness.)

Bottom line, no matter what form they take, all idols are a source. They take the place only God deserves. An idol can serve as your source of happiness, comfort, peace, provision, and so forth. God says, "You shall not make idols for yourselves" (Lev. 26:1). We are the ones who make it an idol. An idol is anything we put before God in our lives. It is what we love, like, trust, desire, or give our attention to more than the Lord. An idol is what you draw your strength from or give your strength to. A believer is drawn into idolatry when he allows his heart to be stirred with discontentment and looks for satisfaction outside of God's will for his life. Again the bottom line is covetousness.

ANSWERED ACCORDING TO COVETOUSNESS

Returning to God's words to Ezekiel, He lamented the fact His own people came for assistance with idols in their heart. They wanted God to give them what they selfishly desired, rather than seek His will. It is not altogether different with teenagers who expect their parents to agree with their ideas, rather than seek the wisdom of their parents, failing to realize that their parents are wiser and only want the best for them.

God's response to Ezekiel is both alarming and sobering. In no uncertain terms He tells Ezekiel that when His own come to Him with covetous hearts: "I the LORD will answer him who comes, according to the multitude of his idols" (Ezek. 14:4). The New American Standard Bible says it this way: "I the Lord will be brought to give Him an answer in the matter in view of the multitude of his idols." It could be read this way: "I the Lord will be brought to give Him an answer in the matter according to his covetous desires."

A STRAYING OF A MAN OF GOD

This is evident in the life of Balaam. He was a great prophet of Jehovah, not a false god, but of the very Lord we serve. His prophetic ministry was so powerful it reached the ears of kings. One king in particular was Balak, king of Moab and Midian.

The people of Moab and Midian were terrified because Israel had just leveled the most powerful nation in the world, Egypt, and now they camped on the plains of Moab. The people reasoned that if Egypt could be destroyed so readily, they would have no trouble doing the same to them. The fear was rampant and reached even to the palace.

The king had a plan. He understood that whomever this great prophet, Balaam, blessed would be blessed, and whomever he cursed, would be cursed. He sent noblemen with a huge offering to Balaam and beseeched him to return with them so he could stand beside the king and curse Israel from the high places of Moab.

Balaam was intrigued: "Lodge here tonight, and I will bring back word to you, as the LORD speaks to me" (Num. 22:8). His response sounds similar to that of most believers today: "Let me pray about this matter and hear what the Lord says."

The Lord comes to Balaam and demands, "Who are these men with you?" In other words, "Why do you even need to pray about this? These men do not have a covenant with Me, but they are asking you to curse My covenant people! Why do you even need to ask?"

There is a message to all of us in this: there are some things we don't have to pray about! We should already know God's desire before we even ask. It displeases me when my teenage sons approach me and ask for something they already know I'll say "no" to. "Why do they even ask?" I mutter to myself after giving them the answer they knew deep down they would hear. They do this because my word is still law, or restrictive, to them in that area of life, rather than their delight.

Returning to Balaam, I imagine the reward offered was huge and the position of honor would be great among the people of Moab and Midian. Did Balaam's desire for money and honor veil his eyes from perceiving sound wisdom?

God, who is merciful, probably thought, *Ok, Balaam, since you didn't get the clue, or really didn't want to, I'll make My will very plain.* So He utters, "You shall not go with them; you shall not curse the people, for they are blessed" (v. 12). Now is this clear? I often find that when God speaks it is precise and clear; we are the ones who muddy and complicate it.

Balaam obeys and the following morning sends the emissaries away with, " 'Go back to your land, for the LORD has *refused* to give me permission to go with you' " (v. 13, *author's emphasis*). Even though he obeys, there is reluctance that can be heard in his choice of words, especially the word *refused*. Picture this: a teenage daughter is invited to the dance by a young man who is really popular but has a bad reputation. She is thrilled to be invited by one so popular and enthusiastically asks her father for permission to go. Out of love and concern for his daughter her father gently denies her request. She's crushed and tells the young man, "I can't go, my parents won't let me." She is really saying: my parents said "no," but I would say "yes." It's her parents who have refused to give her permission. She desires to go, but the word of her parents alone restricts her from her coveted desire. Unfortunately, if she does not receive the heart of her parents, she will eventually find a way to get together with this young man, and more often than not face awful consequences.

Balaam was a prophet with an unhealthy desire for money. Covetousness burned within him. He yearned for the nicer things of life as well as greater social influence. He obeyed, but it was not without reluctance. God's word brought restriction, rather than delight, because it kept him from what he really wanted.

DRAWN AWAY BY OUR OWN DESIRE

The elders of Moab and Midian returned to King Balak and reported, "Balaam refuses to come with us." Yet this didn't deter the king; he immediately sends men of greater position and honor with more money Balaam's way.

Why does Balak do this? I believe demonic forces urged him. Why do I say this? The Bible explains, "But each one is tempted when he is drawn away by his *own desires* and *enticed*" (James 1:14, *author's emphasis*). Notice two things. First, the words *own desires*. Any strong desire we have contrary to God's will is covetousness, which is idolatry. Secondly, notice *enticed;* this is the enemy's part—he entices. But hear this: you can't be enticed by something you don't desire. If you were to offer the drug ecstasy to most people in the church they wouldn't hesitate before refusing you. Why? They have no desire for it. You can't be enticed by something you don't desire. However, you can be enticed by the desires you have not put under the cross! We are enticed by things we covet; or should I say *desire intensely.*

The enemy knew this prophet loved money and recognition and urges this ungodly king to send more of both. These representatives have the power to offer anything Balak possesses by saying, "I will do whatever you say to me." Wow, what an offer! It's one thing to be offered anything your neighbor has, he may or may not have a lot, but it is quite another thing for a king to offer you anything he has—

especially if your weakness is in the areas of the king's strength. Yet, listen to Balaam's response:

> Though Balak were to give me his house full of silver and gold,
> I *could not* go beyond the word of the LORD my God, to do less
> or more. (Num. 22:18, *author's emphasis*)

Most would be inspired by Balaam's obedience. Yet hear again his choice of words, *could not*. Again he is being restricted by the word of the Lord from what he truly desires. Balaam knows what most people who walk through the doors of churches know. *You cannot willfully disobey the word of the Lord and still be blessed.* He also knows what perhaps half of those who attend church know: judgment awaits the willfully disobedient. Yet, sometimes this is just enough information to lead you to trouble, because if you can't get it one way in the will of God, you'll continue to search to find a way to get what you want within the parameters of the "will of God." In explanation, examine Balaam's next statement:

> Now therefore, please, you also stay here tonight, that I may
> know what more the LORD will say to me. (Num. 22:19)

Do you hear this? " . . . what more the Lord will say." Does he think more money is going to change God's mind? Does he think the first time the Lord said "Do not go with them," it was because God wanted him to hold out for a better offer?

Why does he need to pray about this again? Do you see he is still trying to find a way to get what he wants? His passionate desire is overriding any sense of reason. It is no different than the teenage daughter who pesters her father until she gets to go out with the popular boy. Balaam is stubborn, and unwilling to fulfill God's desire with joy because it rages against his covetous heart. Or should I say heart of idolatry? Scripture affirms this with, "Stubbornness is as idolatry" (1 Sam. 15:23 ASV). Hear God's response to Balaam:

And God came to Balaam at night and said to him, "If the men come to call you, rise and go with them; but only the word which I speak to you—that you shall do." (Num. 22:20)

The men were going to call him the next morning because they stayed with Balaam and hoped he'd return with them. So in essence God is saying, "When the men come to call you, go with them, but only the word which I speak to you—that you shall do." Wow, maybe we were wrong in our assessment. Notice it doesn't say, "Now the devil came to Balaam at night and said, 'Rise and go with them,' " nor does it say, "Now a deceiving spirit came to Balaam that night and said . . ." I was joking earlier, but in light of this, it could look like God had him hold out for more money, because now He is the One saying "go."

GETTING WHAT WE WANT

Balaam now has the word of the Lord to go. He rises early the next morning to do what he was instructed by the Lord the night before to do, and watch what happens:

So Balaam rose in the morning, saddled his donkey, and went with the princes of Moab. Then *God's anger was aroused because he went.* (Num. 22:21–22, *author's emphasis*)

Wait a minute! Now the Lord is angry because Balaam is simply doing what God told him to do the night before! We know God is not schizophrenic, so how do we explain this? The answer is found in God's words to Ezekiel. Recall the Lord says when His own come to Him with covetousness in their hearts, "I the Lord will be brought to give Him an answer in the matter according to his covetous desires."

This is what many in the church do not know or understand. If we really want something, if we continue to covet when God has already revealed His desire, quite possibly He will give it to us even when it is against His will, and even if He knows we will later be judged!

At this point you may be shocked; but consider Israel, they wanted a king. Samuel approached the Lord with their request and God let them know His desire was for them not to have a king. He told Samuel the king would take their best sons, daughters, lands, vineyards, and groves, as well as tax them.

Samuel brought this word of the Lord to the people; read their response: "Nevertheless the people refused to obey the voice of *Samuel.*" Notice the Bible does not say they refused the voice of the Lord. Again just like with Moses, they disqualified the messenger by maintaining *their own image of the Lord* so they could have what they wanted. God comforted Samuel in private. "They have not rejected you, but they have rejected Me" (see 1 Sam. 8).

In response God gave them their kings. He even picked them out, with the first being Saul. Just as predicted the kings took their best lands, sons, and daughters and levied taxes. Then these kings eventually led them into Babylonian captivity. God gave them what they earnestly desired!

Consider Israel in the wilderness. They ate the finest food man has ever eaten, manna. Elijah ate just two cakes of it and ran forty days and nights! That is power-packed food!

Yet Israel tired of it and whined for meat. They requested meat from the Lord and we read that God "gave them their request" (Ps. 106:15). Again, they were given their covetous desires. In fact, He miraculously provided it to them:

> He caused an east wind to blow in the heavens;
> And by His power He brought in the south wind.
> He also rained meat on them like the dust,
> Feathered fowl like the sand of the seas;
> And He let them fall in the midst of their camp,
> All around their dwellings.
> (Ps. 78:26–28)

They made a request, God gave it to them by way of the miraculous ("by His power"); He brought into the desert quail enough to feed three million people! Wow, what an amazing miracle, because quail don't live in the desert! Not only this, but they did not have guns or dogs! What a great miracle! Yet, watch what happens:

> So they ate and were well filled,
> For He gave them *their own desire*.
> They were not deprived of their craving;
> But while their food was still in their mouths,
> The wrath of God came against them,
> And slew the stoutest of them,
> And struck down the choice men of Israel.
> (Ps. 78:29–31, *author's emphasis*)

He miraculously grants their desire, but before they were finished His judgment came upon them. He answered them according to the passionate desire of their hearts.

Consider this: a young man is dating a young lady. His parents are troubled, "Son, we are not comfortable with this relationship. We want you to stop seeing her." His youth pastor affirms this, "I want to echo the words of your parents. When I pray about this I'm very uncomfortable. You really should stop seeing this girl." But the young man eventually counters with, "I've prayed and prayed and God told me I could marry her." They marry, and later he wonders why their problems are overwhelming.

Consider this: a man tells his wife he is praying for a particular job position. The wife shares, "I'm uncomfortable with this position. If you get it you'll travel over two hundred days a year. You won't be able to attend church but maybe once a month, and you'll miss the messages God places in the heart of our pastor, not to mention the worship, and any position of serving any longer . . ." The pastor shares similar concerns, but the husband is determined and prays until he gets the promotion. A year later he wonders how he has ended up in a hotel room with a strange woman and is distant from his family.

The list is almost endless. What we must realize is that when we covet something contrary to God's will for us, God will often give it to us; His answer is according to the idols resident in our heart. Ultimately He does this to recapture our hearts.

> I the LORD will answer him who comes, according to the multitude of his idols, that I may seize the house of Israel by their heart, because they are all estranged from Me by their idols. (Ezek. 14:4–5)

The NIV says it like this: "I will do this to recapture the hearts of the people of Israel." The Lord desperately desires to draw us back to His heart. Remember, we are His pursuit, He yearns for us. Though His desire is that none would stray, He will not be mocked. His heart is reserved for those who have given theirs completely. For this reason He seeks to recapture our hearts from any snare of covetousness, which is idolatry, lurking in it.

When the prodigal son asked his father for the inheritance he came as a son, not a stranger or servant but as one of his own family. It is obvious this son did not have the heart of his father, but his own self-seeking motives drove him. The father did not deny his request, even though he knew his son would handle it incorrectly. He still gave him the very large sum of money, and the son ultimately suffered greatly, just as the father knew he would. The good news is the son eventually came to himself and returned to the father. In this reunion he came to know his father's heart like never before.

God ultimately hopes to recapture each and every child who has strayed because of a lack of holy fear. Sadly, just as with Balaam, some never make the adjustment and come to know the Lord's heart; if you read the rest of the account of Balaam he continued in his covetous pursuits and was eventually judged by the sword.

This comparison is brought forward to the New Testament when those who presently lack holy fear are categorized with the children of Israel, Cain, and Balaam (all of whom I've discussed in this chapter). We read this warning:

> I must remind you—and you know it well—that even though the Lord rescued the whole nation of Israel from Egypt, he later destroyed every one of those who did not remain faithful. (Jude 5 NLT)

Jude then describes New Testament believers who profess the grace of God, yet slip back to live a life of covetousness, lust, and disobedience:

> Woe to them! For they have gone in the way of Cain, have run greedily in the error of Balaam for profit, and perished in the rebellion of Korah. These are spots in your love feasts, while they feast with you without fear, serving only themselves. (Jude 11–12)

Notice they are spots in our love feasts, which today could refer to our church services. We must never forget Jesus is coming for a bride (His intimate lover) who has kept herself unspotted from the world's lusts. But Jude says these professing believers "feast with you without fear, serving only themselves." They desire the blessings, and even closeness to the Lord, yet lack the fear of God. They are deceived and their deception will only continue to grow if they do not return to the heart of God with holy fear and love.

WARN AS WELL AS TEACH

Let me turn this around. The writer of Hebrews says, "But we are not like those who turn their backs on God and seal their fate" (Heb. 10:39 NLT). I am convinced the reason you now read this book and are willing to probe your heart, is because you not only desire to walk intimately with God, but desire with all your heart to please Him in deed and truth, not just in intent and word alone. For this reason we are told:

> Therefore, my beloved, as you have always obeyed, not as in my presence only, but now much more in my absence, work out your own salvation with *fear and trembling*; for it is God who works in you both to will and to do for His good pleasure. (Phil. 2:12–13, *author's emphasis*)

Those who walk in holy fear will obey when they sense God's presence as well as when they don't. They are steadfast, even when it looks as though God has abandoned them, which He never will! The Lord is drawn to those who walk in holy fear and empowers them to not only will, but to do His good pleasure. He didn't admonish us to work out our salvation with love and joy, but with fear and trembling. Again, the fear of the Lord is crucial and produces unconditional obedience in our hearts as well as actions.

What I've written in this chapter is sobering, yet Paul tells us that in order to present every believer perfect in Christ we must warn as well as teach (Col. 1:28). Warnings at first glance might not appear positive, yet in the end they are life-saving and produce fruit when heeded. I enjoy hearing happy and optimistic words, but I also realize many will look at ministers on Judgment Day and cry out, "Why didn't you warn me?" These preachers will tremble if they propagated seeker-sensitive or friendly messages, only to be left with bloodstained hands.

I made this comment once in a service and afterward a pastor came up to me irate. He said, "How dare you say someone's blood could be on our hands. That is Old Testament stuff, not grace." I opened my Bible and pointed him to the words of Paul:

> Therefore I testify to you this day that I am innocent of the blood of all men. For I have not shunned to declare to you the whole counsel of God. Therefore take heed to yourselves and to all the flock, among which the Holy Spirit has made you overseers. (Acts 20:26–28)

I will never forget the look of shock his face as he read those words. He'd been in the ministry for years and read these verses repeatedly, yet he saw it for the first time that day. He soberly apologized and we chatted a few minutes longer on the importance of not falling into the trap of being one-sided in our preaching—always emphasizing the positive, or even the negative. We must be balanced and "warn" as well as "instruct."

This is the time period in which Jesus warned that many, including the elect, could be deceived; He said deception would run rampant. We must take heed where we stand, lest we fall. We must draw near with a heart of holy fear, rather than a careless heart easily subject to deception. Our loving Father is for us, and has given to us all things that pertain to life and godliness. He has given us grace, through our Lord Jesus, to live obediently to His will, and it is only through this holy fear that we may have true intimacy!

STUDY QUESTIONS

1. The assertion is made that "without the fear of the Lord . . . an incorrect image is developed, shaped, and molded within our own soul or imagination." As you look back at your faith thus far, was there a time when your image of God was incorrect? If so, in what way was it distorted?

2. The author points out that when we covet something contrary to God's will for us, God will often give it to us. Looking honestly at your own prayer life, is there something you are continually approaching God about which might actually be a covetous desire? Is there an instance in your life when you received something you passionately desired, only to regret it afterwards?

3. In the first question at the end of the first chapter, you were asked what had initiated your desire to read this book. As you consider what you have gained thus far, how have you been challenged? What changes are you beginning to see in your image of God and what it means to please Him in deed and in truth?

CHAPTER EIGHT

TRUE WORSHIP

✠

"A religious spirit is one who uses
My Word to execute his own will."

Deception awaits those who lack the fear of the Lord, while intimacy awaits those who draw near in holy fear. The outward evidence of this is unconditional obedience to the desires of God; not only do we obey, but we have the heart to fulfill His will. We see this repeatedly in the lives of those who walked with God.

Enoch's testimony was that he pleased the Lord. We will draw from the writings of Clement, an early church father, for greater insight. Clement of Rome, who lived in the first century and was a companion to the apostles Peter and Paul, wrote, "Let us take for instance Enoch, who being found *righteous in obedience* was translated, and death was never known to happen to him." The earmark of God's pleasure with Enoch was his obedience.

The next man in Scripture who walked with God in intimate fellowship was Noah. The New Living Translation gives us insight into his life as it records:

> This is the history of Noah and his family. Noah was a righteous man, the only blameless man living on earth at the time. He *consistently followed God's will* and enjoyed a close relationship with him. (Gen. 6:9 NLT, *author's emphasis*)

Just as with Enoch, the earmark of Noah's life was that he consistently followed God's will. In other words, he was obedient to God's desires. They are the antithesis of Balaam who only obeyed out of personal concern for himself. He understood one cannot be blessed and eventually will be judged for blatant disobedience. Balaam perverted God's word in that he sought his own benefit in obedience, rather than obey out of a passion to fulfill all the will of God. The Lord's will was not his ultimate desire, but instead a law.

This was not at all the case with David. Scripture records of his life:

> He [God] raised up for them David as king, to whom also He gave testimony and said, "I have found David the son of Jesse, a man after My own heart, who will do all My will." (Acts 13:22)

The fear of the Lord is when we not only obey, but fulfill all His will. We seek to carry out His wishes as if they were our own. We take His heart's desires on as our own. This is true obedience.

A RELIGIOUS SPIRIT

I will never forget while worshiping the Lord, He gently spoke to my heart, "John, do you know what a religious spirit is?"

Now I've learned that when God asks us a question He is not looking for information; rather He only asks because we don't know, or to expand on the limited revelation we do have. I had written and spoken on what a religious person's behavior is, but my response to His question was, "Lord, I obviously don't know. What is a religious spirit?"

He then spoke to my heart, "A religious spirit is one who uses My Word to execute his own will." His words echoed deeply in my heart for days as many questions continued to be answered.

This is exactly what Balaam did. He sought to obey, yet for his own self-seeking benefit; rather than seeking to carry out the heart desire of God. For this reason the angel of the Lord said to him, "Your way is *perverse* before Me" (Num. 22:32, *author's emphasis*). *Webster's* defines the word *perverse* as "distorted." So it could be defined as distorting or twisting the intention of God's Word, and using it to our own advantage.

TRUE WORSHIP

If you examine the lives of Abraham, Moses, Joshua, David, Esther, Daniel, and others in the Scriptures who walked closely with the Lord you will find this common denominator in all their lives. In the very core of their intimacy with God was genuine heartfelt obedience to His desires. God's cry to every person He had covenant relationship with in the Old Testament was:

> For I earnestly exhorted your fathers in the day I brought them up out of the land of Egypt, until this day, rising early and exhorting, saying, *"Obey My voice."* (Jer. 11:7, *author's emphasis*)

The Lord lamented that His people did not obey, but followed the dictates of their own hearts. They did not take on His heart; rather they were restrained by what He spoke. Consequently they would seek avenues to fulfill their own desires to the level of their own self-imagined boundaries which God would tolerate, and therefore could have no intimate fellowship with Him. Integral obedience is absolutely vital to intimacy. In the New Testament Jesus tells us:

But the hour is coming, and now is, when the true worshipers will worship the Father in spirit and truth; for the Father is *seeking* such to worship Him. God is Spirit, and those who worship Him must worship in spirit and truth." (John 4:23–24, *author's emphasis*)

There is so much within these few statements. First, notice the Father is *seeking* such to worship Him. Recall an earlier chapter when we discussed how passionately He desires us and is pursuing our fellowship. Again, this is brought out by Jesus' statement.

Secondly, He is looking for those who will worship Him in spirit and truth. Let's discuss worship. I will never forget the time when I was reading my Bible and the Holy Spirit shouted on the inside of my heart, "Worship is not a slow song!" My attention was immediately arrested.

So many see worship as just that: a slow song. Consider the order of a typical evangelical service: we come into our meetings and we begin with praise, followed by worship, then announcements, offering, the message, and finally altar ministry. Traditional churches have printed bulletins, while we evangelicals have merely memorized ours, yet we boast of being Spirit-led or free. As for worship, for the few who don't know the difference between praise and worship, praise is the fast songs and worship is the slow ones. It's rather humorous; we were delivered from the hymnals only to be bound to the large screen projectors. So when you say the word *worship,* to most believers the first thing that comes to mind is slow songs on a CD, music video, or in a service.

When the Lord spoke this to me I immediately pushed back my Bible and said, "Lord, I don't know what worship is. Please tell me exactly what it is."

He then said firmly, "It is a life!"

Immediately He gave me an example. He said, "Son, consider this: you get up in the morning and Lisa needs help getting the kids ready for school, but you say that you're too busy. A little later in the morning she needs help and your reply is the same. Then she asks if you can assist her with preparing lunch, but again you reply you're too busy.

That afternoon she asks if you can pick up the kids at school only to get the same response from you again. Again she seeks your assistance to help with dinner and cleaning up afterward; and again only to get the same response of being too busy."

He continued, "That evening after the kids have been put to bed you now want something from her, specifically sex. So you approach her with tender words such as, 'Honey, I love you so much.' "

He then asked me, "What will be her response to your words of love and seeking sexual intimacy?"

I responded, "She would probably say, 'Hit the road Jack!' "

He then said, "You're right, and why would she say that to you?"

I responded, "Because intimate lovemaking begins in the morning and merely climaxes with sexual union in the evening."

In pondering what He spoke I realized that if I did this with my wife my confession of love for her would only be in word, not in deed and truth. A husband who continuously behaves this way with his wife is self-deceived.

The Lord then said to me, "Son, I have many children whose attention I seek all throughout the week, but they ignore Me. I try to get them to minister to the person who lives next door, but they don't listen, or they suppress My leading because they are busy, or want to enjoy their planned pleasure. They will not listen to Me when I ask them to give an offering; or serve in their church, or their community; or minister to their family members, and so forth. Then they come into a service and want something from Me, namely *blessings*, and they begin to sing soft songs with lyrics of their love for Me and they call that worship. That is not worship, it is a slow song!"

I was stunned. I realized my concept of worship was warped. Later I discovered something amazing which I had never noticed before. Allow me to ask you the reader a question: Where do you find the first occurrence of the word *worship* in the Bible? This question is significant, because I've learned that in writing a book whenever you introduce a new term, one which is not familiar to most, you need to do one of three things: give a definition, or offer an example which illustrates what it means, or use the word in such a way that demonstrates its meaning. The first time you find *worship* in Scriptures is in Genesis 22. It reads:

> Abraham said to his young men, "Stay here with the donkey; the lad and I will go yonder and *worship*." (Gen. 22:5, *author's emphasis*)

Abraham was not going up yonder to sing a slow song with Isaac. He was going up there to put the most treasured possession in his life to death, simply because God asked him to do it! So as you can see worship is *a life of obedience*. This explains why God passionately says to His own people who were singing songs to Him:

> Away with your hymns of praise! They are only noise to my ears.
> I will not listen to your music, no matter how lovely it is. Instead,
> I want to see a mighty flood of justice, a river of righteous living
> that will never run dry. (Amos 5:23–24 NLT)

I have been in so many services where the music has been progressive and beautiful, but there was no manifest presence of the Lord. In those situations I usually first search my heart with diligence asking the Holy Spirit, "Have I offended you or sinned?" Most often there is a reassurance deep within my heart that I haven't, so I know the hindrance lies with the people. I will then preach with confidence on the fear of the Lord and obedience. In these atmospheres, almost every time, I witness over 50 percent of the people respond to the call of repentance at the end of the message. I then come into the next service with the same worship songs and worship team, and almost every time the presence of God manifests wonderfully. Why is that? True worship is a life of obedience and out of that life will flow songs of worship, which will delight the heart of God, rather than repulse Him as in the above Scripture. It is no different than my approaching my wife for sexual intimacy after a day of loving her, rather than ignoring her.

WORSHIP IN TRUTH

Jesus tells us the Father is seeking those who will worship Him in spirit and truth. We will cover extensively in future chapters the aspect of worshiping God in *spirit*. Let's now discuss worshiping Him in *truth*. The Greek word for *truth* is *aletheia*. *Vine's* defines this word as: "The reality lying at the basis of an appearance; the manifested, veritable essence of a matter."

I love this definition as it beautifully enhances what Jesus is communicating. He is showing that true worship is found at the base level of a human being which is the heart. To help explain, let me identify and define the three levels of communication.

First is verbal communication, which is the lowest level. Jesus points this out with the example of the father who asked his two sons to go work in his vineyard (Matt. 21:28–31). One son replied, "Sure Dad," but didn't do it. The other son replied, "No way," yet afterward went. Jesus then explained that the one who did the will of his father was the one who initially said "no," rather than the one who said "yes." Thus, showing actions are a higher form of communication than words.

James also shows verbal communication is the lowest level by saying, "Suppose you see a brother or sister who needs food or clothing, and you say, 'Well, good-bye and God bless you; stay warm and eat well'—but then you don't give that person any food or clothing. What good does that do?" (James 2:15–16 NLT). John the apostle confirms this truth as well by saying, "But if anyone has enough money to live well and sees a brother or sister in need and refuses to help—how can God's love be in that person?" (1 John 3:17 NLT).

This can be seen in countless scenarios, one of which would be a man who tells his wife he loves her, yet never spends time with her; or a woman who tells her husband she respects him, yet she doesn't listen to his counsel to stop running credit cards up to their limits. I think you know this list is almost endless. John continues in his epistle:

My little children, let us not love in word or in tongue, but in deed and in truth. (1 John 3:18)

The Amplified Bible records it, "Little children, let us not love [merely] . . . in speech but in deed and in truth." We are to absolutely love in word, but it is hypocritical if there is not deed and truth to confirm our words of love. Notice he says "deed and truth." This describes the two higher levels of communication.

The next level is *deed* or action; however, this is not the highest level of communication, and can easily mislead as actions can be contrary to truth. For example, Paul says, "Though I bestow all my goods to feed the poor, and though I give my body to be burned, but have not love, it profits me nothing" (1 Cor. 13:3). The actions he describes in this verse would appear to be the greatest level of love, yet he said we can actually perform these seemingly glorious deeds without the love of God in our hearts.

This leads to the highest level of communication which is the *heart*. It is the base level of man. This is the level both John and Jesus referred to as *truth*. The thoughts and intents of the heart reveal the truth of our worship, yet they cannot be discerned outside the Word of God. We are told to guard our heart with all diligence, for out of it flow the forces of life. If neglected we can be easily deceived. A heart left to itself outside of the counsel of God's Word and His Spirit is a heart which is deceitful above all else.

God declares to His people, "If you are *willing* and obedient, you shall eat the good of the land" (Isa. 1:19, *author's emphasis*). Notice He doesn't say just obedient, but rather *willing* and obedient. Willingness deals with the attitude of our heart. I can ask my son to do something and he can immediately obey, and appear quite submitted, yet all the while murmuring in his heart. The reality is that he is not obeying in truth, but rather under pretense. John tells us we are to love God and mankind in action as well as truth, which is heart level, "And by this we know that we are of the truth, and shall assure our hearts before Him" (1 John 3:19).

I'll never forget the time when God confronted me on this. I had been working very hard to refrain from any sort of complaining. I had come to realize complaining is an affront to God's character, as complaining says to God, "I don't like what You are doing, and if I were You I would do it differently." It is a lack of holy fear and God hates it; in fact, it destroyed the children of Israel's opportunity to enter into the promised land. So I had not complained for quite some time verbally and was actually becoming proud of that fact. Yet on a particular morning I heard the Holy Spirit say firmly upon awaking, "I hear the complaining of your heart!" I was nailed; I sat there in shock, realizing how deceived I had been in my pride. My worship of God was not in truth and it took the light of His corrective word to expose the error of my heart. I repented quickly and have been relieved that He has not corrected me in this manner since. Thank God for His grace!

Look at *Vine's* definition of truth again in this light. He tells us truth signifies the reality lying at the basis of an appearance; the manifested, veritable essence of a matter. We can so easily drift from truth. I'll give an example. We can pray and sing to the Lord, yet not one word is coming from our heart. The whole while we are singing we are thinking about how hungry we are, how the kids fought that morning, what a great day we have planned after service, and so forth. We can pray and say, "Lord, I am so thankful to You." Yet we've been complaining for days about a difficult situation we are in. Are we really thankful, or have we deep in our hearts been blaming the Lord for not working things out the way we thought He should have? Oh, the list is endless!

To worship God in truth is to not only obey Him, but to delight in what He has asked you to do. It is to speak to Him what is really in your heart, not what you know is the right thing to say. It is not being two-faced with God. I love David's words when he says,

> Trust in Him at all times, you people;
> *Pour out your heart before Him;*
> God is a refuge for us.
> (Ps. 62:8, *author's emphasis*)

I have discovered that when I am gut-honest with the Lord He will draw near. If I'm covering something, it hinders me, and I can't get anywhere in prayer; it becomes an absolute struggle because I'm not connecting with Him. He is seeking those who will draw near in integrity of heart, not pretense. I sometimes wonder when I observe people in services saying, "Thank you Jesus . . . Hallelujah . . . glory to God," if they are just repeating "Christian lingo," or if they are speaking from the base level of their hearts. No different from a husband, who to pacify his wife says with very little heart, "I love you, dear." It's quite different from when he was engaged to her and said with deep passion, "I love you."

Out of a life of true worship, which is obedience from the very core of our being, will flow songs of worship. There are men and women in the body of Christ who are gifted to bring forth songs of praise and worship. They are modern day psalmists. Some are living lives of true worship, while others are worldly and sensual. Those who are defiled can still come up with tremendous songs, because of their gifting, yet lack the holy presence of the Lord as they sing; while the pure carry a glorious presence of God as they minister to Him and to His people from their hearts.

JESUS' PROMISE TO MANIFEST HIMSELF

To worship God in truth is to worship Him from the integrity of our hearts. It is to fear and reverence Him in the truest sense. The psalmist says:

> Happy are those who hear the joyful call to worship,
> for they will walk in the light of your presence, Lord.
> (Ps. 89:15 NLT)

God is seeking those who will hear His call to a life of worship. Those who heed are those who will walk in His presence. They will know Him intimately as He will manifest Himself to them. Jesus says it like this:

A little while longer and the world will see Me no more, but you will see Me . . . He who has My commandments and keeps them, it is he who loves Me. And he who loves Me will be loved by My Father, and I will love him and *manifest Myself to him.* (John 14:19–21, *author's emphasis*)

Those who have His commandments and keep them are those who worship Him in truth, and He promised they would see Him. Recall that *to manifest* means to bring out of the realm of the unseen into the seen; out of the unknown to the realm of the known. In the New American Standard Bible, His words read, "I will love him, and disclose Myself to him." The Amplified Bible records it like this:

Just a little while now, and the world will not see Me any more, but you will see Me . . . The person who has My commands and keeps them is the one who [really] loves Me; and whoever [really] loves Me will be loved by My Father, and I [too] will love him and will show (reveal, manifest) Myself to him. *[I will let Myself be clearly seen by him and make Myself real to him.]* (John 14:19, 21 AMP, *author's emphasis*)

Only those who truly worship Him *really* know Him. He reveals Himself to them as they are His dear friends. This stunned the apostles so one of them spoke up:

Judas, not Iscariot, asked Him, Lord, how is that You will reveal Yourself —make Yourself real—to us and not to the world?

Jesus answered, If a person [really] loves Me, he will *keep My word—obey My teaching;* and My Father will love him, and We will come to him and make Our home (abode, special dwelling place) with him. Anyone who does not [really] love Me does not observe and obey My teaching. (John 14:22–24 AMP, *author's emphasis*)

So you can see it comes down to obedience. Recall what God thundered in my heart: "Worship is a life of obedience to His heart's desires." When we love Him in the truest sense, then He comes to us, not to visit, but to make His abiding place in us. thus revealing Himself.

There are many who are gifted by the Spirit of God, yet they do not keep the words of the Master with all their heart. They are the people who can be most easily deceived. The reason is the presence of the Lord will be sensed to a degree in their gifting, such as their preaching, singing, praying, or other form of ministry. This would be no different from Balaam, who was very gifted in prophecy and as a result would experience a degree of the presence of the Lord whenever this gift operated, yet he was far from the heart of God.

The deception is that these people can easily assume that the presence of the Lord that is on them in ministry is His approval of their lives, and mistake that presence for intimacy with Him. It would be little different from a good man who hired someone to work for him. That person could incorrectly assume that just because they are in the employer's presence daily it means they are intimate with him. This, as you know, would be an incorrect assumption. Jesus says many professing to know Him are going to:

> stand outside and knock at the door, saying, "Lord, Lord, open for us," and He *[the Lord]* will answer and say to you, "I do not *[intimately]* know you, where you are from," then you will begin to say, "We ate and drank *in Your presence*, and You taught in our streets." But He will say, "I tell you I do not know you, where you are from. Depart from Me, all you workers of iniquity." (Luke 13:25–27, *author's emphasis*)

If you read this in conjunction with Matthew's account (Matt. 7:21–23) you will discover the ones who say this are those who did miracles in Jesus' name. They were gifted, yet assumed the presence of the Lord that accompanied the gifting equated to His presence of approval or intimacy. You can see the shock of these who professed to know Him, yet were turned away. It is so important that we understand there is a difference between His abiding presence and His presence that accompanies ministry.

You can see Jesus' response to Judas (not Iscariot) in the above verse showed that those who worship Him in truth are those whom He will seek out to make His dwelling place. This is most remarkable as it speaks of His abiding presence. I love the words He uses: *home, abode, special dwelling place.* In these words lie the remarkable difference between the Old Testament and the New Testament saints. The Old Testament saints did not have the privilege of being the abiding place of God. The abiding place of God was the "Most Holy Place" in the tabernacle or temple. Yet we see a parallel. God's presence was rare and almost nonexistent in the tabernacle during Eli's days, because of his and the people's self-gratifying ways. Yet His presence was strong in the days when His people obeyed Him with diligence.

It is no different today. Those believers who worship Him in spirit and truth—obey Him with passionate hearts—are those who experience His abiding presence. These are the ones He chooses to reveal Himself to. Oh, what a glorious fellowship we have awaiting us. How could any believer ever flirt with disobedience or worldliness when we have such a treasure awaiting us?

He has promised to make His home, abode, special dwelling place with us, and in so doing He will manifest or reveal who He really is. Oh, the thought of such a glorious promise, and it is not for the future only, but for now! These are some of my favorite words in the Bible, that this glorious King would desire to "manifest Himself," or make Himself known to you and me personally. In future chapters we will happily explore how He actually does this. However, in the next chapter we will first discuss another crucial and needed virtue He seeks in those He inhabits.

STUDY QUESTIONS

1. As you examine the lives of such characters as Enoch, Noah, Abraham, Moses, David, Esther, Daniel, and others in the Scriptures,

you find the common denominator in all their lives was a genuine heartfelt obedience to God's desires rather than their own. What would happen in your life if you were to implement that type of obedience today?

2. Reflecting on the author's humorous statement, "Praise is the fast songs, worship is the slow ones," did you identify with that assessment? The message he ultimately received from the Lord regarding worship, was "It is a life." How does that statement affect the need for changes in your life?

3. As you think about what Jesus said in Luke 13:25–27 and Matthew 7:21–23, how would you describe the difference between His abiding presence and His presence that accompanies ministry?

CHAPTER NINE

WITH WHOM GOD DWELLS

✠

The power twins of the kingdom are
the Fear of the Lord and Humility.

I n this chapter we will explore another crucial element in coming
close to the One who so earnestly desires our fellowship. Our
flagship Scripture calls us to, "Draw near to God and He will draw
near to you." Yet let's examine what we read before and after this
amazing invitation:

> Therefore He says: "God resists the proud, but gives grace to the
> *humble*." . . . Draw near to God and He will draw near to you . . .
> *Humble* yourselves in the sight of the Lord, and He will lift you
> up. (James 4:6–10, *author's emphasis*)

God's heart cry is sandwiched between two exhortations of humility; and for good reason, for God says,

> Thus says the High and Lofty One who inhabits eternity, whose name is Holy; I dwell in the *high* and holy place, with him who has a contrite and *humble spirit*, to revive the spirit of the *humble*. (Isa. 57:15, *author's emphasis*)

James says if we humble ourselves in God's sight, then He will lift us up. Up where? God tells us through the prophet Isaiah: to *the high and holy place!* He looks for a people to inhabit, not visit. James invites us to more than a visit; we are invited to dwell in His presence continually and as Isaiah says, it is only available to the humble.

OUR IGNORANCE OF HUMILITY

Many in the body of Christ do not understand humility or its power; they view it as being weak, wimpy, spineless, or even religious. Yet it is a fact that often the truly humble are mistaken for being arrogant! Consider David, who at his father's request visits his older brothers who were in battle against the Philistines. He arrives and notices all the soldiers, including his brothers, in a strange new battle position: hiding behind rocks in fear of Goliath the giant. He learns this has been going on forty straight days. David then asks the men in no sheepish tone, "Who is this uncircumcised Philistine, that he should defy the armies of the living God?" (1 Sam. 17:26).

This infuriates his oldest brother Eliab. He more than likely thinks, *My little brother is not only a brat, but he's full of himself.* So Eliab in turn snaps back at David with, "I know *your pride* and the insolence of your heart" (1 Sam. 17:28, *author's emphasis*). The NIV records his words, "I know how *conceited* you are."

Wait, who was proud? Only a chapter earlier the prophet Samuel came to Jesse's house to anoint the next king and this firstborn son didn't make the cut. Both Jesse and Samuel assumed Eliab was the one because he was probably the tallest, strongest, and smartest of Jesse's sons, but God firmly said, "I have rejected him" (1 Sam. 16:7 NIV). There is only one reason God rejects a person, and that is pride. The very pride Eliab accused David of, resided in himself, yet God boasted about David's humility by saying that he was a man after His own heart (Acts 13:22), and David was the furthest thing from being weak, wimpy, or spineless.

David shakes off this verbal assault and meets the giant with great confidence, letting him know he is about to lose his head. Then David runs toward the enemy camp, kills Goliath, and takes his head.

Let me further prove how often we really don't understand humility. The book of Numbers, which is one of the first five of the Bible, belongs to a group we call the *Pentateuch*. We read in this book:

> Now the man Moses was very humble, more than all men who were on the face of the earth. (Num. 12:3)

Wow, what a statement! If we're honest we'd admit that we would love this said of us, but we wouldn't dare say it! Why? Only an arrogant person would say that about themselves. But, who wrote the book of Numbers? The answer: Moses! Wow!

We'd never consider a man humble who said he was humble, let alone the most humble on the earth! Can you just imagine a minister standing up before a Christian conference saying, "You all, I'm humble, so let me tell you about it." He would be sneered and laughed at and called a heretic, yet hear what Jesus says:

> Come to me, all you who are weary and burdened . . . and *learn from me*, for I am gentle and *humble* in heart, and you will find rest for your souls. (Matt. 11:28–29 NIV, *author's emphasis*)

So in essence we have missed the true meaning of humility because we've thought it meant to never speak of ourselves and to live as unworthy worms, yet that is the farthest from truth.

HUMILITY DEFINED

Humility has three aspects. First, our obedience to God; second, our utter dependence on Him; and third, our view of ourselves. Let's look briefly at each.

First, our obedience; immediately after James writes about humility he follows it with, "Therefore submit to God" (4:7). This links obedience and humility. The Lord always gives His own people His promises and plans. "For I know the thoughts that I think toward you, says the Lord, thoughts of peace and not of evil, to give you a future and a hope" (Jer. 29:11). These promises are His will and paint within us a prophetic picture of where we're to go. We earnestly desire their fulfillment as it is He who places these desires in our hearts (see Ps. 37:4). In our hearts we glimpse where He's taking us, and our understanding determines a logical path to follow. However, quite often He will lead us in directions that appear completely opposite of logic. True humility acknowledges God's wisdom and directives as far above our own, and chooses to obey even when we don't understand. Proverbs 3:5 says, "Trust in the Lord with all your heart and lean not on your own understanding."

Abraham waited years for the promise of Isaac to manifest, and as time passed there would be a logical progression of his marriage and the resulting children. Abraham could begin to glimpse the promise of being the Father of a multitude. But then God changes all that when one night He tells Abraham to journey three days and then put Isaac to death! It didn't make sense! Can you imagine his struggle to obey? This was a painful command and made absolutely no sense in regard to the promise! Yet out of humility Abraham chose to obey even when he didn't understand.

The Bible contains many more examples of this when God instructs or allows circumstances to occur which appear opposite to what He's shown us, yet by obedience we'll see His promise fulfilled in a way outside our understanding.

OUR COMPLETE DEPENDENCE ON GOD

Second, humility can be defined as our complete and utter dependence on God. David appeared arrogant, yet he knew his ability came from God. In his own words, "The LORD, who delivered me from the paw of the lion and from the paw of the bear, He will deliver me from the hand of this Philistine" (1 Sam. 17:37). His brothers trusted in their own ability, which is why when they compared themselves to David, they were older and stronger. David's strength was in his faith and obedience.

We see this in Caleb and Joshua. They were two of twelve leaders chosen to go and check out the promised land. After forty days the twelve returned to give Moses and the people the report of the territory. The words of ten of the leaders were, "We arrived in the land you sent us to see, and it is indeed a magnificent country—a land flowing with milk and honey. Here is some of its fruit as proof. But the people living there are powerful, and their cities and towns are fortified and very large'" (Num. 13:27–28 NLT).

Once these men spoke, the congregation went into an uproar. Caleb then quieted the people and with firm confidence exhorted them. "Let's go at once to take the land," he said. "We can certainly conquer it!" (v. 30 NLT).

The other leaders quickly snapped back, "We can't go up against them! They are stronger than we are!" (v. 31 NLT).

Scripture then tells us: "And all the congregation said to stone them [Caleb and Joshua] with stones" (Num. 14:10).

In the eyes of the people and other leaders, Caleb and Joshua were overconfident and bigheaded. The leaders, who said they could not take the land, were realists. They sized up the situation and knew it was utterly impossible for them as former slaves to invade such a powerful and fortified nation. After all, they were only protecting their wives and children (see Num. 14:3). These leaders appeared to be humble, caring for the nation, which included the lives of the elderly and weak. Caleb and Joshua seemed so conceited they didn't consider the welfare of the helpless ones.

Yet, hear where their confidence came from: "Do not rebel against the Lord, and don't be afraid of the people of the land. They are only helpless prey to us! They have no protection, but the Lord is with us! Don't be afraid of them!" (Num. 14:9 NLT). Joshua and Caleb's utter dependence was on God's ability, not their own. They knew it was His will for them to go into that land and conquer. They might have appeared to be bigheaded, while their fellow leaders were seen as realistic. But it was God who separated the humble from the proud.

Humility or a complete dependence upon God's grace, is exemplified in the life of Paul. He says of himself:

> There is nothing in us that allows us to claim that we are capable of doing this work. The capacity we have comes from God. (2 Cor. 3:5 TEV)

And again:

> Now I am glad to boast about how weak I am; I am glad to be a living demonstration of Christ's power, instead of showing off my own power and abilities. (2 Cor. 12:9–10 TLB)

This was a progression in Paul's life: the longer he lived the more dependent he became on God's grace and the less he relied on his own strengths, talents, or abilities. The more he emptied himself in his submission to Christ, the bolder and stronger he became in his resolve to glorify Christ.

HOW WE VIEW OURSELVES

This leads to the third aspect of humility, how we view ourselves. When first saved, Paul humbled himself by forsaking all his accomplishments and achieved status prior to meeting Jesus; he called them rubbish. For most, it's not difficult to count the life we lived before knowing Christ as garbage.

But what about our accomplishments in Christ after our salvation? This is often an entirely different story. Concerning these feats he stated, "Brethren, I do not count myself to have apprehended; but one thing I do, forgetting those things which are behind *[what God had done through him since being saved]* and reaching forward to those things which are ahead" (Phil. 3:13, *author's emphasis*).

Years after his conversion Paul was ordained an apostle (see Acts 13:1–4). He was given an abundance of spiritual revelations and wisdom that afforded him again the opportunity of achievement. He birthed churches all over Asia and Eastern Europe. We glimpse his humility in 56 A.D. in his letter to the virgin church he started in Corinth. He was ten years away from death, a seasoned veteran in the service of Jesus. Yet hear his words:

> For I am the least of the apostles, who am not worthy to be called an apostle. (1 Cor. 15:9)

Do you hear the humility in these words? I want to point out; this is not a false humility. Counterfeit humility knows how to use politically correct words in order to appear humble, yet there is no lowliness of heart or mind. This is deceptive and untrue. But in writing Scripture under the inspiration of the Holy Spirit you cannot lie! He would not have been permitted to write such a statement if he didn't really see himself as such. So when Paul said he was bottom of the barrel of the apostles, it wasn't politically correct jargon, but rather true humility.

However, look at Paul's next statement: "I labored more abundantly than they all" (1 Cor. 15:10). Who are they all? The answer is all the other apostles! Wait. Is Paul bragging? It now sounds as if he is talking out of the other side of his mouth. How can he say he is the least of all the apostles and then follow it with, "I've done more than all of them"? At first it sounds arrogant, and as if he didn't mean what he first said, but it is not. It precedes another declaration of Paul's dependence:

Yet not I, but the grace of God which was with me. (1 Cor. 15:10)

He followed his assessment as the least with an acknowledgment that all he'd done had only been by God's grace. He was able to separate himself from all the accomplishments; he was fully aware all he'd achieved flowed from God's ability through him.

Paul's self-description as "the least of all the apostles" is hard to swallow. Both in his day and throughout church history, he'd been esteemed as one of the greatest apostles. Now consider what Paul said to the Ephesians seven years later in 63 A.D., three to four years prior to his departure. In those seven years, since the letter to the Corinthians, he accomplished more than at any time period in his life. He here describes himself:

> To me, who am *less than the least of all the saints*, this grace was given, that I should preach among the Gentiles the unsearchable riches of Christ. (Eph. 3:8, *author's emphasis*)

Seven years earlier he called himself "the least apostle" and now he describes himself as lower than "the least of all the saints"! What?! If anyone could boast it was surely Paul, and remember, when writing Scripture you cannot lie; you cannot write religiously correct jargon. He really saw himself this way!

This progression continued for we find that just prior to his death he wrote a letter to Timothy in which he stated:

> Christ Jesus came into the world to save sinners, of whom I am chief. (1 Tim. 1:15)

Now he's not least of the apostles, or even least of all the saints, but he sees himself as chief of all sinners. Notice he did not say, "I *was* chief," rather, "I *am* chief." And he was the one who had the revelation of being a brand new creation in Christ; old things passed away, and all became new! (See 2 Cor. 5:17.) He never lost sight of how great a debt he owed the Savior.

The longer Paul served, the smaller he viewed himself as his humility progressively grew. So could this be why the grace of God increased proportionately the older he became? For James tells us that God "gives grace to the humble" (James 4:6). Could this also be why God revealed His ways so intimately to Paul that it baffled the apostle Peter? God says through Isaiah that He dwells with, not visits, those who are humble. When we dwell with Him, we become intimate with Him.

THE POWER TWINS

Now we come to the place where we meet the power twins of the kingdom; they are the *Fear of the Lord* and *Humility*. Recall, in recent chapters we clearly observed that the fear of the Lord is the beginning of an intimate knowledge of Him, yet now we see the same is true with humility. The psalmist declares,

> The *humble* He teaches His *way.*
> (Ps. 25:9, *author's emphasis*)

God reveals his ways to the humble, yet just a few verses later we find:

> Who is the man that *fears the Lord?*
> Him shall He teach in the *way* He chooses.
> (Ps. 25:12, *author's emphasis*)

In essence, those who fear the Lord are truly humble, and the truly humble fear the Lord. Recall that Moses knew God's ways, yet Israel only knew Him by how their prayers were answered, which were His acts. Moses both feared the Lord and was very humble. Do you see the connection? Israel lacked the fear of the Lord (Deut. 5:29), as well as humility (which we saw in the above example of Joshua and Caleb).

The psalmist links the fear of the Lord with humility as almost insep-arable. We see this repeatedly in Scripture. One example would be:

> The *fear of the Lord* is the instruction of wisdom, and before honor is *humility*. (Prov. 15:33, *author's emphasis*)

The kingdom of darkness has its power twins as well. They are just the opposites of the *Fear of the Lord* and *Humility*; they are *Rebellion* and *Pride*. We see them contrasted in Proverbs:

> The reward of *humility* and the reverent and worshipful *fear of the Lord* is riches and honor and life. Thorns and snares are in the way of the *obstinate* and *willful*; he who guards himself will be far from them. (Prov. 22:4–5 AMP, *author's emphasis*)

Do you see how humility and the fear of the Lord are linked as well as contrasted with pride and rebellion? Jesus humbled Himself more than any other human or angelic being. Therefore He was highly exalted more than any other (see Phil. 2:8–9). He also delighted, above all virtues, in the fear of the Lord; therefore, the Spirit of God's presence with and upon Him was without measure (see Isa. 11:2–3; John 3:34).

In contrast Lucifer, who was the anointed cherub, now known as Satan, lifted himself up through pride and became rebellious, more than anyone before or after him. Therefore, he was brought down to the "lowest depths of the Pit." (See Ezek. 28:14–17; Isa. 14:12–15.)

Keep in mind, Scripture shows repeatedly the dwelling place of God is the high places, and the dwelling place of demonic forces is the lower parts. You will see over and over throughout Scripture pride and rebellion associated with the low, and humility and the fear of the Lord with the high. To be lifted up is to dwell with God in intimacy!

THOSE WHOM GOD CHASES

God resists the proud and rebellious (James 4:6), but He is attracted to those who fear Him—the truly humble. In the Old Testament there were a group of people serving or worshiping God as Scripture prescribed. They were bringing lamb and bull sacrifices, burning incense in the Holy Place, and bringing grain offerings. Yet God said that in His eyes their sacrifices were like killing a man; their offerings were like offering Him pig's blood; and their incense, which is a type of prayer and praise, were like blessing an idol! He then told them why:

> Because, when I called, no one answered, when I spoke they did not hear; but they did evil before My eyes, and chose that in which I do not delight. (Isa. 66:4)

What does He not delight in? Sacrifices that are not accompanied by obedience! (See 1 Sam. 15:22.) In other words, any form of worship void of the fear of the Lord.

The Lord hit these "worshipers" hard. He cut their feet out from under them. Can you imagine the shock of these people? They think they are serving and pleasing Him, only to find out He is repulsed by their worship. However, in regard to His people, the Lord never roots out where He does not intend to plant; He never tears down where He does not intend to build. So He then encourages by telling them what attracts Him:

> This is the one I esteem: he who is humble and contrite in spirit, and trembles at my word. (Isa. 66:2 NIV)

The Hebrew word for *esteem* is *nabat*. *Strongs* defines this word as "to look intently at; to regard with pleasure, favor or care." So in essence God is saying, "This is the person I regard with pleasure, favor, and pay close attention to." To put it simply He's saying, "I'm after this person; he's who I'm chasing." Tommy Tenney, a contemporary author and teacher, has what I consider to be one of the greatest book titles of our generation, *The God Chasers*. That perfectly describes the hearts of those who love God. It is one thing to chase

God. However, it is an entirely different thing to have God chasing you! Yet this is exactly what God is saying here.

Consider David. God instructs the senior prophet of Israel, Samuel, to go to Jesse's house, even at Samuel's protest, for he feared Saul's wrath. Yet, God still commands him to go, because He is after one of Jesse's sons. The prophet goes through all seven of the oldest boys and finally the Lord in a nutshell says to him, "No Samuel, it is not these elder boys, but the little ruddy one out there in the fields with the sheep; that's the one I'm chasing!" (author's paraphrase).

Why was God chasing David rather than his other brothers or all the other men of Israel? The answer is found in the above verse. He favors and is after those who are humble, contrite in spirit, and tremble at His Word. The contrite in spirit are those who are quick to repent in their commitment to be submitted to divine authority. Another translation records it, "I am pleased with those who are humble and repentant, who fear me and obey me" (TEV). A contrite spirit is another form of true humility and the fear of the Lord. So in essence He is communicating that He chases those who are humble and fear Him; those who walk in the virtue of the power twins of the kingdom! This is why we are told,

> He has no use for conceited people, but shows favor to those
> who are humble. (Prov. 3:34 TEV)

And again:

> Oh, how great is Your goodness,
> Which You have laid up for those who fear You . . .
> You shall hide them in the secret place of Your presence.
> (Ps. 31:19–20)

This is why we are told in the New Testament to "clothe yourselves [ourselves] with humility" (1 Peter 5:5 NIV) and to "live your [our] lives as strangers here in reverent fear" (1 Peter 1:17 NIV). God, the Holy Spirit, is exhorting us with these words through Peter that we may enter into sweet communion with Him, which is His heart's passion for us as dear children.

The choice is ours. God has paved the way for us to walk with Him, and given us His grace to do it. What a wonderful God and Father we serve! Now it's up to us to hear and heed His call to His inward chamber where He manifests Himself. In the next several chapters we will discuss how He actually does it!

STUDY QUESTIONS

1. In this chapter, the point is made that even though humility is generally misunderstood to be weak, wimpy, and spineless, the truly humble are often mistaken to be arrogant. As you reflect on this, can you think of people you've written off as arrogant, who were actually quite humble? If so, what can you learn from that incorrect assessment?

2. Reflect on the three aspects of humility—obedience to God, total dependence on Him, and our view of ourselves—and the biblical examples of each. If you were to confess to one of these as your greatest challenge, which would it be?

3. In Isaiah 66, a group of people were serving and worshiping God by the letter of the law—bringing proper sacrifices, burning proper incense, and making on the proper offerings. Yet, the Lord did not delight in their worship due to their lack of obedience. In what ways can our worship be displeasing to God, even when it is led by gifted, talented leaders?

CHAPTER TEN

INTIMACY
WITH THE
HOLY SPIRIT

✠

I believe the Holy Spirit is one of the most
ignored persons in the church.

Now we come to the section of the book I have longed to discuss; how the Lord actually draws near to us. First of all let me reiterate, He longs for you with greater intensity than you for Him. Recall Moses' words, "For he is a God who is passionate about his relationship with you" (Ex. 34:14 NLT).

Recently while deep in prayer, before fully realizing what I was saying, I cried out, "Lord, if I can't have intimate fellowship with You here on this earth then please take me home to Heaven with You!" My knees shook a little as my words poured forth from my heart. I knew I meant what I'd said, yet almost immediately my mind screamed, "What did you just ask for?" My sense of reasoning questioned whether I should request such things.

A few hours later I caught a plane to Phoenix, Arizona, sat in my seat, grabbed my Bible out of the briefcase and just opened it. The first verse my eyes made contact with read as follows,

> O LORD my Rock:
> Do not be silent to me,
> Lest, if You are silent to me,
> I become like those who go down to the pit.
> (Ps. 28:1)

I about jumped out of my seat. What were the chances of my eyes coincidentally falling upon this Scripture? It dealt exactly with what I had questioned just a few hours earlier. I knew it was a word from God as my heart was racing.

David says we are no better off than a sinner headed for hell if God doesn't speak to us. I carry the New Living Translation with me so I looked it up, and it matched what I had prayed that morning. It reads, "For if you are silent, I might as well give up and die." This was precisely what I had cried out. As many times as I had read this verse, I had never seen it in this light before.

Immediately I knew I had not prayed contrary to God's will but by the Holy Spirit. This again affirmed to me that God does not want to be silent with us; rather He desires earnestly to communicate with us. One of my very favorite Scriptures contains these words penned by David:

> My heart has heard You say, "Come and talk with Me." And my
> heart responds, "Lord, I am coming." (Ps. 27:8 NLT)

Can you hear the yearning of God's heart? He is inviting each of us by saying, "Draw near, I want to commune with you, to share My heart and show you great and mighty things which you know not!"

This should describe every believer's life, "Draw near to God" and if we do, He guarantees, "He will draw near to you." We determine the level of our intimacy, not Him. He has already opened the door that leads to His private chambers; He is waiting, calling us to come. It is up to us to respond, and the closer we come the more He reveals Himself and His desires. Yet again look at James's words just prior to this great invitation:

> Or do you think that the Scripture says in vain, "The Spirit who dwells in us yearns jealously"? (James 4:5)

He longs for us, yet jealously. The past several chapters we have seen that He will not share us with the covetous desires of this world. For this reason James says, "Do you not know that friendship with the world is enmity with God? Whoever therefore wants to be a friend of the world makes himself an enemy of God" (James 4:4). This is no different from a wife saying to her unfaithful husband, "You cannot have me along with your mistress; so choose! If you pick her, you have rejected me and I'm leaving." The Lord is no different; He will not share us with the world. He is to be the passion of our hearts or He will not disclose Himself to us.

THE SPIRIT WHO DWELLS IN US YEARNS

Earlier we discussed extensively His longing for us; but now we need to focus on the word *Spirit*. It is most significant that Scripture records, "The Spirit who dwells in us yearns . . ." Notice it does not say, "Jesus who dwells in us yearns . . ." Jesus is not here on earth, He is seated on the right hand of Majesty on High, and He has been there for almost two thousand years. On the day Jesus left, the angels spoke the words to His disciples, "Men of Galilee," they said, "why do you stand here looking into the sky? This same Jesus, who has been taken from you into heaven, will come back in the same way you have seen him go into heaven" (Acts 1:11 NIV). He was physically taken up in a cloud out of their sight, and we're promised He'll return the same way.

Now don't get me wrong, our wonderful Savior Jesus yearns for us, but the One who has been among us since shortly after His departure is the Holy Spirit, and He is the specific person of the Godhead identified in this verse. Yet He is in many ways overlooked by those who call upon the name of Jesus. In fact, I believe the Holy Spirit is one of the most ignored persons in the church. Think of it; how often would you drive twenty minutes with someone in your car and not say one word to them the entire ride, yet how often we do this with Him. We contemplate our day, or listen to Christian music or radio stations while driving and so often don't even acknowledge His company. We fail to recognize His companionship at home, in the office, and the countless other places that occupy our time; yet if questioned, we would certainly acknowledge His existence and His dwelling in our hearts.

OUR IMAGE OF THE HOLY SPIRIT

One of the reasons for the lack of recognition of His presence and companionship is our image of the Holy Spirit; it's mystical because of the way we have written and preached about Him. In fact, if I had a dollar for each time I've heard the Spirit of God referred to as an "it," I would be financially rich. Unfortunately, by many He is viewed as a "holy entity" rather than One who is Most Holy, and desires to be your closest friend. If we only meditated on the Scripture we would come to know that He has a mind (Rom. 8:27), as well as a will (1 Cor. 12:11), and emotions that are described by His love for us (Rom. 15:30). He speaks (Heb. 3:7); in fact He does it clearly (1 Tim. 4:1). He teaches (1 Cor. 2:13), can be grieved (Eph. 4:30), insulted (Heb. 10:29), and lied to, just as any human being.

Our first impression of Him is usually a picture of a dove. But why is He pictured as a dove? He never manifested once as a dove! In all four Gospels it is recorded that John the Baptist saw the Spirit of God descending upon Jesus, "like a dove" (Matt. 3:16; Mark 1:10; Luke 3:22; John 1:32). That doesn't make Him a dove. I have heard statements made about men and women such as "She ran like the wind," or "He's strong like an ox." That does not make that woman wind, or the man a four-footed animal. They are human beings.

Someone else may say, "Yes, but John the apostle saw the Holy Spirit as lamps of fire when He beheld the throne of God." Yes, that is true for he wrote, "Directly in front of his throne were seven lighted lamps representing the seven-fold Spirit of God" (Rev. 4:5 TLB); but this same John also wrote, "And I looked, and behold . . . in the midst of the elders, stood a Lamb as though it had been slain . . . Then the elders and others in the throne room sang to the Lamb, 'You are worthy to take the scroll, and to open its seals; for You were slain, and have redeemed us to God by Your blood out of every tribe and tongue and people and nation' " (see Rev. 5:6–9). It's quite clear he is speaking of Jesus, but our perception of Him is not an animal! We certainly know Jesus to be a person in whose image we are created; we are not created in the image of an animal!

The Holy Spirit is a person, and we have been created in His image. Oh yes, His image! We read in Genesis, "Then God said, 'Let Us make man in Our image, according to Our likeness'" (Gen 1:26). It doesn't say, "I will make man in My image." No, it was the Father, Son, and the Holy Spirit creating man in unison. We are very aware of the Father and Son's role in Creation, but Scripture also clearly states, "The Spirit of God has made me" (Job 33:4), and again, "You send forth Your Spirit, they are created" (Ps. 104:30). So when God said, "Let us make man in Our image," the Holy Spirit was certainly included. We are created in the image of the Father, Son, and Holy Spirit. He is a person, the third person of the Godhead, not a mystical wind or flighty bird.

How could Mary be impregnated by the Holy Spirit if we were not created in His image? Yet Scripture records, "But while she was still a virgin, she became pregnant by the Holy Spirit" (Matt. 1:18 NLT). Later the angel of the Lord said to Joseph, "What is conceived in her is from the Holy Spirit" (Matt. 1:20 NIV). If the Holy Spirit was a "thing" or an "it" how could a man be formed in Mary? She was impregnated by the Spirit of God. It takes two beings of the same image to create normal offspring.

I hope you are seeing that the Holy Spirit is a person, in fact a most wonderful person. For this reason Paul says to believers:

> The grace of the Lord Jesus Christ, and the love of God, and the *communion of the Holy Spirit* be with you all. Amen. (2 Cor. 13:14, *author's emphasis*)

Notice he says, "The *communion* of the Holy Spirit be with you." For years I've studied this word *communion* because knowing God intimately is my passion. I've looked it up in about every Greek dictionary I could get my hands on. The following are some of the major defining words:

- Fellowship
- Sharing together *or* social intercourse
- Partnership *or* joint participation
- Close mutual association
- Intimacy

There are other words used to define *communion* but they closely resemble at least one of the definitions listed above, so I chose these. Let's look at each one separately and meditate on them.

FELLOWSHIP

The first word *fellowship* is defined in *Webster's* dictionary as *companionship or company*. It is also defined as *the quality or state of being comradely*. You would never expect to find companions who refrain from interacting with each other; both keep each other informed in regard to what they are currently doing or planning to do. They are comrades and there is continuous communication between them. This relationship between the Holy Spirit and His servants is exemplified over and over again in the book of Acts. The following is just a sample from one of Paul's statements,

> And now I am going to Jerusalem, drawn there irresistibly by the Holy Spirit, not knowing what awaits me, except that the Holy Spirit has told me in *city after city* that jail and suffering lie ahead. (Acts 20:22–23 NLT, *author's emphasis*)

You can see from his own words the continual communication between Paul and the Holy Spirit. They were comrades together in life, travel, and ministry.

The same is true of every servant of the Lord in the New Testament. No matter where they went He was with them and communicated to them as they looked to Him. He was their companion. Philip, another disciple, left a citywide meeting and journeyed into the desert, yet he wasn't alone or at a loss for what to do, for "The Spirit said to Philip, 'Go near and overtake this chariot' " (Acts 8:29).

Peter in the midst of trying to figure out a difficult vision didn't have to rely on His own knowledge of the Scriptures for he heard the voice of the Spirit say, "What God has cleansed you must not call common." Then to further direct, " . . . *the Spirit said* to him, 'Behold, three men are seeking you. Arise therefore, go down and go with them, doubting nothing; for I have sent them' " (Acts 10:19–20, *author's emphasis*).

You see the companionship of the Holy Spirit with Paul's entire team for Luke records, "Now when they had gone through Phrygia and the region of Galatia, they were *forbidden by the Holy Spirit* to preach the word in Asia. After they had come to Mysia, they tried to go into Bithynia, but *the Spirit did not permit them*" (Acts 16:6–7, *author's emphasis*).

I could cite several more examples. However, the point I'm making is that New Testament servants were very aware of the Spirit of

God's constant companionship with them; it was never a spooky or out of the ordinary occurrence to interact with Him. They expected His involvement in their lives just as we would expect any other person's involvement in our lives if we lived with them 24/7.

People ask me if I get tired of hotel rooms in all my travels. I reply, "Honestly, I never get bored of them." In fact, I've been in some of the most beautiful cities in the world and have had no desire to sightsee because I'm enjoying His companionship so much that I don't want to lose that time. In the past, before really understanding and experiencing the companionship of the Holy Spirit, I would be most unhappy when alone. I needed people around me constantly. Now, I find myself longing for solitude so I can easily listen and speak with Him.

This is His passion, to commune with you! Take a moment and close your eyes and think about the Holy Spirit being your companion or comrade. For the Word of God declares, may "the *fellowship* of the Holy Spirit be with you." Or meditate on this: "May the *companionship* of the Holy Spirit be with you." Or again, "May the *company* of the Holy Spirit be with you." Let these words expand in your heart to open the door of intimacy between you and your Maker.

SHARING TOGETHER

The second definition, *sharing together* or *social intercourse,* describes the exchange of thoughts or feelings. The richest times I have with my inner circle of friends are when we get into conversations and share with each other the deepest or most intimate things of our hearts. In those times we become vulnerable and share things that someone who does not really know us may misunderstand or mock. However, we know this is not the case with our dearest friends; they will do neither, as they know our heart and will not misinterpret what we are sharing. Paul exemplifies this similar relationship with the Holy Spirit when he writes, "In the presence of Christ, I speak with utter truthfulness—I do not lie—and my conscience *and the Holy Spirit* confirm that what I am saying is true" (Rom. 9:1 NLT). The Holy Spirit knew Paul's heart, as did Paul know His heart. There was a closeness that developed from them sharing together their core thoughts and feelings.

Again this is why the fear of the Lord is so important. The Lord will not share His innermost thoughts with those who do not hold them precious, just as we would not cast our pearls before those who would pervert them. Simply put, we would never share the deep things of our life with those who do not have our heart; God is no different.

An Old Testament saint cries out, "Can you search out the deep things of God?" (Job 11:7). Yet because of the open door of intimacy with the Holy Spirit that the new covenant brings, Paul excitedly says, "But God has revealed them to us *through His Spirit*. For the Spirit searches all things, yes, the *deep* things of God" (1 Cor. 2:10, *author's emphasis*). Notice it is through His Spirit. He is the person of the Godhead who shares with us the intimate or deep things of God! Wow, doesn't that excite you?

So pause again, close your eyes, and meditate on the very fact that the Holy Spirit desires this kind of intimacy with you. He longs to show you His deepest thoughts and feelings and to hear yours. For the Word of God states, "May the *sharing of the thoughts and feelings of the Holy Spirit* be with you."

PARTNERSHIP

The third definition, *partnership* or *joint participation*, is beautifully exemplified by the testimony of the leaders of the early church. They wrote in their letter,

For it seemed good to the Holy Spirit, and to us. (Acts 15:28)

They distinctly showed the Holy Spirit's view as well as their own. It was a joint participation in the decision; they were partners in king-dom work. This can be mirrored in the Old Testament when God came to Abraham to discuss His plans for Sodom. Abraham was permitted to interject his perspective and God finalized His decision after hearing Abraham's counsel.

This is also seen a few times with Moses as well. The Lord in His anger was ready to destroy the children of Israel and would have done so had it not been for the counsel of Moses. He had to remind God of His own promises and reputation; as a result of Moses' input we read in one account, "So the Lord changed His mind about the harm which He said He would do to His people" (Ex. 32:14 NAS). Moses and Abraham were both partners of God, yet they didn't have the continuous communion we have been given today under the new covenant's provisions; it's staggering when you think of it.

We see clear evidence of the Holy Spirit's role as our senior partner when we hear Paul's words spoken to the leaders of Ephesus:

Therefore take heed to yourselves and to all the flock, among which the *Holy Spirit* has made you overseers, to shepherd the church of *God*, which He purchased with *His own blood*. (Acts 20:28, *author's emphasis*)

In this verse we can distinctly see the different persons of the Godhead, yet their perfect unison. The *Holy Spirit* is the first person spoken of, and He is the One who made them overseers. Then the Father is mentioned in the phrase *church of God*, and finally we see the Son's role as it was *His own blood* which purchased us; three different persons, yet one God. This is difficult to comprehend, yet we have a natural example that minutely illustrates this. We know water as three different forms—ice, liquid, and steam—yet all one molecular structure. So is the Godhead three different persons, yet perfectly one.

Again it is interesting to note that the Holy Spirit was the person of the Godhead who had placed these leaders in their positions. This is also made clear when the elders of a different church, Antioch, sought the Lord. As they did, "the Holy Spirit said, 'Now separate to Me Barnabas and Saul for the work to which I have called them.' " Then they prayed and laid hands on these two men and we read,

"So, being *sent out by the Holy Spirit*" (Acts 13:2–4, *author's empha-sis*). He was the person of the Godhead working with these men to glo-rify Jesus.

From these couple of examples we see a definite partnership in which the Holy Spirit is the leader or senior partner. I must empha-size this again: it is His desire that you and I be co-laborers with Him, yes, partners! We clearly read this in Paul's letter to the Corinthians when he writes, "For we are God's fellow workers" (1 Cor. 3:9). *Fellow* means *comrade* or *associate*. The King James Version brings it out clearer by saying, "For we are labourers together with God." Wow, again I ask, what comrades do you know who don't interact and work together?

Take another few moments and ponder the Holy Spirit's desire to be your senior partner. For the Word of God states, "May the *part-nership* of the Holy Spirit be with you," or again, "May the Holy Spirit *jointly participate* with you in all things."

CLOSE MUTUAL ASSOCIATION

The next definition is *close mutual association*. This is best described by giving experiences I've had over the years with great men and women of God. I recall the first time I met Dr. David Cho, who pas-tors one of the largest churches in the world in Seoul, Korea. It was his first visit to my home church. At the time I was one of the assis-tant pastors, and it was my responsibility to transport him during his visit. I had been doing this for several years, so I had previously picked up close to a hundred ministers, for many came to our church. However, this would be different, for when he got into my car the first time, the presence of the Lord came into my car. Almost imme-diately I started crying, tears were running down my face. I was very quiet as I didn't want to disturb him before ministering, yet I even-tually felt compelled to speak. I said soberly and softly, "Dr. Cho, God is here, in our car." He smiled and nodded.

I later thought how much this man has written and preached on the communion he enjoys with the Holy Spirit. I then recalled others I had picked up over the years who also emphasized and lived in close relationship with the Holy Spirit. Even though I transported close to a hundred ministers, there were only a few I could remember whom when I met, I immediately came into contact with the Holy Spirit. One of those was a lady named Jeanne Wilkerson, a minister who spent years in intercessory prayer, and has since gone to be with the Lord. When she climbed into the church vehicle the first time I met her, my mouth must have remained open in awe for the entire ride. I had a hard time focusing on driving. I realized I was in the presence of a woman who not only knew about God, but really knew him intimately. She spoke much of the Holy Spirit, and His presence was evident and strong every time I was with her.

Recently I spoke at a four-thousand-member church in the Midwest part of the United States. I preached about the Holy Spirit in the Sunday morning service and that night when we returned I was supposed to get the platform forty-five minutes into the service. Well, I didn't get the microphone until two hours after the service because the Holy Spirit had other plans. He ministered to so many, it was amazing! Finally before I was given the platform the pastor, who is no soft or weak man (he can bench-press over five hundred pounds), came to me in tears saying, "John, in the eight years that I have pastored this church, I have never felt the presence of God so strong!"

I immediately replied, "There is a reason for that; and it's because we talked about the Holy Spirit this morning, and whenever you talk about Him, He will manifest."

This close mutual association can be seen in marriages. There are some male ministers who often speak of their wives. They frequently include them in their messages or speak of them when in conversation if they are not present. They are frequently together not only in private, but in the public's eyes as well. So when you think of the minister you also think of his wife. (The same is true if the wife is the minister.) I am asked frequently about Lisa when she is not with me as I speak and write of her often. However, there are other ministers who even though they are married, rarely talk about their wives and you see them together infrequently. When you mention those minister's names you will not think immediately of their wives.

The same is true of the Holy Spirit. There are certain children who have a close mutual association with the Spirit of God. When you speak of them, you think of the Holy Spirit, because these men or women consciously minister as junior partners with Him and continuously acknowledge Him, therefore He manifests in their ministries. The result is that Jesus receives more honor, because the Spirit of God glorifies Jesus.

The Holy Spirit wants to be in close mutual association with you. If you honor Him then He will manifest, but if you don't it will be little different than the minister who has no intimacy with the wife he has been married to for years. Not only will he and his wife be distant, but they will be distant in the public's eyes as well. So ponder this: "May the *close association* of the Holy Spirit be with you."

INTIMACY

The final definition in the list above is the word *intimacy*. This word best defines communion, as it sums up the previous four categories we have discussed. In fact, one of Webster's definitions of *communion* is *intimate fellowship or rapport: communication*. Intimacy can only be developed by communication, which is the avenue to a strong friendship. One version of the New Testament reads: "The intimate friendship of the Holy Spirit be with all of you" *(The Message)*.

Again, it all comes down to friendship; this is the end goal of communion. The Spirit of God desires to be your friend. He yearns for your fellowship. He desires to teach you what He knows, and His knowledge is infinite! He is God; there is nothing hidden or mysterious to Him. There is no knowledge He doesn't possess. As Isaiah says,

"Who has directed the *Spirit of the Lord,* or as His counselor has informed Him? With whom did He consult and who gave Him understanding? And who taught Him in the path of justice and taught Him knowledge, and informed Him of the way of understanding? (Isa. 40:13–14 NASB, *author's emphasis*).

The answer, no one, because He is God!

I'll repeat it again: He is God! His wisdom, knowledge, and understanding are limitless, and He yearns to teach you what He knows. Think of it; when you know something of great value, you passionately desire to share it with those you are close with and love. He is no different. He wants to share with you what He knows! Do you see what is available to you? Have you been missing out because you have not pursued the person of the Godhead who resides within you? Have you tried to develop your relationship with Jesus apart from the Holy Spirit?

Too often many in the church attempt to draw near to Jesus apart from an intimate relationship with the Holy Spirit. I contemplated this recently and the thought came to me that in the days of Jesus' earthly ministry often the Jews wanted a relationship with God apart from Jesus. They made statements such as, "We are not illegitimate children . . . The only Father we have is God himself.' " (John 8:41 NIV), and "We are Moses' disciples. We know that God spoke to Moses" (John 9:28–29). They were confident in their relationship with God, which they really did not possess. Their confidence came from the fact they knew His Word (Scripture) given through Moses. Yet, did they really? They refused to receive from the very Word made flesh who stood in their midst.

Even so today many believers want a relationship with Jesus apart from the Holy Spirit. Yet, He is the One standing in our midst, and no one comes to know Jesus apart from Him; and to further complicate matters, the Spirit of God is easier to ignore than Jesus was for the Jews because He is not flesh and blood as Jesus was.

Jesus says, "If you really knew me, you would know my Father as well" (John 14:7 NIV). Jesus was simply saying, "The Father is not here, He is in heaven, but if you come to know Me you will know My Father because We are one." Well the same is true of the Holy

Spirit. Jesus is no longer here, He is in heaven; but if you come to know the Holy Spirit, you will know Jesus because they are one! That is why He is also known as the "Spirit of Christ" (1 Peter 1:11; Rom. 8:9).

ANOTHER ONE JUST LIKE ME

Just prior to leaving the disciples Jesus said to them,

> If you love Me, keep My commandments. And I will pray the Father, and He will give you another Helper, that He may abide with you forever—the Spirit of truth, whom the world cannot receive, because it neither sees Him nor knows Him; but you know Him, for He dwells with you and will be in you. I will not leave you orphans; I will come to you. (John 14:15–18)

There is so much in these few statements. First of all, again notice Jesus speaks of obedience, "Keep My commandments," followed by the words, "*And* I will pray the Father, and He will give you . . ." the companionship of the Holy Spirit. He directly relates receiving the Holy Spirit with obedience to His Word, hence, the fear of the Lord. Peter affirms this by saying, "And we are His witnesses to these things, and so also is the Holy Spirit whom God has *given to those who obey Him*" (Acts 5:32, *author's emphasis*). (Again, notice the partnership, two different witnesses were mentioned, the disciples, and secondly the Holy Spirit). Peter says that God gives the Holy Spirit to *those who obey Him*. So again, the foundation of intimacy is the fear of the Lord. Why have we not preached this more readily in our messages?

Returning to John 14, Jesus says that the Father will give those who fear God "*another* Helper." There are two Greek words translated into our English word *another* in the New Testament. If we examine them we will come to know more about the Holy Spirit. The first Greek word is *allos*, which means "another of the same sort." The other word is *heteros*, which means "another of a different sort."

An example that would illustrate the difference of these words is as follows: Let's say you ask for a piece of fruit, and I give you a peach. Upon finishing it, you ask again for another piece of fruit, and I then give you an apple. I have truly given you another piece of fruit, but a different sort. Yet if I give you another peach, then I have given you another fruit of the same sort; it is exactly like the one I just gave you. This explains the difference between *heteros* and *allos*.

The Greek word Jesus uses is *allos*—another of the *same sort*. Jesus is saying, "The Holy Spirit is just like Me." In fact, the Greek word for Helper is *parakletos*. This word comes from two different words: *para* which means "to the side of" and *kaleoo* which means "to summon." Hence, the word *parakletos* means *one who is called to another's side to aid him*. This word was originally used in a court of justice to denote a legal assistant, counsel for the defense, an advocate; then, generally, one who pleads another's cause, an intercessor, or advocate. Interestingly enough this word is used only one time in the epistles, and that was to identify Jesus (1 John 2:1). So just as Jesus ever lives to be our advocate or intercessor, so also the Holy Spirit is our advocate as well. He is called alongside to aid us.

Jesus is communicating to His disciples, "Exactly the way I have been with you is the way He will be to you." I frequently hear people say, "Oh, if I could have only walked with Jesus, I would have asked so many questions." Well, would they have? The very fact that they make such statements only reveals their lack of intimacy with the Holy Spirit. If they don't fellowship with the Spirit of God, what makes them think they would have done differently with Jesus? In fact, Jesus made this astounding statement:

"Nevertheless I tell you the truth." (John 16:7)

Before I complete His statement let me interject that this preface to His statement has always amazed me. He has walked with them for three and a half years. He has never told them one lie, or deceptive thought. Everything He has told them over those years has always come to pass. Yet, what He is about to share with them is so mind boggling that He has to preface it with, "Guys, what I'm about to say is not a lie, but the truth!" So let's continue to see this mind-blowing statement:

It is to your advantage that I go away; for if I do not go away, the Helper will not come to you; but if I depart, I will send Him to you. (John 16:7)

Wow, stop and think about these words. He says it is better for them that He goes away. Now you can understand why He had to preface this statement with, "Guys, I'm telling you the truth." In the time He had been with them He had taught them the most profound things of the kingdom anyone had ever heard. He healed their sick, raised their dead, cast out tormenting spirits, paid their bills and taxes, and this was only the beginning. Yet now He is saying it is best for you that I leave! Why? His answer is if He left He would send us the Helper.

Think of it, if Jesus remained on earth and we wanted to fellowship or ask Him questions, we would have to catch a plane to Tel Aviv, rent a car, drive out to the countryside of Galilee, and then find Him. This wouldn't be too difficult because there would be thousands around Him. However, you would have to wait for all the thousands who were there before you to leave, before you could make your way to the middle where He was. But even then you would be delayed because Peter is so outspoken he dominates all the conversations. Besides him, there are James and John, the sons of thunder; they're not so quiet themselves, and then there are the other disciples who have been waiting for the opportunity to ask what has been on their heart. Besides all that, Jesus does have to sleep six to eight hours a night, tend to His personal needs, and eat periodically.

However, the beauty of the Holy Spirit residing inside of us is that He doesn't have to sleep. You can speak with Him any time of the day or night, and you don't have to wait for others to finish. You have His complete and undivided attention at all times. In fact, ten thousand people can speak to Him intimately at the same moment! He has the ability to personally communicate with all of us who are hungry. But it doesn't stop there; it gets even better, for Jesus continues:

> Oh, there is so much more I want to tell you, but you can't bear it now. When the Spirit of truth comes, he will guide you into all truth. He will not be presenting his own ideas; he will be telling you what he has heard. He will tell you about the future. He will bring me glory by revealing to you whatever he receives from me. All that the Father has is mine; this is what I mean when I say that the Spirit will reveal to you whatever he receives from me. (John 16:12–15 NLT)

When the Holy Spirit speaks to us, in essence it is Jesus speaking to us, who actually is the Word of the Father to us. Oh yes, even though they are three different persons, each with their own mind, will, and emotions, yet they are absolutely one. You will never find them differing, and you will always find them one in purpose, plan, and execution of will. Recall the clear declaration of the Scripture: "Hear, O Israel: The LORD our God, the LORD is one!" (Deut. 6:4).

THE THREE LEVELS OF RELATIONSHIP

In the above Scripture Jesus told His disciples there was so much more He wanted to reveal to them, but they couldn't bear it. They were not able to grasp the more intimate things of God through their own natural senses.

Recall after Jesus was raised from the dead: He appeared to ten of the disciples; Thomas wasn't present. After hearing the others testify of seeing Jesus alive, Thomas said, "Unless I see in His hands the print of the nails, and put my finger into the print of the nails, and put my hand into His side, I will not believe" (John 20:25).

Jesus later appeared to all of them. He immediately told Thomas to put his finger in His hand and his hand in Jesus' side, and believe.

Thomas then cried out, "My Lord and my God!" Jesus then said something to Thomas, which I didn't understand for the longest time:

> "Thomas, because you have seen Me, you have believed. Blessed are those who have not seen and yet have believed." (John 20:29)

It used to be that I felt Jesus was a little hard on Thomas, because He didn't give him much hope after he had already repented and cried out, "My Lord and my God!" My reasoning was wrong due to my ignorance and incorrect understanding. Later the Holy Spirit brought enlightenment to what Jesus was communicating. He wasn't being hard on Thomas; rather He was just making a statement of fact. Jesus was simply conveying that those who know Him through their physical senses, can never know Him to the depth of those who know Him by their spirits, therefore the latter are more blessed.

Look at the apostle Paul. He never walked with Jesus like Peter and the others; rather he came to know Jesus by the Holy Spirit's revelation. He wrote:

> But I make known to you, brethren, that the gospel which was preached by me is not according to man. For I neither received it from man, nor was I taught it, but it came through the revelation of Jesus Christ . . . But when it pleased God, who separated me from my mother's womb and called me through His grace, to reveal His Son in me, that I might preach Him among the Gentiles, I did not immediately confer with flesh and blood, nor did I go up to Jerusalem to those who were apostles before me; but I went to Arabia, and returned again to Damascus. (Gal. 1:11–17)

As time went on Paul was able to go to a depth in a relationship with the Lord that none of the original apostles attained. Peter even made mention of this by writing:

This is just as our beloved brother Paul wrote to you with the wisdom God gave him—speaking of these things in all of his letters. *Some of his comments are hard to understand.* (2 Peter 3:15–16 NLT, *author's emphasis*)

Wow! Peter walked with the Master Himself three and a half years in the flesh, and Paul never did, yet Paul is giving insight into Jesus' nature and ways to the measure that even Peter had a difficult time understanding. Why? Because more than likely Peter constantly dealt with the memories of what he had seen and heard, and this hindered him from going into deeper intimacy with Jesus. That is why Jesus said, "Oh, there is so much more I want to tell you, but you can't bear it now. When the Spirit of truth comes, He will guide you into all truth."

A weak example of this (please understand it is not the full reason, but it will help shed light) would be those who fall in love over the Internet without ever meeting each other personally. This happens often, and it can easily become a stronger love than those who know each other in person.

In fact, to show how strong this can be, let me show you how it can even destroy a marriage. I recall one evening after a service I walked up to a man who seemed heavy in heart. He had two babies in his arms. Concerned, I asked, "Is everything okay?"

He said, "No, my wife left me recently to run away with a man she met on the Internet."

He then went on to tell me that she left not only him but the six children whom they had together for a man she had never met in person. They fell into a deep love over the Internet and it was so strong she left even her own children.

Getting back to the positive, over time I've observed those who fall in love with each other through a long-distance relationship sometimes end up having a deeper level of intimacy than those who continually courted in person. The reason again is that they were able to go beyond the physical and grew close in their souls. Many times when people meet in person they are dominated by the physical aspects, and beauty or exterior mannerisms blind them to the true person.

As I stated in the previous chapter, just as there are three levels of communication, verbal, deed, and heart; there are also three levels of relationship, or of knowing another. The lowest is the natural or physical level. Unfortunately this is the level that motivates many marriages, and once the physical loses its luster the two grow more independent. He often dives deeper into his sports, hobbies, ministry, and so forth, while she gravitates toward shopping, friends, ministry, and so forth. It's most sad.

Next would be the soul or personality of the person. This is the level in which David and Jonathan were strongly connected. We read: "The soul of Jonathan was knit to the soul of David" (1 Sam. 18:1). David in lamenting over his death cried out, "I am distressed for you, my brother Jonathan; you have been very pleasant to me; your love to me was wonderful, surpassing the love of women" (2 Sam. 1:26). David never knew Jonathan in a perverted way, there was no physical attraction at all between the two; but they were connected at a deeper level than the physical, and it was shown by his statement of Jonathan's love being better than a woman's. Their knowledge of each other was on a higher level, the soul. Understanding this level of soul relationship to be higher than the physical explains why people can leave their families for people they have only met by phone, letter, or Internet.

However, the highest level of knowing someone is the spiritual level. That is why Paul says,

> The Spirit searches all things, even the deep [intimate] things of God. For who among men knows the thoughts of a man except the man's spirit within him? In the same way no one knows the thoughts of God except the Spirit of God. We have not received the spirit of the world but the Spirit who is from God. (1 Cor. 2:11–12 NIV)

This is the level on which Paul came to know Jesus. Although Peter also came to know Him on this level, he most likely reverted back at times to the memories of knowing Him on the different other levels when they walked together in the flesh. For this reason Paul makes this very clear point:

> Therefore, from now on, we regard no one according to the flesh. Even though we have known Christ according to the flesh, yet now we know Him thus no longer. (2 Cor. 5:16)

If we are to go to a level of knowing God intimately we must realize that the greatest blessing He has given us is not to reveal Himself to us by the flesh but by His Spirit.

Wow! Are you getting excited as I am? What a wonderful Lord we serve. He yearns to make Himself known to us in the deepest way. He is the one who first desired this intimacy. Is your heart now crying out in hunger for the same?

STUDY QUESTIONS

1. Have you ever prayed a "please-take-me-home-to-Heaven-to-be-with-you" prayer? What were the circumstances when you did?

2. Many in the church attempt to draw near to Jesus apart from an intimate relationship with the Holy Spirit, even when they know that no one comes to know Jesus without the Holy Spirit. Why? Have you found this to be true in your own life?

3. As you meditate on the partnership role of the Holy Spirit, how does His presence influence your confidence in speaking your heart to God? Is there really anything you can hold back?

CHAPTER ELEVEN

THE PROMISE
OF THE FATHER

✠

You will never be blessed with something you don't believe.

I came to know Jesus Christ as Savior through a fraternity brother at Purdue University in 1979. Once I turned from my own ways and confessed Jesus Christ as my Lord I knew I was born into the kingdom of God. Scripture tells us, "If you confess with your mouth the Lord Jesus and believe in your heart that God has raised Him from the dead, you will be saved. For with the heart one believes unto righteousness, and with the mouth confession is made unto salvation" (Rom. 10:9–11).

There was no question I was saved. My heart bore witness to it, and Scripture confirmed it. Yet, I was living my new life lacking something, and for several months it eluded me as to what it was. The Lord seemed distant, even though I knew I was His child. When I read the Scripture it seemed I was in a cloud; it was difficult to comprehend, and I was only getting a limited amount of understanding, even though I read it diligently. I also lacked the ability to walk a victorious life over my adverse circumstances, and it seemed I was helpless to the strong current of peer pressure that came as a university student.

As time passed I began to meet people who seemed to have a much closer walk with the Lord than I did. They talked of Him in a beautiful and personal way. I was baffled. What were they doing that I wasn't? Why would God give them this closeness that I couldn't seem to find? They seemed to have strength and insight into the Lord's ways I just couldn't get. Then as I studied my Bible I realized there was a further encounter with the Lord that I had not experienced.

THE PROMISE OF THE FATHER

Let's take a look at what I discovered from the Scripture. Right before Jesus was taken to heaven we read:

> And being assembled together with them, He *commanded* them not to depart from Jerusalem, but to wait for the Promise of the Father, "which," He said, "you have heard from Me; for John truly baptized with water, but you shall be baptized with the Holy Spirit not many days from now." (Acts 1:4–6, *author's emphasis*)

Jesus told those who believed not to go anywhere, preach, start churches, or fulfill their callings until they first received the "Promise of the Father," which was in His own words the baptism of the Holy Spirit. The word *baptized,* which Jesus uses in this verse is from the Greek word *baptizo*, which means "to immerse, submerge; to make overwhelmed." Jesus was communicating that there would be an immersion of the Holy Spirit they didn't have yet; even though they believed in His resurrection, confessed His Lordship, and were His own faithful followers who were heaven bound.

One of the first things that stood out to me was the fact that receiving the infilling of the Holy Spirit was not a suggestion, option, or recommendation—it was a *command!* A command is given for our benefit, protection, or the good of the kingdom. We are not to take His commands lightly, for our sake as well as the kingdom's.

This Promise of the Father that they were commanded to receive unbeknownst to them would occur only ten days after Jesus was taken up. Interestingly, Jesus appeared to five hundred believers after being raised from the dead (1 Cor. 15:6), but only one hundred and twenty were in the Upper Room ten days after He left them. I firmly believe most of the five hundred started out waiting for the Promise, but as time passed by, waves of people left because of impatience, doubt, unbelief, or other reasons, until there was just a fraction remaining. Sadly, almost four out of five did not do as Jesus commanded.

Those who stayed were of one accord; they were dead to their own agendas. They had not taken lightly or made excuses for what Jesus commanded. I firmly believe their attitude was to stay as long as it took, just because the Master said to stay. Once God had remaining only those who took Jesus' command seriously we read:

> When the Day of Pentecost had fully come, they were all with one accord in one place. And suddenly there came a sound from heaven, as of a rushing mighty wind, and it filled the whole house where they were sitting. Then there appeared to them divided tongues, as of fire, and one sat upon each of them. And they were all filled with the Holy Spirit and began to speak with other tongues, as the Spirit gave them utterance. (Acts 2:1–4)

The day was called "Pentecost," which is not a term originated in the New Testament, but one of the major feasts of Israel. Notice they were *filled* or *baptized* with the Holy Spirit, just as Jesus foretold. This was the Promise of the Father, and was accompanied by them speaking in *other tongues.*

With some today the term *tongues* is confusing or mystical purely because of ignorance. When the scriptures speak of *tongues*, which I will do as well, it is only speaking of a language that is not recognizable to your understanding. We use this word outside of Biblical conversations as well. If you are with a foreign person who speaks English and you want to know what his primary language is you may ask him what his *mother tongue* is. In asking this question you are merely seeking to know what language he first learned from his parents when growing up.

The noise of the rushing mighty wind was the wake of the Holy Spirit making His initial entrance into the temples He had always desired to dwell in. Again, Scripture does not say He was wind; rather wind was the manifestation of His entrance.

OPPOSITE WAYS

At this point let me interject this interesting observation. Satan and his cohorts always do things opposite to or in perversion of God's ways. Whenever the Holy Spirit makes His initial entrance He does it in such a way that it can't be missed. People would *see* and *hear* His manifestation when He filled them. We will see this in other accounts in the book of Acts. Yet when the Holy Spirit leaves, He does it quietly. Recall when Delilah said to Samson that the Philistines were upon him and he jumped up and said,

> "I will go out as before, at other times, and shake myself free!"
> But he *did not know* that the LORD had departed from him.
> (Judg. 16:20, *author's emphasis*)

Samson did not know the Lord left because the Spirit of God always leaves quietly. However, whenever demons enter in, they do it quietly, but when they leave many times they do it with a manifestation of some sort (you will see this throughout the Gospels).

THE PROMISE IS FOR ALL

Now let's return to the day of Pentecost. There were Jews visiting Jerusalem from every nation on earth for the feast. When the city heard the noise of the rushing wind, multitudes came to where the disciples were. These visitors were in shock as they heard the uneducated disciples speaking of the wonderful works of God in their own languages. The amazed visitors cried out, "Whatever does this mean?"

Peter took advantage of their shock and stood up to preach Jesus to all present. Toward the end of his message he said,

> This Jesus God has raised up, of which we are all witnesses. Therefore being exalted to the right hand of God, and having received from the Father the promise of the Holy Spirit, He poured out this which you now *see* and *hear*. (Acts 2:32–33, *author's emphasis*)

Notice, he said the promise of the Holy Spirit was something they could *see* and *hear*. Say to yourself: "see and hear." It is important that we remember this for the upcoming verses.

The gathered crowd was cut to the heart and asked what they should do. Peter responds:

> Then Peter said to them, "Repent, and let every one of you be baptized in the name of Jesus Christ for the remission of sins; and you shall receive the gift of the Holy Spirit. For *the promise is* to you and to your children, and *to all who are afar off, as many as the Lord our God will call.*" (Acts 2:38–39, *author's emphasis*)

Notice carefully, the Promise, which they *saw* and *heard, is to all who are afar off, as many as the Lord our God will call.* Exactly what these disciples received in the Upper Room has been promised to all who call upon the Lord, which includes you and me!

At this point I would like to briefly walk you through every record of people receiving the Holy Spirit in the New Testament. There are four other occurrences. Make a note of two things. First, in every account except one, it was a separate experience from receiving Jesus Christ as Lord. Second, in every case bystanders could *see* and *hear* an outward manifestation of people receiving the infilling of the Holy Spirit.

SAMARIA

Philip went to a city in Samaria and proclaimed Jesus. Multitudes came out to hear the things he spoke. There were tremendous miracles as "unclean spirits, crying with a loud voice, came out of many who were possessed; and many who were paralyzed and lame were healed" (Acts 8:7). The outreach was amazingly powerful and there was great joy in the city, and we read,

> When they believed Philip as he preached the good news of the kingdom of God and the name of Jesus Christ, they were baptized, both men and women. Simon himself believed and was baptized. (Acts 8:12–13 NIV)

The people believed the good news of Jesus Christ and were baptized in water. So according to Scripture they were now reborn into the kingdom of God. Yet as we continue to read we find:

> When the apostles in Jerusalem heard that Samaria had accepted the word of God, they sent Peter and John to them. When they arrived, they prayed for them that they might receive the Holy Spirit, because the Holy Spirit had not yet come upon any of them; they had simply been baptized into the name of the Lord Jesus. (Acts 8:14–16 NIV)

Further confirmation of already being born into the kingdom of God is given again by the statement that they had been "baptized into the name of the Lord Jesus." There is no question, they had been delivered from the kingdom of darkness and were now in the family of God. Yet, even though they were now born-again believers, they still had not been baptized with the Holy Spirit.

You may question how they were able to be saved since Scripture clearly states, "No one can say that Jesus is Lord except by the Holy Spirit" (1 Cor. 12:3). That is true, we cannot confess the lordship of Jesus without the Holy Spirit's influence, yet this is altogether different from being filled with Him. At the moment of conversion we are sanctified, sealed, and indwelt by the Holy Spirit (see 1 Peter 1:2; Eph. 1:13; Rom. 8:9–11), but we are not filled with His presence until we ask the Father in Jesus' name. For Scripture says,

> If you then, being evil, know how to give good gifts to your children, how much more will your heavenly Father give the Holy Spirit to those who ask Him! (Luke 11:13)

From His words "your heavenly Father," we see this promise is only given to those who are already His children. Along these same lines, Jesus later says that "the world cannot receive" the Spirit of truth (John 14:17). From Jesus' words we see it is a separate experience from the new birth into the kingdom.

Let's continue with the people of Samaria:

> Then they laid hands on them, and they received the Holy Spirit. And when Simon *saw* that through the laying on of the apostles' hands the Holy Spirit was given, he offered them money, saying, "Give me this power also, that anyone on whom I lay hands may receive the Holy Spirit." (Acts 8:17–19, *author's emphasis*)

These believers received the Holy Spirit after already being saved. We are not told specifically that the people spoke in tongues; however, why would Simon offer them money? The Scripture says he *saw* that they had received the Holy Spirit. There was an obvious manifestation, and that would be none other than seeing them speaking in tongues because it is congruent with what happens with the other infilling experiences in the New Testament.

Reviewing this scriptural account of Samaria, we see first of all, that receiving the Spirit of God's infilling was a separate experience from conversion, and second, that bystanders *saw* an outward manifestation.

EPHESUS

The apostle Paul and his team came to Ephesus and found some disciples. The first question he asked them was,

> "Did you receive the Holy Spirit when you believed?" (Acts 19:2)

This should also be the first question we ask those who've been recently converted. Why would we want people to live even an hour without intimacy with the Lord and the power to be witnesses of Jesus (see Acts 1:8)?

These disciples had not heard of the Holy Spirit, they had only been baptized in water by John the Baptist. So Paul and his team told them of salvation that comes through Jesus Christ. Continuing we read,

> When they heard this, they were baptized in the name of the Lord Jesus. (Acts 19:5)

Now according to Scripture they are definitely born-again into the kingdom as they have confessed the lordship of Jesus and have been water baptized. Continuing we find:

> And when Paul had laid hands on them, the Holy Spirit came upon them, and they spoke with tongues and prophesied. (Acts 19:6)

Again they spoke in tongues and prophesied the moment the

Spirit of God filled them, and again bystanders could *see* and *hear* the manifestation of the Promise of the Father in those who received.

To prophesy means to "speak by divine inspiration." Peter prophesied on the day of Pentecost when he spoke the brilliant message that brought thousands into the kingdom. He proclaimed the Word of God without any preparation or previous study; it was spoken by inspiration. These men in Ephesus had little understanding of the ways of God prior to being filled with the Holy Spirit, and now they are speaking by inspiration the Word of God once filled.

This same thing happens to every person who gets filled with the Spirit of God. The *Teacher* comes to live in us, and the things of God become clearer. Before being baptized with the Spirit, the Word and ways of God were a blur to me. Not so afterward; the Bible opened up to me personally. I have witnessed numerous times those, who after living as a believer for long periods of time without the Holy Spirit, say after being filled with the Holy Spirit, "I had so many questions, and now they are all answered," and also, "The Bible has become so clear to me."

Along these same lines I have heard diligent students of the Scriptures who were born-again believers, yet not filled with the Holy Spirit, comment on Spirit-filled believers' knowledge of the Scriptures. They may study three times as much, yet they are taken back by a Spirit-filled believer's understanding. In hearing their comments I simply respond, "It's simple, those who are not filled don't have the full illumination of the Holy Spirit." But they can, because being filled with the Spirit is God's promise to all who call upon the name of Jesus! God is so good to us!

So again, as with the people of Samaria, the believers of Ephesus receiving the Spirit of God was a separate experience from their conversion, and again bystanders *saw* an outward manifestation.

THE APOSTLE PAUL

In Acts 9, Saul, whom we know as Paul, was traveling on the road to Damascus intending to persecute believers. When he came close he saw a blinding light from heaven and heard the voice of the Lord asking,

"Saul, Saul, why are you persecuting Me?"

Saul immediately asked who it was, and the Lord responded, "I am Jesus."

Saul then asked, "Lord, what do you want me to do?"

He was told to go to Damascus and there he would be given instructions.

At this point I believe he is born again. My reason for this is twofold. First, after the Lord said, "I am Jesus," Saul confessed Him as "Lord." Secondly, Saul fasted and prayed for three days, then Ananias came to him and clearly said,

> "*Brother* Saul, the Lord Jesus, who appeared to you on the road as you came, has sent me that you may receive your sight and *be filled with the Holy Spirit*." (Acts 9:17, *author's emphasis*)

Notice the word *brother*. He was a believer of Jesus Christ and confessed Him as Lord and had been praying three days. So after already being born-again, Ananias prayed for him to be filled with the Holy Spirit.

Now it does not say that Saul spoke in tongues here. However, he himself clearly tells us in his letter to the Corinthians, "I thank my God I speak with tongues more than you all" (1 Cor. 14:18). When did he start speaking in tongues? When Ananias laid hands on him and prayed (Acts 9:17).

CORNELIUS AND HIS HOUSEHOLD

There was a Roman officer named Cornelius. He, his household, and friends would become the first Gentiles to be born again. Cornelius had been fasting and praying often and one afternoon an angel appeared to him and told him to send for Peter.

Once Peter came a few days later, Cornelius had gathered his loved ones and they were ready to hear his message. Peter began to preach Jesus and before he could finish we read:

> While Peter was still speaking these words, the Holy Spirit fell upon all those who heard the word. And those of the circumcision who believed were astonished, as many as came with Peter, because the gift of the Holy Spirit had been poured out on the Gentiles also. For they heard them speak with tongues and magnify God. (Acts 10:44–46)

The Jews would have nothing to do with the Gentiles in regard to religious and even most social matters. They were excluded from the covenants of promise, without hope, and without God (see Eph. 2:12). So what happens here blows away the Jews who were with Peter. They were astonished that these Gentiles had received salvation and the Holy Spirit.

This is the only incident in the Bible where people actually get saved and receive the Holy Spirit at the same time. I personally believe, and I realize you can challenge this, that God did this because He knew these Jews would not have prayed for Cornelius and his loved ones to receive either Jesus or the Holy Spirit, as they would have altogether doubted they could be saved. Think of it, there is no immediate miraculous outward evidence of a person who is born-again. So even though these people would have accepted the Word as Peter preached it, and confessed Jesus, the Jews would not have believed their conversion could be possible.

However, when God filled them with the Holy Spirit and they began to speak in tongues, just as these same Jews did when they were filled, they could not deny that God had poured out His salvation to the Gentiles.

This occurrence shows beyond a doubt that the reality of a person receiving the fullness of the Holy Spirit is the outward manifestation of speaking in tongues. Another translation records, "the gift of the Holy Spirit had been poured out upon the Gentiles, too. And there could be no doubt about it, for they heard them speaking in tongues and praising God" (Acts 10:45–46 NLT). How did they know? "For, they heard . . ." They saw and heard the Promise of the Father!

TONGUES WILL CEASE

You may now be questioning: Yes, that is all true for the early disciples, but doesn't the Bible say that tongues will cease when that which is perfect comes? Yes, it does. Yet has the perfect come? Some may say, "Yes, the perfect was the Bible, and now that we have it we don't need tongues." Well let's look at Scripture to see if that interpretation is correct. Paul writes,

> Love never fails. But whether there are prophecies, they will fail; *whether there are tongues, they will cease;* whether there is knowledge, it will vanish away. For we know in part and we prophesy in part. But when that which is perfect has come, then that which is in part will be done away. (1 Cor. 13:8–10, *author's emphasis*)

First of all, we are told that when that which is perfect comes not only will tongues cease, but knowledge (*revealed* knowledge, to be exact) will vanish away as well. That certainly hasn't happened yet. So let's continue to read in order to find out exactly when the time period is that "the perfect has come."

> For now we see in a mirror, dimly, *but then* face to face. Now I know in part, *but then* I shall know just as I also am known. (1 Cor. 13:12, *author's emphasis*)

Notice he says twice, "but then." That is referring to the time when the perfect has come. Two things identify that time. First, we will see the Lord *face to face.* Are you seeing Him face to face right now? Are you seeing His resurrected body, with eyes that are flames of fire and hair that is white as wool, and His face shining like the sun? The second indicator is, "I shall know just as I also am known." Do you know Him as He knows you? The answer to these questions is obviously, no! He is speaking of the time when we shall be with the Lord in our own glorified bodies. That is when the perfect will come.

So since that which is perfect has not yet come, then tongues have certainly not ceased yet. As we continue in future chapters I will show you that one of the main reasons for tongues is for greater intimacy with God on this earth!

DO ALL SPEAK WITH TONGUES?

Someone else may question, "I believe in tongues, but not every believer is able to receive them, for the Scripture even asks, 'Do all speak with tongues?' and the answer to that is no." This again is a gross misunderstanding of what Paul is asking. To put this question to rest, which has robbed so many of God's Promise, we must first establish that the New Testament speaks of four different categories of tongues. Two are for public ministry, and two for personal fellowship with God. We should briefly review each to adequately answer this question: *Is it God's will that all His children speak in tongues?*

TONGUES WHICH ARE A SIGN TO UNBELIEVERS

This first set of tongues is for *public* ministry. In using the term *public* I speak of ministering to another person, or a group of people. Paul writes about them,

> Therefore tongues are for a sign, not to those who believe but to unbelievers. (1 Cor. 14:22)

These tongues occur when the Holy Spirit transcends our intellect and gives us the ability to speak another language of this earth that we have not previously had any training or ability to speak. This is given as the Spirit of God wills; we cannot just decide to operate in it, and we most often do not even realize when we are functioning in it. We are just aware that we are speaking in tongues, but don't realize we are speaking a known language of this earth.

Let me give an example. Recently I was preaching a service in a large church in Colorado. One of my staff members was in the meeting sitting in one of the back rows. She spends much time in prayer and intercession and felt as if the Lord wanted her to pray for me as I preached. So the entire service she thought she was merely praying softly in unknown tongues (which I will get to shortly). After the service a gentleman sitting in the seat in front of her turned to her and said, "You speak very good French, in fact, with a perfect accent."

She informed him that she did not speak French.

He then, in amazement, said to her, "I am a French instructor, and you were praying for that man in perfect French the entire time he was preaching, and you were quoting Scriptures in your prayers and immediately after you quoted the Scripture, the man then said in his message to turn in our Bibles to the exact Scripture you had just prayed!"

Needless to say he was most touched, and she was most excited. It was a sign to this man that what I was preaching was indeed the Word of God.

This tongue manifested with the disciples on the day of Pentecost. Scripture records,

> Now there were staying in Jerusalem God-fearing Jews from every nation under heaven. When they heard this sound, a crowd came together in bewilderment, because each one heard them speaking in his own language. Utterly amazed, they asked: "Are not all these men who are speaking Galileans? Then how is it that each of us hears them in his own native language? . . . [a list of the nations represented is then given, which I've omitted] . . . we hear them declaring the wonders of God in our own tongues!" (Acts 2:5–11 NIV)

Again, these tongues are a sign to the unbeliever. They were a sign to the French teacher above, as well as to these educated men from all over the world in this Scripture. This sign got their attention and it opened their heart to the Word of God.

I have heard numerous cases of believers speaking the Word of God to people in foreign languages they've never learned, and it is a sign confirming the message of God's love. In every case, there is tremendous ministry that results from this wonderful sign.

TONGUES GIVEN FOR INTERPRETATION

This second category of tongues is also for public ministry. These tongues are heavenly languages; there are no dialects like them on earth. This is true for the rest of the categories I am about to define.

You may now be questioning the fact that there is more than one language or dialect in heaven. Consider this possibility: the book of Revelation tells us that in heaven Jesus will give to the person who overcomes "a white stone with a new name written on it, known only to him who receives it" (Rev. 2:17 NIV). Also we are told of Jesus Himself that "His eyes were like a flame of fire, and on His head were many crowns. He had a name written that no one knew except Himself" (Rev. 19:12). So if no one else knew these names then it can only be that there are different languages in heaven.

These tongues fall into one of the nine categories of gifts of the Holy Spirit listed in the twelfth chapter of First Corinthians. It reads as follows:

> . . . to another different kinds of tongues, to another the interpretation of tongues. (1 Cor. 12:10)

Notice these tongues must have interpretation, not translation. Why? Because they are heavenly languages that are not known to the natural world.

I recall a meeting in Singapore. I was asked to minister in one of the largest churches in the nation and it was my first of several visits. Before I was given the platform to preach, the crowd, which was very large, was silent after a period of singing beautiful songs of worship. All of a sudden a man began to speak a language of heaven. It was so loud and clear, yet he had no microphone. He was located somewhere in the balcony of this huge auditorium, yet everyone could hear the clarity and authority that was in his voice. It was as if heaven amplified it.

As he spoke my inner man was leaping with joy while my outer man froze in reverence. It seemed every hair on my arms and legs were at attention and my heart racing in this holy atmosphere. Once he was finished, the interpretation came and the word of the Lord given through that tongue and interpretation was exactly what I was about to preach that night. I was amazed. God gave not only myself, but this entire congregation confirmation that what I was bringing that night was from Him.

These tongues when interpreted are similar to prophecy. For this reason Paul says, "He who prophesies is greater than he who speaks with tongues, unless indeed he interprets, that the church may receive edification" (1 Cor. 14:5). Again, by this verse you can see these tongues are given for public ministry to the church; and they are the category of tongues Paul was referring to when he asked, "Do all speak in tongues?" So let's read this verse now in context:

> And God has appointed these in the church: first apostles, second prophets, third teachers, after that miracles, then gifts of healings, helps, administrations, varieties of tongues. Are all apostles? Are all prophets? Are all teachers? Are all workers of miracles? Do all have gifts of healings? Do all speak with tongues? Do all interpret? (1 Cor. 12:28–30)

Do you notice that Paul is speaking about ministry giftings that God has set in the church? Certainly *not all* are apostles, or prophets, or teachers, or pastors, or have gifts of miracles and healings, and all *do not* have the ministry gift of speaking in tongues or interpretation of heavenly tongues. Why is that? The answer is found in the following:

> Therefore tongues *[tongues for a sign]* are for a sign, not to those who believe but to unbelievers . . . if the whole church comes together in one place, and all speak with tongues *[tongues for*

interpretation], and there come in those who are uninformed or unbelievers, will they not say that you are out of your mind? (1 Cor. 14:22–23, *author's emphasis*)

Before I answer our question, let me point out that these two verses clearly show the difference between the two public tongues. He first writes that tongues are a sign to unbelievers. This is speaking languages of this earth in which we have never been trained. An unbeliever who knows these languages clearly sees that there is no possible way we could speak those words except by miraculous intervention of the Lord. So it is a sign to the unbeliever.

Then Paul talks about the whole church coming together and speaking in tongues at the same time. This is clearly the tongues that are the languages of heaven. The reason I know this is that all the disciples on the day of Pentecost were all speaking in different earthly languages the wonderful works of God. They did not have to be interpreted, for the unbelievers knew what they were saying. He is talking in this verse about speaking to the church in the heavenly tongue that needs to be interpreted. If not, then no one would understand. As you can see, there is no need for all to speak in tongues otherwise the uninformed or unbelievers would think we were crazy.

So the answer to this question "Do all speak in tongues?" which has been so misunderstood by many, is simple. God is selective when it comes to ministry gifts He places in the church, because not all need to operate in it. But He is *not* partial, and I repeat, He is not selective, in what He gives to each of us believers for our own personal walk. The following two categories cover the gift of tongues in regard to our personal relationship with Him.

TONGUES FOR PERSONAL PRAYER

The next two categories of tongues are for personal prayer, and are the Father's provision to every Christian who believes. We can see them represented in the following verses:

> For if I pray in a tongue, my spirit prays, but my understanding is
> unfruitful. What is the conclusion then? I will pray with the spirit,
> and I will also pray with the understanding. I will sing with the spirit,
> and I will also sing with the understanding. (1 Cor. 14:14–15)

Notice Paul is specifically identifying these tongues as prayers, not tongues that minister to the church. We are also told in this same chapter, "He who speaks in a tongue does not speak to men but to God" (1 Cor. 14:2). When we speak in one of the two public tongues we are speaking to unbelievers (tongues for a sign), or to the church (tongues for interpretation); but when we pray in tongues we speak to God, not to men. Do you see the difference?

In the above verse Paul tells us of two different ways to pray, one in your own understanding, which for me would be English. The other way is to pray in tongues, which is my spirit praying, led by the Holy Spirit. The same is true for singing songs of worship, "I will sing with the spirit, and I will also sing with the understanding."

Jude identifies personal praying in tongues by saying,

> But you, beloved, building yourselves up on your most holy faith,
> praying in the Holy Spirit. (Jude 20–21)

Notice when we pray in tongues that we build ourselves up, whereas when we speak in tongues to the church and interpret, we edify or build up the church (1 Cor. 14:5). God desires both, and both are very important.

In the next chapter I will discuss in much greater depths this category of tongues. You will discover that it is vital to walking intimately with our Lord. I call this category of tongues, "The language of intimacy."

TONGUES FOR INTERCESSION

The last of the four categories of tongues is for intercession, which is when we stand in the gap in prayer—pleading for another in need.

> Likewise the Spirit also helps in our weaknesses. For we do not know what we should pray for as we ought, but the Spirit Himself makes intercession for us with groanings which cannot be uttered. Now He who searches the hearts knows what the mind of the Spirit is, because He makes intercession for the saints according to the will of God. (Rom. 8:26–27)

There are times we are at a loss for what to pray. The New Living Translation brings this out the best by saying, "For we don't even know what we should pray for, nor how we should pray."

I don't know all that is going on with my loved ones or others in need, but the Spirit of God does. My mother lives in Florida, and I live in Colorado. Suppose she is in a situation that requires divine assistance, yet she doesn't realize it or can't reach me? How would I know what to pray, let alone that she even needed prayer?

The very first time I saw this Scripture become a reality to me was back in my university days. I had only been a believer for two years but was so hungry to tell others of Jesus; so I began a campus Bible study that targeted fraternity and sorority students. We had approximately sixty attending the study. One night I taught on the Holy Spirit. I simply walked through Scripture and showed them the will of God. There was a girl in the study who was taught that she received the Holy Spirit automatically when she was born again and that tongues had passed away. How sad that her teachers didn't believe the Scriptures, but believed their mentors who were blinded as well. Yet, that night when she saw what the Bible said about it, she believed and was filled with the Holy Spirit immediately, along with several others.

Early the next morning I was awakened by an intercom page from one of my fraternity brothers telling me I had a visitor. I quickly dressed and walked out to the foyer of our house to greet this same young lady whose sorority was right across the street. She was glowing and said, "John, I'm sorry to wake you, but I couldn't wait to tell you about what just happened this morning."

She told how she was awakened by the Holy Spirit that morning at five o'clock and felt an urgency to pray in her heart. She knew something was very wrong, so she found a secluded place and began to pray in tongues. She said it became more and more intense as she was aware she was in a battle. So she asked the Lord as she was praying who it was that God was having her intercede for. All she heard in her heart was that it was an older man and that his life was in jeopardy. She prayed for an hour and then felt a peace come to her heart.

Almost minutes later an urgent phone call came for her roommate, who was also a believer. Her roommate took the call only to find out that her grandfather, who was very dear to her, had just suffered a massive heart attack at five o'clock that morning, and his life was miraculously spared. They were able to stabilize him just minutes before the call, which was exactly when she felt the peace to stop praying.

She was beaming. All her Christian life she was told tongues passed away, because they were no longer needed. What had she missed because someone didn't just believe the Scriptures? You could never convince her otherwise now. She is forever settled that praying in tongues is a necessity for us believers today.

I have seen this countless times. One of the neatest examples of tongues for intercession is a situation that happened to Esther, our Australia office manager. She is a great prayer warrior as well as a minister. Back in the nineties, when she was in Bible school, one morning while doing her housework she just lifted her hands and said, "Lord, I don't have anything to pray about today, so if You need me here I am."

She said all of a sudden a tremendous burden hit her to pray. She bent over in her living room and tongues just gushed out of her with great intensity. She kept seeing in her spirit a Chinese man kneeling on a dirty floor moving his hands in circular motions as if cleaning it. As she was praying she felt the urge to cry out, "Get up! Get up! Get up!" After praying for quite some time she felt a release in her heart and went back to her housework.

Approximately five months later a New Zealand man who is a missionary to China came to their Bible school and was sharing a story of a Chinese pastor who was being persecuted in prison in mainland

China along with another pastor. The other pastor looked at this Chinese pastor and told him that God was going to release him from prison. With this in their hearts they went about their daily prison cleaning chores.

Soon afterward the guard decided to send all the prisoners back to their cells except for this pastor. He was now alone in this room cleaning the floor when he suddenly heard a voice intensely saying, "Get up! Get up! Get up!" Not being able to ignore what he heard, he stood up and walked to the door. Amazingly it was unlocked so he opened it and walked undetected right out of the secured prison, and when he got outside there was a taxi sitting right in front of it. He got in and was driven away.

Esther was so excited to think that this could have been what she was praying about months earlier. So she went up to the missionary (whom she had never met before in her life) after he spoke, and found out it was the exact day in her prayer journal that she had been praying in her living room.

Also one of the Bible school leaders came up to Esther and the missionary. He too had remembered a burden that the Holy Spirit placed on him months earlier to pray for a man in need. As he prayed in urgent tongues he too vividly saw a Chinese man in prison. The missionary pulled out a group photograph of the Chinese church and the Bible school leader pointed to the man whom he saw while praying in tongues. Needless to say it was the senior pastor from the prison!

Esther and the Bible school leader then compared notes in their prayer journals and found out it was the exact same day! God had confirmed to them both they had been a huge part in seeing that man freed as a result of their obedience to pray.

How Will We Believe?

What if Esther had have been taught that tongues passed away with the emergence of the Bible? What if she had been taught that tongues are not for everyone? How many are missing out today because they have believed what man has taught over what the Bible teaches?

One of the greatest tragedies I have observed in my years of ministry is that so many Christians interpret the Word of God through their experiences, rather than allowing the Word of God to dictate their experiences. God is not limited to our experiences; He is so much greater!

In my search for the infilling of the Holy Spirit I met numerous well-meaning Christians who tried to deter me from speaking in tongues. A few months after receiving Jesus as my Lord, I was brought to a leaders meeting of the campus ministry that printed the material that was used to lead me to salvation. I will always be grateful to that group.

However, in the meeting, I was in for a shock. The president asked each leader to share what their number one prayer request was for the semester. One young man said that he was praying for a "B" average. Another shared he was praying for his roommate's salvation. Then they came to me and I simply said, "I would like to receive the Holy Spirit like they did in the Bible, when they spoke in new tongues."

As soon as I said these words, the main leader quickly and nervously said, "John, we'll talk about this after the meeting."

We never did. However, my fraternity brother who led me to the Lord pulled me aside after the meeting and said, "John, they don't believe in speaking in new tongues."

As a new believer, I looked at him in amazement and said, "What, they don't believe what is in the Bible?"

This took me back, because my former denomination based their doctrine mostly on what man taught, rather than the Scriptures. In fact we were encouraged not to read Scripture but to allow our pastor to interpret for us. I attended church for nineteen years and thought I was on my way to heaven, when in reality I was on my way to hell. So when I found God's plan for salvation in Scripture through my fraternity brother, I made up my mind that I would believe the Word of God whether I understood it or not! That is the fear of the Lord, and the fear of the Lord is the beginning of under-standing (see Ps. 111:10).

BLESSED OR IGNORANT

I have good news; it is God's will for you to be filled with His Spirit and to pray in the languages of heaven! If fact if you want to hear God's heart cry for you, it is as follows:

"I wish you all spoke with tongues." (1 Cor. 14:5)

You may say, "Those are Paul's words to the Corinthians."

No, we are clearly told: "Above all, you must understand that no prophecy in Scripture ever came from the prophets themselves" (2 Peter 1:20 NLT), and that "All Scripture is given by inspiration of God" (2 Tim. 3:16). Simply put, these are not Paul's words to the Corinthians, but the Lord's words to us, for the Word of God "lives and abides forever" (1 Peter 1:23). It is God saying to His children, "I wish you all spoke in tongues!"

You will never be blessed with something you don't believe. I want to say this again: God is not moved by our reasoning, need, or feel-ings; rather by our faith. You will see over and over Jesus saying to people, "Be it done to you according to your faith." Faith simply believes that what God says He will do, He will do. Faith comes by hearing God's words, not man's incorrect beliefs.

It is so important that we preach and believe truth, rather than experience. Experience is a wonderful confirmer of truth, but is not to be a teacher of truth. The Holy Spirit is our Teacher and He will never speak contrary to what the written Word of God states. When we believe the Word of God, then we will see and experience. So many have it backward; they want to experience, then believe. That again, describes the words of Jesus to Thomas. We have a choice: to base our faith on others' experiences, or on the Word of the One of whom it is recorded:

God is not a man, that He should lie, nor a son of man, that He should repent. Has He said, and will He not do? Or has He spoken, and will He not make it good? (Num. 23:19)

In conclusion, the Holy Spirit says to all of us concerning praying in tongues, "I do not want you to be ignorant" (1 Cor. 12:1). He then goes on to discuss what we have written about in this chapter and more. Then at the conclusion of discussing all these matters He clearly says:

But if anyone is ignorant, let him be ignorant. (1 Cor. 14:38)

In other words, He is saying to us through Paul, "I have made My will clear to you on the matter of tongues. If you choose to remain ignorant, then you will be ignorant and will not be blessed with My provision." I'm sure He was grieving when He moved upon Paul to write this, as He foresaw the people, who years later, would make this a matter of discussion (this was not even a question in the days of the early church).

Again, He is sadly saying to us that we can stay in our ignorance, but if we do, His final comment on the matter is:

Do not forbid to speak with tongues. (1 Cor. 14:39)

Here is a warning, if you ever hear someone attack tongues he is in direct disobedience to the Lord. God knew some in the latter days would either in ignorance or stubbornness tell His sheep that speaking of tongues had passed away, or that it's not of God.

It is my prayer that you will see the wonderful provision God has given His children as we move into the next chapter and discover the wonderful language of intimacy the Holy Spirit gives those who believe.

(Note: If you have not received the infilling of the Holy Spirit, turn to Appendix B; I would like to lead you in a prayer to receive.)

STUDY QUESTIONS

1. In the opening of this chapter, the author reflects on his young faith as a college student. He describes living a new life, but feeling that something was lacking even though he was diligently reading Scripture. Can you identify with that situation in your own past, or maybe even in your life now?

2. As you consider this study on what it means to speak in tongues, how are your beliefs being challenged? How are you affected by the news that it is God's will for you to be filled with His Spirit and to pray in the languages of heaven?

3. You have been reading this book for a reason—an experience or event has prompted you to explore what it means to draw near to God. Could it be that He has provided a means to draw closer through what you are studying now? Could the gift of tongues for personal and intercessory prayer be the next step in your walk with the Lord?

CHAPTER TWELVE

THE LANGUAGE
OF INTIMACY

✢

The wisdom or counsel of God is deep water and
is often a mystery to the natural mind.

I've written this again and again, but to make sure it becomes real in
the very core of your being, I'll keep repeating it: *God passionately
desires intimacy with you.* He yearns for your fellowship. Not only does
He desire to interact with you, but for that interaction to be lush and rich.

COMMUNING WITH GOD ON HIS LEVEL

In order for this abounding communion to become a reality He has
made a way for us to fellowship with Him on His level! Allow me to
explain. Scripture tells us:

> For he who speaks in a tongue does not speak to men but to God.
> (1 Cor. 14:2)

We know that Paul is not referring to either category of public tongues, for both are people speaking to people the Word of God in languages that are unfamiliar to the deliverer. In this Scripture Paul is referring to when we pray or commune with God. When we *pray* in tongues we speak directly to God, not to men. Paul also wrote, "The Holy Spirit helps us in our distress. For we don't even know what we should pray for, nor how we should pray" (Rom. 8:26 NLT). Again, two distinct hindrances to communing with God: often we don't know what to pray; or secondly, how to do it.

This is best illustrated as follows. If I were to walk into the office of the president of the United States, could I communicate with him on his level? The answer is obviously no; he would have to come down to my level of understanding. He knows so much more than I know about the affairs of the nation, including all the security issues that are not made available to the public. He knows of the many plans and projects of the nation along with the terms and codes that have to be kept secret; because if they fall into the hands of the wrong people, they could threaten national security.

To parallel this, when I walk into the King of the universe's office— His throne room—if I only pray out of my understanding, then our communication is limited! I cannot talk to the Lord on His level because He knows far more than I do. The only way He can communicate with me is to come down to my level of understanding. As in our example above, He knows so much more than I do concerning the affairs of the universe that include the mysteries, kept secret for various reasons, one reason is to insure the mysteries do not fall into wrong hands. This is clearly seen in Paul's admonition:

> We speak of God's secret wisdom, a wisdom that has been hidden and that God destined for our glory before time began. None of the rulers of this age understood it, for if they had, they would not have crucified the Lord of glory. (1 Cor. 2:7–8 NIV)

Even though this specifically speaks of the wisdom of the crucifixion and resurrection of the Lord Jesus and glories that followed, it is just one example of God making sure His wisdom doesn't fall into the wrong hands. But there are others. (See Matthew 7:6.) Scripture tells us that we are in a war, and the enemies we fight are principalities, powers, rulers of darkness, and spiritual demonic forces (Eph. 6:12). In a natural war there has to be a secret communication between those fighting together. The same is true for the Commander of the hosts of the Lord and His kingdom warriors. What a fabulous secret communication link-up the Lord has given His children for the good of the kingdom and our protection. The enemy is clueless as to what we are petitioning the Father for when we speak in tongues. Demonic forces can be devising a plan to attack us or loved ones, but as we pray in tongues, all of a sudden a barrage of angelic assistance shows up to the demons' surprise. As a result the demons flee in terror before their attacks can prosper.

THE MAIN PURPOSE

Our prayer language in tongues is not only for keeping critical knowledge from getting into the wrong hands. Its main purpose is intimacy. My wife and I have been together so long and have become so close that we have developed communication that is unique to us. She can say things to me in the midst of a room full of people that no one else would understand. We've developed a language of intimacy. This is not only so with husbands and wives, but with all who have close relationships. It can be between lifetime friends, those who have worked together for years, those who went to war together, and so forth. Bottom line, there is a language of friendship that is formed that is unique to them.

In a similar way, God has given us a way to intimately communicate and fellowship with Him on a deep level; a level that our natural unredeemed minds could never reach. The psalmist foresaw it and wrote, "Deep calls unto deep at the noise of Your waterfalls" (Ps. 42:7). This communication is compared to living waterfalls. Jesus tells that out of our hearts " ' . . . will flow rivers of living water.' But this He spoke concerning the Spirit, whom those believing in Him would receive" (John 7:38–39). Our intimate communion with the Lord is likened to flowing living waters. Oh, what the Holy Spirit has given us! The ability that He has granted us! It's staggering to think about.

Let's further explore as it gets even better. Paul went on to say about a believer who prays in tongues,

> . . . for no one understands him; however, in the spirit he speaks mysteries. (1 Cor. 14:2)

What does Paul mean by *mysteries?* The Greek word is *musterion.* W.E. Vine, who is an expert in Greek New Testament words, writes about this word: "In the New Testament it denotes, not the mysterious (as with the English word), but that which, being outside the range of unassisted natural apprehension, can be made known only by divine revelation, and is made known . . . to those only who are illumined by His Spirit. In the ordinary sense a 'mystery' implies knowledge withheld; its Scriptural significance is truth revealed."

So here is one of the many benefits of praying with tongues. God the Holy Spirit knows what the mind of Jesus and the Father are since they are all One. He also knows what we lack since He is our constant Companion. So He mediates by giving us the words in the language of heaven to ask, seek, or commune in a perfect manner. Oh, how wonderful! You may be thinking: *but I don't understand what I am saying when I pray in tongues.* Yes, and for this reason Paul says,

> Therefore let him who speaks in a tongue pray that he may interpret. For if I pray in a tongue my spirit prays, but my understanding is unfruitful. (1 Cor. 14:13–14)

So whether it's a request, intercession, or simply communing with God; if I ask the Holy Spirit to bring illumination to my understanding of what He is giving my spirit to pray, He will do it! Now not only my spirit enjoys the fellowship, but my soul as well.

STEWARDING REVEALED MYSTERIES

Many times, in this fellowship, revelations of the Lord come from Scriptures that all of a sudden come alive, and these are the truths that I have written and taught over the years of ministry. However, there are so many more that I have not yet taught.

You may wonder why I haven't taught them. The reason is the time is not right, or God wanted something else said and emphasized to His people. When we speak as ambassadors of the kingdom we must remember we speak as oracles of God, and there are things that He wants to be spoken, and other things that are not to be spoken at that particular time.

I will never forget when I learned this the hard way. I was meeting with a man of God who was very well known in his part of the world. I had heard of his ministry and admired him and longed to meet him. Another pastor arranged for us to meet. I was so excited. So we met for dinner one night—the pastor, the man of God, and our wives. At the dinner I shared the most profound revelations God had given me that I could think of, and I did it in order to impress the man of God. (I wasn't consciously thinking this at the time, but in retrospect I know that was my motive—how immature.)

We were driven back to our hotel that night by the pastor. My wife and I were exhausted; it had been a long day. However, as tired as I was, I had a very uncomfortable feeling in my spirit. I knew the Lord wanted me to pray, so I told my wife to go on to bed without me. She did, and I headed out to the balcony of our hotel room. As soon as my foot crossed the threshold I heard the Holy Spirit say sternly in my heart, "So, the king showed all the treasures in his house tonight!"

My heart sank to my feet. I was utterly shocked as well as ashamed. I knew the Holy Spirit was referring to Hezekiah's mistake. There were people who visited him that he wanted to impress and we read:

And Hezekiah was pleased with them, and showed them the house of his treasures—the silver and gold, the spices and precious ointment, and all his armory—all that was found among his treasures. There was nothing in his house or in all his dominion that Hezekiah did not show them. (Isa. 39:2)

After showing them all his treasures the prophet Isaiah brought Hezekiah a rebuke from the Lord. I felt the same way. I knew I had spoken that night the truths or treasures God had shown to me to impress this man.

God then said to me firmly, "Son, I've not revealed My precious truths for you to go around and spew out whenever it seems best for you. They are not given to impress! You are a steward of what I reveal to you and you are not to speak it unless I prompt you."

I quickly repented and asked for forgiveness and the burden lifted and I immediately went to bed with peace. His mercy is amazing!

If we are wise we choose our inner circle of friends to be those who will not carelessly tell what is intimate between us to just anyone. Close friends are wise with how they handle what they know about each other. If a friend repeatedly violates this we then have to back off what we share with them, knowing it is no longer held as precious. It is the same with the Lord's secrets. If we desire for Him to share His heart, we must be sensitive to what and when He wants us to share.

DRAWING OUT THE COUNSEL OF GOD

When I pray or commune with God in tongues, I find that ideas, revelations, wisdom, or teachings simply come to my mind. The best way I know how to describe it is they just bubble up like trapped air being released from the depths of the sea and surfacing. The ideas bubble up from deep within my inner man and surface in my mind or understanding. Scripture tells us:

The spirit of man is the candle of the LORD, searching all the inward parts of the belly. (Prov. 20:27 KJV)

We must keep in mind that the Holy Spirit does not speak to our

heads, but to our spirits. That is the part of our being that He illu-
minates. As we pray in the Spirit and ask for interpretation, the wisdom or counsel of God bubbles up from our hearts to the realm of
our understanding or mind. Scripture tells us,

> Counsel in the heart of man is like deep water, but a man of
> understanding will draw it out. (Prov. 20:5)

What is counsel? It is wisdom that is applied to a specific situation.
Why do people go to counselors? To get the wisdom—which is a mystery to them—they need for a certain circumstance.

Notice the only one who can draw out the counsel of God, which
is likened to living water coming from a deep well, is the person of
understanding, or the one who knows the ways of "The Counselor."
The Holy Spirit knows all mysteries (unrevealed counsel, knowledge,
and wisdom) of the kingdom. Again in reviewing what Jesus cried out:

> "He who believes in Me, as the Scripture has said, out of his heart
> will flow rivers of living water." But this He spoke concerning the
> Spirit, whom those believing in Him would receive. (John 7:38–39)

According to Proverbs the water coming out of our heart is the
counsel or mysteries of God, and Jesus tells plainly that its source is
the Spirit of God. He is the fountain of living water (see Jer. 2:13).
Now read carefully what Paul says,

> We speak the wisdom [or *counsel*] of God in a mystery . . . that
> we might know the things that have been freely given to us by
> God. These things we also speak, not in words which man's wis-
> dom teaches but which the Holy Spirit teaches, comparing spiri-
> tual things with spiritual. (1 Cor. 2:7, 12–13, *author's emphasis*)

So the wisdom or counsel of God is deep water and is often a mystery to the natural mind. Yet Jesus tells us this living water will come
forth by the Holy Spirit. How? Paul tells us clearly:

> For he who speaks in a tongue does not speak to men but to
> God, for no one understands him; however, in the spirit he
> speaks *mysteries*. (1 Cor. 14:2, *author's emphasis*)

There it is! That is how a person, who possesses understanding, draws out the counsel of God. How often I have come to places in Scripture that were a puzzle to me. I have unanswered questions that come to mind. The understanding is a *mystery* to me. Most always I simply say, "Holy Spirit I don't understand this, would You please show me . . ." Then I simply pray in tongues and either at that time or a while later, after I've ceased praying in tongues and left the prayer closet, the revelation of the hidden truth bubbles up into my mind or understanding. Oh, how wonderful it is!

Numerous times I've been writing a book and hit what seemed to be a dead end. The direction I am to continue is a *mystery* to me. I then get up from my chair and start praying in tongues and in a matter of time, usually minutes later, the wisdom comes forth like a dam breaking open, and I type for several more hours.

When I was a single man it was a *mystery* whom I should marry. Over the years of being a single Christian man there were three girls I liked very much, but after spending time praying in the Spirit I knew God was saying a definite "no." Then I met Lisa and for one month I prayed every day in tongues for thirty minutes concerning our relationship. God gave me a very strong go ahead in those times of prayer, and afterward many confirmations. But I have to say, I knew beyond a doubt before the confirmations that she was the one because of the clarity, accompanied by peace, which came while praying in tongues.

There have been times when I've been at a loss for understanding what has transpired in my life or the life of someone close to me. It's a *mystery* to me. I simply ask the Holy Spirit to please show me His wisdom or view on the circumstance. Sure enough after a time of praying in tongues, if it was information that He wanted me to have, it comes.

I have had situations where a certain member of my family has needed prayer and it was hidden to my own understanding, but the

Spirit of God came on me to pray for this family member in tongues, and then later I found out the divine assistance or prevention of harm that was given.

Mysteries are things that are hidden to our natural mind. It could be where I'm to go to church, what ministry I am to be a part of, what house to buy, how to pray effectively for the president or other leaders, or how to pray effectively for my pastor. As you know, the list is endless.

PEACE IN KNOWING GOD'S DIRECTION

The area of *mystery* that seems to weigh down most believers is direction. That is the primary reason people go to counselors. But have I got great news for you! You will never have to worry over what to do again. God promises, "If any of you lacks wisdom *[what to do]*, let him ask of God, who gives to all liberally" (James 1:5). We can ask perfectly! How? By praying in tongues about our situation. I have been in jams before where I've not known what to do, and then prayed in tongues, and every time an inspired idea came bubbling up from my heart and it was the wisdom I needed for the situation.

This is how we have functioned in the ministry over the years. When I've lacked direction for what to do, I have prayed in tongues for a period of time and all of a sudden divine inspired ideas begin to flow. My wife and I began the ministry years ago; every major decision we've made has come through praying in the Spirit. Today we have over thirty employees with offices in three continents. God has given us the privilege of touching millions of lives with His Word and presence. We've not had to borrow any money in fourteen years and now have substantial physical and personnel assets to help us effectively serve God's people. The reason is all because God says,

> I am the LORD your God, Who teaches you to profit, Who leads
> you by the way you should go. Oh, that you had heeded My
> commandments! Then your peace would have been like a river,
> And your righteousness like the waves of the sea. (Isa. 48:17–18)

I can honestly say our peace has flowed like a river. We have been in times where it seemed like we should be in utter panic in judging the circumstances that surrounded us. Yet as we prayed in tongues and committed our works to Him, peace has abounded in our lives. In regard to praying in tongues we read,

> For with stammering lips and another tongue He will speak to this people, to whom He said, "This is the rest with which You may cause the weary to rest," And, "This is the refreshing." (Isa. 28:11–12)

Those who have no peace have no rest. The rest that He speaks of in this verse is a result of the peace that flows like a river. I could give countless stories from over the years to illustrate this point, but one specific situation comes to mind. It would have been very easy for me to lose all peace because I was at a loss for what to do. This situation occurred when I traveled to Mexico to preach an evangelistic meeting. I flew to the city of Monterey for a one night outreach. It was to be held in an auditorium in the downtown area. I had prayed all day in tongues and saw a vision in my spirit of a bright light streaming from the sky down on top of the auditorium in which we were to meet that night. The Lord spoke to my heart and said, "This is My glory which will manifest tonight."

That evening the pastor who coordinated the meeting and I drove to the hall with excitement. His church had done much to prepare for the outreach. When we arrived fifteen minutes before the meeting was to start I noticed that an angry looking man, who had two armed guards accompanying him, approached the pastor. He spoke to him in Spanish, and I could tell it wasn't in a nice tone. The pastor then came over to me and said, "John, you're not going to be able to preach tonight."

I said, "Why not?"

He said, "That man is a high ranking government official, and there is a law which states you cannot preach the gospel in Mexico unless you are a Mexican citizen. It is a law that is hardly ever enforced, but this man insists on the fact that we obey it. If you don't, you could get in some serious trouble. In fact, he wants to speak with you immediately."

I immediately thought of Peter and John who were told by leaders not to preach the gospel, yet they didn't obey since it was contrary to the Word of God. So I said to the pastor, "There is no way this man is going to stop what God showed me would happen this afternoon in prayer! Will this affect your church? Because if it doesn't I'm going to go ahead and preach once he leaves. I didn't come all the way down here to sit and do nothing! But if this will have adverse effects on you, then I won't preach."

He said, "John, this man can create a lot of trouble for our church, so I think it is best we do what he says." I conceded to the pastor's counsel and we walked over to the government official.

The first thing this man did was look at me and then gruffly asked, "Do you speak Spanish?"

"No sir," I replied.

He then said, "I have one thing to say to you. You will only speak to these people about tourist-related activities." He then turned and continued to speak sternly to the pastor in Spanish; the whole while the guards with guns were staring at us with very intimidating looks on their faces. Once this government official was through warning the pastor, they left.

The pastor seemed very shaken and apologized to me for not being able to minister, and went into the auditorium to make final preparations for the meeting.

At this point, I was very upset. I knew I needed the counsel of God; what to do was a *mystery* to me. So I stepped out of the auditorium and noticed a semiprivate place where I could pray. (I was in the downtown area so there was no place completely private.) I knew the way to draw out the counsel of God was to pray in the Spirit. So I began to speak boldly in tongues. A few people walked by, but I figured they probably thought I was a foreigner walking around speaking to myself.

Within moments of speaking in tongues the peace of God began to fill my soul. I continued for fifteen minutes or so and all of a sudden the thought came bubbling up from my heart; I heard, "Put away your

Bible and speak to these people about the greatest Tourist who has ever visited Mexico."

I leaped with excitement and cried aloud, "That's it, that's it; he told me all I could speak about are tourist-related activities! I'll tell them about Jesus, the greatest Tourist who has ever visited Mexico."

I hurried back into the auditorium. However, the service had already started and the pastor was in the front greeting the audience. His wife who was in the back of the auditorium said, "John, Pastor wants you to come to the front."

I went up and he looked at me and said in a whisper, "God told me to tell you to do whatever He has instructed you to do."

I then said, "Folks, I was told by a government official that I could only speak to you about tourist-related activities. So I am here to tell you about the greatest Tourist who has ever visited Mexico, Jesus."

The believers in the crowd cheered with excitement. I then preached the next sixty minutes the Word of God. When I was through I called all those forward who were willing to forsake their own lives and commit themselves to the lordship of Jesus.

As many came forward I suddenly noticed a police officer walking into the back of the auditorium headed straight for the platform. I thought to myself, *I must get these people saved before I get arrested.* I recalled Peter and John who preached at the beautiful gate and were arrested before they could even tell the people how to receive Jesus. So I quickly prayed with the people who came forward to be saved. After praying with them I noticed that the policeman walked past me on the side of the stage and went through the rear curtain on the platform. Immediately I felt relief as I now could minister to the people.

I then told the people they could go with the counselors who would minister further to them. As they walked off the platform I noticed a man who was crippled. I then heard the Holy Spirit speak to my heart, "He is the first one I want to heal. Stop him and pray for him immediately."

I did exactly what He told me and after praying for him I said, "Now sir, please drop your crutch."

He looked at me as if to say, I can't do that, but with my further prompting he did. Then I took him by the hand and we began to walk together. He started out slow, but got faster and faster until we eventually were running together.

The place went wild with excitement. People started coming down from all over and there were hundreds of them at the platform. Many were healed by the power of the Holy Spirit. I'll mention a few. We prayed for a woman who was deaf and the Lord opened her ears. She wept so profusely that her light blue blouse became dark blue in the front from the stream of tears that were pouring down from her face. God healed the eyes of another woman, and cancer in another.

We then prayed for a five-year-old boy and he was healed. We ministered to the people for over an hour; it was beautiful and many were weeping with joy. At one point I noticed there were people there with cameras, but didn't pay much attention to them.

I left the country the next morning and returned to the United States. A week later the pastor flew to the U.S. to meet with me. He said, "John, I had to come and share this with you in person." He began to tell me that the government official sent two undercover agents that night to the meeting and their instructions were to arrest me if I preached.

They arrived as I was praying for the crippled man. When they saw him walk one said to the other, "Do you think this is real?"

His partner replied, "I don't know, but let's go closer and check it out." The pastor knew of their conversation because one of his ushers overheard them and stayed close.

The two officers came forward and witnessed the miracles. When the lady's ears opened, one said, "I think this is real."

Then they saw the five-year-old boy healed by the power of God and they looked at each other and said, "This is real!"

The pastor then said to me, "John, those men who came to arrest you then came forward and asked you for prayer, and they both got saved that night!"

Needless to say the pastor and I rejoiced in my office; but that wasn't all. He then held up the city's newspaper and showed me an article that was done the day after our meeting. The article stated the officials claimed I was a fraud and illegally taking money out of the country, but they reported seeing people getting healed and did not witness money being taken. Interestingly enough, I felt in my heart not to take any offerings, and our ministry paid for the airplane ticket. We did not take one cent out of the country for those meetings.

How wonderful the Holy Spirit is. How can anyone live through these times without His guidance? If I wasn't able to pray in tongues that day in my room and that night around the flagpole I would have left Mexico frustrated by not fulfilling God's purpose. The pastor wouldn't have let me preach due to the intimidation of the government official. However, because of praying in other tongues, the will and wisdom of God, which was a *mystery* to us, manifested. I was able to intercede for the pastor according to the will of God, which resulted in him hearing God's voice, and the Lord gave me the wisdom concerning how to walk through the resistance. To Him be all the glory!

Oh, how the enemy has fought this in the church. He fears it, for this is God's direct line of communication with His saints and demons are unaware of what transpires. There are times we have situations or desires on our heart that we are able to articulate in our own understanding, but much more, there are other times we have situations that we cannot articulate in our own understanding and need the aid of the Holy Spirit's words. For this reason Paul says, "What is the conclusion then? I will pray with the spirit, and I will also pray with the understanding" (1 Cor. 14:15).

BUILDING OUR INNER MAN

In recent times my heart has cried out for God's people to enter into greater intimacy with the Holy Spirit for reasons such as the above examples. Our response to His cry for nearness will become more and more crucial. As time progresses it will not be enough to have only an understanding of the Scriptures, which even the Pharisees possessed. We must develop sensitivity to what the Spirit of God is *saying*, rather than only what He *has said*. Jesus lived this way. He said, "By myself I can do nothing; I judge [*make decisions*] only as I hear" (John 5:30 NIV, *author's emphasis*). The Amplified Bible brings this out much clearer by saying:

> I am able to do nothing from Myself [independently, of My own accord—but only as I am taught by God and as I get His orders] . . . [I decide as I am bidden to decide. As the voice comes to Me, so I give a decision]. (John 5:30 AMP)

Jesus lived so sensitively to the Holy Spirit's direction and voice that He repeatedly acknowledged His dependence. He said, "The Son can do nothing of Himself, but what He sees the Father do" (John 5:19). Again He says, "The words that I speak to you I do not speak on My own" (John 14:10). As His followers we are told in no uncertain terms, "He who says he abides in Him ought himself also to walk just as He walked" (1 John 2:6).

As He was, even so, should we be responsive to the Spirit of God. In fact, I personally believe God's desire is for us to become more aware of His realm than of what is transpiring around us in the natural world. Praying in tongues builds our inner man that we may be sensitive to the Holy Spirit. Again, we are told,

> He who speaks in a tongue *edifies* himself. (1 Cor. 14:4, *author's emphasis*)

The Greek word for *edifies* is *oikodomeo*. Its pure definition is "to build a house." This is interesting in the fact that our bodies are the temples of the Holy Spirit. Paul specifically tells us that "you are God's building" (1 Cor. 3:9). We are His house. Therefore when we pray in tongues we are enlarging our dwelling place for the Holy Spirit. We are giving Him more room to occupy. Of course this is not in a physical sense, but figuratively; for W. E. Vine tells us this word, "signifies 'to build,' whether literally or figuratively."

So when we pray in tongues we enlarge our ability to contain His presence and power within our lives. We are strengthening our inner man so that we are more easily led by the Spirit of God, rather than our natural minds.

Mr. Vine also tells us this word is used metaphorically in the sense of "promoting the spiritual growth and development of character of believers." In a similar sense the apostle Jude tells us in his epistle:

> But you, beloved, building yourselves up on your most holy faith, praying in the Holy Spirit. (Jude 20)

The Greek word for *building* in this verse is *epoikodomeo*. The definition of this word is "to build upon." This again implies the continual act of building up our spirits. Paul told believers that they were God's building, and he by the grace of God laid the foundation in bringing them to Christ, but then clearly says, "Let each one take heed how he builds on it" (1 Cor. 3:10).

Today so many believers' spirits are weak, as they have not built their inner man. They are quicker to see things through natural eyes rather than through the eyes of their heart. They are quicker to believe what they hear with their natural ears, rather than what the Spirit of God is saying to their hearts. Their outer man dominates their lives. Their inner man can be compared to a person who sits around all day on a couch, watching TV and eating potato chips. Oh they may be diligently working in life and ministry, but their inner man is neglected. These believers often say to me, "Why don't I ever seem to hear God?" The reason is very simple. Again, God communicates to our spirits, not our heads. "The spirit of a man is the lamp of the LORD" (Prov. 20:27). If our inner man is not built up then we are not able to hear clearly.

Paul told the Hebrew believers he had so much more to say but couldn't since they'd become dull of hearing (Heb. 5:11). These people were not in need of hearing aids; rather their inward man had digressed to become insensitive to spiritual things. So in essence, this group of people was doing the very opposite of building; they were becoming more dull in their hearts to hearing the Word of the Lord. This very principle applies to those who neglect the building of their inner man. Without a strong inner man, we are hindered in our intimacy with God! For this reason Paul boldly states, "I speak in tongues more than you all" (1 Cor. 14:18). He continues to the Hebrews:

But solid food belongs to those who are of full age *[spiritually mature]*, that is, those who by reason of use *[practice]* have their senses exercised to discern both good and evil. (Heb. 5:14, *author's emphasis*)

Notice he mentions their senses; these are not the outer but inward senses. Also note that he tells us that by using, or as the original states, through practicing, we strengthen our inward senses to discern what is of God and what is of the evil one.

Just as we have five natural senses we have five spiritual senses. Scriptures give us a sampling. As you read each of the following, ask yourself if you could do any of the things mentioned with your natural senses. This will help you conclude the writers are speaking of spiritual senses not natural ones:

TASTE –

Oh, *taste* and see that the LORD is good. (Ps. 34:8, *author's emphasis*)

How sweet are Your words to my *taste*,
Sweeter than honey to my mouth!
(Ps. 119:103, *author's emphasis*)

Your words were found, and I *ate* them, and Your word was to me the joy and rejoicing of my heart. (Jer 15:16, *author's emphasis*)

TOUCH –

Come out from among them and be separate, says the Lord. Do not *touch* what is unclean, and I will receive you. (2 Cor. 6:17, *author's emphasis*)

Depart! Depart! Go out from there, *touch* no unclean thing; go out from the midst of her, be clean, you who bear the vessels of the LORD. (Isa. 52:11, *author's emphasis*)

SMELL –

Now thanks be to God who always leads us in triumph in Christ, and through us diffuses the *fragrance* of His knowledge in every place. For we are to God the *fragrance* of Christ among those who are being saved and among those who are perishing. To the one we are the *aroma* of death leading to death, and to the other the *aroma* of life leading to life. (2 Cor. 2:14–16, *author's emphasis*)

And walk in love, as Christ also has loved us and given Himself for us, an offering and a sacrifice to God for a sweet-smelling *aroma*. (Eph. 5:2, *author's emphasis*)

Indeed I have all and abound. I am full, having received from Epaphroditus the things sent from you, a sweet-smelling *aroma*, an acceptable sacrifice, well pleasing to God. (Phil. 4:18–19, *author's emphasis*)

Sight –

For with You is the fountain of life;
In Your light we *see* light.
(Ps. 36:9, *author's emphasis*)

The *eyes* of your understanding being enlightened; that you may know what is the hope of His calling, what are the riches of the glory of His inheritance in the saints. (Eph. 1:18–19, *author's emphasis*)

For in that He put all in subjection under him, He left nothing that is not put under him. But now we do not yet see all things put under him. But we *see* Jesus. (Heb. 2:8–9, *author's emphasis*)
If therefore your *eye* is good, your whole body will be full of light. But if your *eye* is bad, your whole body will be full of darkness. If therefore the light that is in you is darkness, how great is that darkness! (Matt. 6:22–23, *author's emphasis*)

Hearing –

Then Elijah said to Ahab, "Go up, eat and drink; for there is the *sound* of abundance of rain." (1 Kings 18:41–42, *author's emphasis*)

He who has *ears to hear*, let him *hear!*" (Luke 14:35, *author's emphasis*)

He who has an *ear*, let him *hear* what the Spirit says. (Rev. 2:7, *author's emphasis*)

In regard to our inward man growing dull and insensitive to the Spirit of God Jesus made this clear by saying:

Therefore I speak to them in parables, because seeing *[outer man]* they do not see *[inner man]*, and hearing *[outer man]* they do not hear *[inner man]*, nor do they understand. And in them the prophecy of Isaiah is fulfilled, which says: "Hearing you will hear *[outer man]* and shall not understand *[inner man]*, and seeing you will see *[outer man]* and not perceive *[inner man]*; for the hearts *[inner man]* of this people have grown dull. Their ears are hard of hearing *[inner man]*, and their eyes they have closed *[inner man]*, lest they should see with their eyes *[inner man]* and hear with their ears *[inner man]*, lest they should understand with their hearts *[inner man]*." (Matt. 13:13–15, *author's emphasis*)

The spiritually mature develop their inward senses to discern spiritual things—what's of God, and what's not. This development is determined by the use or training of the believer's senses. We all have natural senses and some individuals are more developed than others merely through training. For example, there are people who've developed their sense of taste to discern the quality of wines. Through practice they can taste and tell the wine's year, whether it was an early or late crop, the abundance or lack of rainfall that year, and so forth.

Others have trained their eyes to determine the value of precious stones. To the untrained eye the stone may appear flawless, but the trained eye can tell the quality of cut and color, the number of minor or major flaws, and the clarity rating.

There are sound technicians, musicians, conductors, and so forth, who have trained their ears to hear sounds and melodies. They can tell if one instrument in an entire orchestra is out of sync. They have through the years trained their sense of hearing to recognize harmony.

There are those who have trained their sense of smell. They can tell you the top note and undertones of a fragrance and name the full bouquet of spice, floral, and citrus in any perfume.

These individuals chose to heighten their natural senses. It wasn't that they were more gifted; they were determined to develop what they had; it didn't just happen, they focused their attention to this end.

By now you are probably thinking of many other examples that illustrate how we can train our outer senses. The same principle applies to the spirit. You can be a believer for years and not develop your spirit. Scripture tells us that John the Baptist "grew and became strong in spirit" (Luke 1:80). Paul told Timothy to give himself entirely to spiritual development so "that your progress may be evident to all" (1 Tim. 4:15). How do we build our inner man? Scripture is clear: through the written Word of God (1 Peter 2:2; Acts 20:32), obedience to His word (Heb. 5:9), and praying in tongues (1 Cor. 14:4; Jude 20).

THE IMPORTANCE OF DEVELOPING OUR SPIRITS

Why is it so important to develop our inward senses? We are freer to commune with the Holy Spirit if our spiritual senses are developed. He can speak more intimately to us on many levels. To explain, let's look again at the natural. If all five of your senses were not working it would be impossible for me to communicate with you. I could shout, but you wouldn't hear; tap you on the shoulder, but you wouldn't feel; hold up a sign, but you wouldn't see, and so forth.

Recently my dad, who is in his eighties, needed a hearing aid, but didn't want one. We'd all be together talking and having dinner and I would notice he looked like he was somewhere else. I'd raise my voice, "Did you get that, Dad?" He looked puzzled as if to say, "What did you say?" I realized he wasn't enjoying any of our conversation because his sense of hearing was dull. (I'm glad to report he now has a hearing aid!) The same is true in the spirit. If your senses are dull you only get part of the conversation at best! I often hear people say, "God doesn't seem to speak to me on an intimate level." Well, again, chances are good their inward senses are underdeveloped. We must settle this issue; God wants to speak to us more than we want to hear from Him, but too often we—like the Hebrew believers—become "dull of hearing" (Heb. 5:11).

You strengthen what you use, and weaken what you do not use. While praying in the Spirit our inner man prays, and natural understanding or flesh is denied. It is a form of fasting our natural reasoning in order to enter into unhindered communion with God. I encourage you to not only pray in the Spirit, but to believe God for the interpretation and train yourself to listen as you pray.

Many mornings I will spend over an hour just praying in tongues. Once I've gone past wandering in my mind, which is more quickly subdued if I sing songs of worship, or pour my heart out to Him first, I find it easy to focus on the spiritual. Usually the sense of the Lord's nearness overshadows any natural concerns or obligations. I then find in these times that ideas, revelations, and wisdom will bubble up into my understanding. I've learned the wisest thing to do is write these things down as I pray and then the Holy Spirit will move on to other things.

In my early years while praying with the Spirit I experienced much frustration because I would at times think of natural things while praying in tongues. For example, as I prayed, ideas would come for titles of new books, a desire to contact people I hadn't talked to in a while, a gift for someone, how to spend ministry finances, and so forth. I eventually learned that this most often was the inspiration and direction of the Holy Spirit. I soon began to make note of these ideas and noticed that as soon as I did they would leave my mind and other ideas would surface. I would then put these things into action and see the blessing of God on them. I realized that while praying in tongues the Holy Spirit would not only bring people or nations to mind, but would give me direction for things He desired me to do. Again, it is a way to communicate with God on a much greater level.

LIVING IN THE REALM OF THE SPIRIT

I personally believe this is how Paul wrote a good portion of his epistles. He would make comments such as, "For though I am absent in the flesh, yet I am with you in spirit, rejoicing to *see* your good order and the steadfastness of your faith in Christ" (Col. 2:5, *author's emphasis*). He didn't see them with his natural eye, because he clearly said he was not physically there. Again to the Corinthians he stated, "For I verily, as absent in body, but present in spirit, have judged already, as though I were present" (1 Cor. 5:3 KJV). How could Paul be present with, and behold what the Corinthian and Colossian believers were doing and saying, yet not be there physically? We must remember we are spirit beings, and there is no distance or barriers in the realm of the Spirit of God. Those whose spirits are built up in the Lord become more aware of things that are transpiring, so they can more effectively pray or minister to those in need. Recall in the last chapter, our Australian office manager's Bible school leader picked out the Chinese pastor among his many church members in the picture without having ever seen him!

Paul would simply see things in his spirit that were going on in the different churches as he prayed in tongues; then address these things in letters and ship them off. During my travels and while praying in tongues I have seen things my family members or staff are going through. I then pick up the phone and many times already know the news before I am told. However, because I've prayed in the Spirit I've been prepared as to what to say and how to handle the situation.

While in Africa I met a man who was a tribal warrior in Kenya. He came to know Jesus years ago, and still remains among his people to minister to them. His Christian name is John and he periodically travels out of Africa to minister. In his most recent trip to the U.S. he stayed with a couple I also know. During his three-week stay he would give periodic reports of his family back in Africa. A little puzzled, the couple he stayed with asked how he knew so much of what was going on with his wife back home because they knew his family didn't have a phone; in fact, there wasn't a phone in their entire village in Africa. He then said something to this effect: "This is what Paul did with the churches of Asia. They were his family in the Lord because he spiritually birthed them, and when apart, as he prayed, he was with them in spirit beholding their order; he could even write to them about their affairs. I am only doing what God has given every believer the ability to do through the power of the Holy Spirit. This is how I keep up with my family's activities, and I do this whenever I'm away from them."

The reason I give John's testimony is that it perfectly lines up with the Word of God. Why should we be surprised by this? Paul mentioned it not once, but a couple of times in the New Testament. This African man hasn't had anyone tell him that Scripture is not true, or has passed away, as so many in America have been told. Why have we drawn back from what Jesus paid so great a price to provide for us? Why are we not building our inner man so that we can be more effective servants and children of our dear Lord and Savior Jesus?

It is not too late! No matter if you are ten or eighty-five years old; whether you have been born-again recently or decades ago; you can build your inner man through praying in tongues, and ask for the interpretation as you pray that your understanding may receive the benefit of the wonderful communion of the Holy Spirit. There is so much He desires to reveal to you; you only have to still your outer man and draw near in your heart to the One who knows all. What an invitation; don't pass it by!

STUDY QUESTIONS

1. Have you experienced situations where the gift of tongues has helped you better understand how God was working in your life? What illumination, peace, or refreshing did you receive?

2. The author writes about the need to properly steward the mysteries God reveals, pointing to Hezekiah's example (Isa. 39:2) and his own situation with a well-known pastor. How important is it for you to wait on the Lord's proper timing to reveal to others what He has revealed to you? Is there a real desire to impress others that needs to be controlled?

CHAPTER THIRTEEN

FULL ASSURANCE OF FAITH

✠

God does not respond to our need, He responds to our faith!

Over the years I've met numerous sincere believers who are filled with the Holy Spirit, love and fear God, and abstain from sin, yet they too ask, "Why is it that I just don't hear from God or experience His presence?" I can sense the frustration with these saints, as they are doing all they know to do, but are misconnecting in prayer. In speaking with them for just a few moments we usually discover the reason for their struggle. Most often there is one answer, and it is found in the following verse:

> Therefore, brethren, having *boldness* to enter the Holiest by the blood of Jesus, by a new and living . . . let us *draw near* with a true heart in *full assurance of faith*, having our hearts sprinkled from an evil conscience and our bodies washed with pure water.

Let us hold fast the confession of our hope without wavering, for
He who promised is faithful. (Heb. 10:19–23, *author's emphasis*)

First, the writer tells us that we can come to the Holiest, where the
Lord dwells. Recall that the moment Jesus gave up His Spirit on the
cross, the veil in the temple was rent from top to bottom. God moved
out and was getting ready to move into His new temple, the born-
again human being. So now when we draw near we seek Him within,
rather than trying to blindly imagine entering a throne room that is
millions of miles away; for to connect with the Spirit of God within,
is to be in the throne room with Jesus and the Father.

Notice the writer tells us that we are to come with *boldness*. How
can we draw near with such confidence? Simply because He has
already paved the way for us to come into His presence through His
royal blood that He shed on Calvary. We've had our conscience
cleansed from the tyranny of condemnation resulting from sin, and
now we can come with full assurance into His presence.

It is *not* a hit-and-miss scenario. It's a fact; God says if we draw
near, He will draw near to us! However, the key reason for the
struggle of most is found in the statement, "full assurance of faith."
We must come in faith! For Scripture clearly tells us:

But without faith it is impossible to please and be satisfactory to
Him. For whoever would come *near to God* must [necessarily]
believe that God exists and that He is the rewarder of those who
earnestly and diligently seek Him [out]. (Hebrews 11:6 AMP,
author's emphasis)

Hear these words: "without faith it is impossible to please Him."
Take a few moments and let these words sink deep within your heart.

"I'M JUST LOOKING FOR SOMEONE TO BELIEVE!"

I will never forget the time when I was only a few years old in the
Lord, single and living in an apartment in North Carolina. One

morning while in a deep sleep I found myself jumping up in my bed to a seated position and the words came crying out of my mouth, "I'm just looking for someone to believe!"

I looked at my alarm clock and discovered it was 4:00 A.M. I was in such a deep sleep I had to check myself to see where I was and what had just happened. I turned on the light next to my bed and noticed that my sheets were soaking wet from where my body had lain, yet I had no fever or any sickness of any sort. I was stunned as well as in awe, for I realized God had just spoken out of my mouth, but I then thought: *Why wasn't it more profound? I know He is looking for people to believe.* I was tired, so I immediately fell back to sleep.

The next morning when I awoke I kept hearing the entire morning: *I'm just looking for someone to believe . . . I'm just looking for someone to believe . . . I'm just looking for someone to believe . . .* About midmorning, all of a sudden it hit me. I spoke aloud to myself, "It is profound!"

From that moment I began to ponder the following two questions: *What grieved Jesus the most?* (not what angered Him more than anything else, that of course would be the hypocritical Pharisees) and *What pleased Him the most?* First, He was most grieved by people who just didn't believe that He would do what He said He would do! To put it simply—their lack of faith. This, in reality, is what faith is; it believes God says what He means, and He means what He says. God is not a man to lie, rather He backs His Word with the honor of His name. He swears by Himself, since there is none higher. So when we doubt Him, we insult His integrity.

Let's take a look at this. Listen to the disappointment of Jesus in the following Scriptures; these are a few just from the book of Matthew (I've chosen Today's English Version as it gives the best feel of His tone):

"What little faith you have!" (Matt. 6:30–31 TEV)

The disciples went to him and woke him up. "Save us, Lord!" they said. "We are about to die!"

"Why are you so frightened?" Jesus answered. "What little faith you have!" (Matt. 8:25–26 TEV)

At once Jesus reached out and grabbed hold of him and said, "What little faith you have! Why did you doubt?" (Matt. 14:31 TEV)

Why are you discussing among yourselves about not having any bread? What little faith you have! (Matt. 16:8 TEV)

Do you hear the disappointment and sadness in His tone with each of these? However, the incident that most amazes me is when the disciples could not cast a demon out of an epileptic boy. Hear what Jesus said to His own staff:

"How unbelieving and wrong you people are! How long must I stay with you? How long do I have to put up with you? Bring the boy here to me!" Jesus gave a command to the demon, and it went out of the boy, and at that very moment he was healed. (Matt. 17:17–18 TEV)

He certainly didn't hold back His feelings. His tone goes beyond disappointment, on disgust, and sadness and borders on righteous anger!

Afterward the disciples asked Him why they couldn't cast out the demon. Jesus simply said,

It was because you do not have enough faith. (Matt. 17:20 TEV)

GOD RESPONDS TO OUR FAITH

Everything we receive from the Lord is through faith. There is a truth I've discovered that many in the body of Christ are ignorant of, and that is, God does not respond to our need, He responds to our faith! Stop and ponder that statement for a moment. I could give countless examples to illustrate this from Scripture, but allow me just two. First, on a certain day Jesus was teaching many leaders in a house and we read:

> And the power of the Lord was present to heal them. (Luke 5:17)

I love how Scripture specifically tells us that God's power was present to heal these leaders. It informs us that at least one of those leaders, but most likely several, needed to be healed, yet none of them received. Why? None of them had faith to receive it.

However, there were a group of men who brought a paralyzed man to the house in a stretcher but couldn't get in because there were so many, so they brought him up on the roof and tore open the tile and lowered the man down on ropes before Jesus. We then read:

> When He *saw their faith* . . . He said to him, "I say to you, arise, take up your bed, and go to your house." Immediately he rose up before them, took up what he had been lying on, and departed to his own house, glorifying God. And they were all amazed, and they glorified God and were filled with fear, saying, "We have seen strange things today!" (Luke 5:20–26, *author's emphasis*)

Jesus saw their faith. The paralytic, along with those carrying him, knew that the Lord was good for His word. They more than likely knew what God had already spoken to His people, and that was to "Forget not all His benefits: Who forgives all your iniquities, Who heals all your diseases" (Ps. 103:2–3). The leaders on the other hand, were amazed when they saw the paralytic healed and they glorified God; yet not a single one of them was healed. Why? Because we cannot receive, even what God desires us to have, unless we receive it by faith! The Father's will was for those sick leaders to receive, yet they didn't! God responds when we believe, which is reflected by our moving forward upon what He says.

In another incident a Greek woman came to Jesus. She pleaded with Him to heal her daughter of demonic oppression. Jesus said to her,

> First I should help my own family, the Jews. It isn't right to take food from the children and throw it to the dogs. (Mark 7:27 NLT)

He called her a dog. She could have been insulted and stormed away. Yet, she somehow knew His character. So she immediately came back with:

> That's true, Lord, but even the dogs under the table are given some crumbs from the children's plates. (Mark 7:28 NLT)

She knew she was in the presence of the Son of God, and believed He was a good God with no shortage of power. She was determined, for she knew that all she had to do was stay with her request and she would not be denied. She stayed in faith, and for that Jesus said,

> For this saying go your way; the demon has gone out of your daughter. (Mark 7:29 NKJV)

When she came to her house she found her daughter completely healed. Again, Jesus responded to her faith, not her need, for her first request was uttered out of need, but her reply to His initial answer was fueled by her faith.

FAITH IS THE KEY TO RECEIVING EVERYTHING

This principle applies to everything in the kingdom. In fact James is bold enough to state that when we come to God in prayer we must do it:

> . . . in faith, with no doubting, for he who doubts is like a wave of the sea driven and tossed by the wind. For let not that man suppose that he will receive anything from the Lord. (James 1:6–7)

Wow, listen to those words again: "let not that man suppose that he will receive *anything* from the Lord." Meditate on this for just a moment. Think of the words *not receive anything*. That is a definitive statement with no gray areas, no exceptions! God is making sure we get this point-blank! He responds to faith, nothing else!

This is why so many have not received the Holy Spirit. They do not ask in faith. Scripture asks us:

> This only I want to learn from you: Did you receive the Spirit by the works of the law, or by *the hearing of faith*? (Gal. 3:2, *author's emphasis*)

This goes along with what James says. You cannot receive *any-thing* from the Lord if you do not approach Him in faith, which would certainly include His Spirit. So many times I have met with hungry believers who do not speak in tongues. They know there is more and they are seeking, yet after hearing the Word of God on the Holy Spirit's infilling, they say to me, "I prayed once to receive and nothing happened." Or when they ask to receive they do it with a "maybe so" attitude. They do not have the determination the Greek woman above had. They do not come with full assurance! They do not come with boldness! God expects us to know His will, for we are told, "Therefore do not be unwise, but understand what the will of the Lord is" (Eph. 5:17); then once we know it, ask with faith and confidence.

In regard to drawing near to God for intimacy this very same principle applies. So many times when believers approach the Lord they do so hoping they will connect with Him. (I'm not speaking of the biblical word *hope,* which is a "confident expectation," but the "maybe so" hope that has evolved in our English language.) Believers often speak words into the air hoping they will be heard. This attitude is not faith and will not access the presence of God. Again, we are told, "Without faith it is impossible to please Him, for he who comes to God must believe that *He is*" (Heb. 11:6, *author's emphasis*). The writer is telling Hebrew believers that when you approach God you must believe *He is*. In other words, that He will be there; He will hear, and He will answer!

James says, "Let not that man suppose that he will receive any-thing from the Lord; he is a double-minded man" (James 1:7–8). A double-minded man is one who approaches God, yet questions being in His presence. He may even wonder if God notices his coming.

A symptom of being double-minded is drifting thoughts. Let me explain. In services many times when people have come to the front to be led in prayer after a message I tell the musicians to stop playing. The reason being that even though the music is just instrumental, many will sing the words of the familiar songs, and they will not be focused on the Lord. James says, "Draw near to God and He will draw near to you . . . purify your hearts, you double-minded" (James 4:8). How can we be seeking God when our minds aren't even focused on Him? Can you imagine approaching a friend in a similar manner?

People are easily distracted because they hope they will connect with God when drawing near. No, you must believe *He is*, you must believe *He is* there; you must believe that *He is* listening and will respond; and He deserves your undivided attention. Faith gives the assurance that *He is* giving you His full attention, because you know He has promised, and He cannot lie; if you draw near, He in turn will come close. Oh, the excitement in my heart at this moment is almost uncontainable. What a wonderful God we serve. He will respond to us if we approach Him in faith!

HOW DO WE GET FAITH?

Now we must address the question that is asked so often: How do I increase my faith? This has been asked for years, in fact, right back to the apostles:

> And the apostles said to the Lord, "Increase our faith." So the Lord said, "If you have faith as a mustard seed, you can say to this mulberry tree, 'Be pulled up by the roots and be planted in the sea,' and it would obey you." (Luke 17:5–6)

Notice first that He says, "If you have faith as a mustard seed." A seed is something very small, but contains within it the potential of growing into a huge tree. So before we talk about having faith developed into a huge fruit-bearing tree, we must first ask, how do we even get the seed? That question is clearly answered in the following verse:

So then faith comes by *hearing, and hearing* by the word of God. (Rom. 10:17, *author's emphasis*)

It is so simple. The seed of faith comes by hearing God's Word. Notice also he says, *by hearing, and hearing.* Sometimes it can happen by just hearing once, but often the seed is deposited in our hearts by hearing over and over. That is why many hungry believers will listen or read a message containing the Word of God repeatedly. I've had numerous people come to me and say, I read one of your books several times, or watched the video message five times and on the fifth time it exploded in me. At that moment is when the seed was deposited and took root!

It's so simple we can easily miss it by complicating it. The seed of faith comes by merely hearing the Word of God spoken or written by inspiration of the Holy Spirit. How sad today that we have so many sermons being preached, so many books being written, yet so little of the Word of God being spoken. The first book I wrote was turned down by a major publishing house because, in their words, "It was too preachy." Too much Scripture, too much of what God says. I guess they wanted something that would appeal to men's emotions or even their flesh.

How sad, but that is the pressure many ministers are yielding to today. We now have "seeker friendly" churches, where the people who attend don't bring their Bibles, because they don't need them. They listen to a nice or funny "speech" that will help them in their busy pleasure-seeking lives. When I ponder the state of our western church, the whole thing is ironic to me, for in the past two years our ministry has sent fifty thousand Bibles to leaders of the underground church in China because they are so desperate for the Word of God. Bibles are so scarce in China that leaders will give pages of the New Testament to elders and ask them to memorize their portions so that they will always be able to speak the Word of God if their Bibles are confiscated by the authorities.

These men and women know the value of the written Word of God.

Yet in our western churches, we are trying to come up with messages that bring entertainment to the soul and comfort to the flesh, instead of messages from the Word of God that bring transformation to the soul and bring death to the flesh. In hearing these messages we may laugh and even shed a tear because of a touching story, but what happens when sin comes knocking at the door of these seekers' lives? Will they have the strength to stand up to it? What happens when they need to know the will of God in a crucial situation—will they know how to pray, or what to ask for? Will they have the faith of those who received in the Gospels? The scenarios are endless!

I'm glad that publisher rejected my first book, because if he had accepted it he may have asked his editors to weaken the message, and the multitudes that have been strengthened by it would have been denied. (The book eventually was published.) The ironic thing is that the owner of the publishing company eventually released the head of his publishing company, and hired a man who had a heart after God. The new publisher hired a staff who had a similar passion to see God's messages proclaimed to His people. This new man approached me and asked if he could publish my next book. I ended up writing five books for this same publishing house, four of which became best sellers; yet more than that, we continue to receive countless testimonies of lives, families, and churches that have been changed. To God be all the glory!

I share this with you because there is a famine in the land, not of bread and water, but of the Word of God (see Amos 8:11). In the American church at large we have so little of the Word of God being preached. I didn't say we don't have messages, because we have an enormous number of books, videos, and audio tapes, but what we've lacked is the Word of God. Why is it that I can go to nations in Africa and Asia and see people who have far fewer resources than we Americans, yet receive so easily from God and have so much more faith and fruit in their lives? It's simple. They are hearing the word of the Lord, not seeker-friendly or legalistic messages!

I promised God I would never yield to the press
sages that please people, instead of the messages t
ing. Paul says, "Am I now trying to win the appr
God? Or am I trying to please men? If I were sti
men, I would not be a servant of Christ" (Gal. 1:1
started out servants of Christ, but now are slaves
tions or audiences? They are now bound by the
those they supposedly lead what they want.

Faith comes by hearing, and hearing by the Wo
Word of God that deposits the seeds of faith wi
leaders we must give the Lord's people what they
think they need. We must feed them the eternal
able to build them up and give them an inheritan

Many leaders are coming to the forefront
claiming the pure and unadulterated Word of (
the trap of pleasing men and are now becomin
are newly arising. They are calling God's people
is God at this time emphasizing intimacy with
simple. He wants you to have the faith to live i
with Him, because you can't have intimacy
seeding His people with His Word to draw near
of it all!

HOW DO WE INCREASE OU

We now come to the question of how we increa
to His disciples:

> If you have faith as a mustard seed, you can s
> tree, "Be pulled up by the roots and be plant
> it would obey you. And which of you, having
> or tending sheep, will say to him when he ha
> field, "Come at once and sit down to eat"? B
> say to him, "Prepare something for my suppe

and serve me till I have eaten and drunk, and afterward you will eat and drink"? Does he thank that servant because he did the things that were commanded him? I think not. So likewise you, when you have done all those things which you are commanded, say, "We are unprofitable servants. We have done what was our duty to do." (Luke 17:6–10)

used to baffle me that Jesus went from speaking of faith as a right into a servant's role with his master. It seemed that Jesus 't congruent, but I knew that couldn't be true. Then one day Holy Spirit opened my eyes.

rst, He tells us that faith comes in seed form. Seeds are very l, but contain within them the potential of growing into huge . So it is not enough just to have a planted seed, but seeds be cultivated to reach their destiny. The second part of His er contains the key to making the seed of faith grow into fruitful trees. In other words, the kind of faith that will ot mulberry trees, remove mountains, or take us into the very nce of God!

y does a servant farm or tend flocks for his master? The ulti-goal is to get food on his table. What Jesus is asking is: Why a servant tend crops or flocks, then come in and not finish the y putting the food on his master's table? To be successful he to complete *all* of what he has been asked to do. Not finish-uld be compared to having a seed that you plant, water, and e; but just before it comes to the time of harvest, you destroy ut of neglect allow the fruit to rot.

s is speaking of our obedience to Him. He is the Master, and His servants in His fields. If we want to see our seeds of faith o fruition and produce, then we must be obedient servants in are asked to do. Notice His words, "So likewise you, when you one all those things which you are commanded." These words n He is speaking of our obedience, and that is the key to see-r faith increase.

PARTIAL OBEDIENCE IS DISOBEDIENCE

It is not enough to partially obey, or to start out obedient only to draw back. This is the error many in the Bible fell into. One specific example would be King Saul. He was expressly told by the word of the Lord to go and utterly destroy all Amalek—kill every man, woman and child, as well as every animal. Nothing that had breath was to be left alive.

Saul doesn't respond, "I won't do it!" Too often we limit disobedience to merely the obvious—blatant rebellion. Yet this is far from accurate. Another thing Saul does not do is agree, and then later change his mind. Most of us understand this form of disobedience as well. Nor does Saul neglect to make it a priority and eventually disobey out of neglect or forgetfulness. Most will admit that behavior would not be obedient, but would excuse it because of its good intentions. More than likely all would agree these scenarios represent disobedient behavior patterns, but let's turn our attention to Saul's actions.

He immediately gathers his army and attacks—killing every man, woman, infant, and nursing child. Tens of thousands are put to the edge of the sword by Saul and his great army. However, Saul spares the king of Amalek. Why? I believe he was conforming to the culture of that time. If you conquered a nation, and took their king alive and made him slave in your palace, he would be a living trophy.

Saul also slaughtered thousands of animals. Yet, he spares the best of the sheep, oxen, fatlings, lambs, and all that was good, and gives it to his people so they can sacrifice to God and do the "scriptural" thing. Imagine how the people must have seen this. While they sacrificed these doomed animals to Jehovah they thought, "What a godly king we have, he always puts the Lord first."

But God has a very different take on it. He laments to Samuel, "I greatly regret that I have set up Saul as king, for he has turned back from following Me, and has not performed My commandments" (1 Sam. 15:11). Saul has killed tens of thousands and spared only one. He did 99.9 percent of what was commanded of him. Most of us would see obedience in his mission, yet God sees disobedience. In fact, a few verses later He calls it rebellion through the prophet. This tells us that partial obedience is not obedience at all in the eyes of God. In fact, *almost* complete obedience, even 99 percent, is not considered obedience, but rather rebellion. How often do we hear this: "Why don't you look at all I have done? You're just focusing on the little that I didn't do!" Saul could have said that for sure. Though this is in line with human reasoning it is not in line with the divine!

INTIMACY IS DIRECTLY PROPORTIONAL TO OUR FAITH

If you continue to follow Saul's life you will notice a steady deterioration of his faith. You will also notice he progressively becomes more distant from the Lord. His intimacy level wanes because of the fact that our ability to have intimacy with God is directly proportional to our faith. In regard to this the apostle John says,

> This is how we will be confident in God's presence. If our conscience condemns us, we know that God is greater than our conscience and that he knows everything. And so, my dear friends, if our conscience does not condemn us, we have courage in God's presence. (1 John 3:19–22 TEV)

Our ability to have intimacy with God is directly proportional to our faith, and our faith is proportional to our obedience to Him. Now let me make this point clear. I'm not speaking of disobedience that is immediately followed by confession and repentance. David's sin was much greater than Saul's, but he immediately repented. His faith did not fail nor did his ability to have intimate fellowship with the Lord. Saul, on the other hand, continued in seeking his own benefit to protect and enhance what he perceived to be his. His heart was not after God's, as David's was.

A good example of this in everyday life would be the dynamic of a husband and wife. If either becomes self-seeking and does not submit to the other, trust and intimacy is lost. A husband can say, "Hey, I pay the bills, put food on your table, a roof over your head, and buy you clothes. What's wrong with me having a girlfriend on the side?" He can say, "I love you," and even say that he is taking good care of her, but I guarantee you their intimacy level will rapidly deteriorate because of his disobedience in just the one area.

We can ask, "Lord, I attend church regularly, I pay my tithes, I read the Bible and pray, why is my faith so weak?" Well, let me ask a question: How are you treating your wife? God says, "Husbands, likewise, dwell with them with understanding, giving honor to the wife, as to the weaker vessel, and as being heirs together of the grace of life, *that your prayers may not be hindered*" (1 Peter 3:7, *author's emphasis*). Our communion with God is hindered because we are not obedient in all areas. Recall Jesus words, "So likewise you, when you have done *all* those things which you are commanded." Partial obedience will never "increase our faith"! This same principle applies to how wives treat husbands, children treat parents, or even how parents treat their children.

Another question that could be asked: Are you a man or woman of your word? Scripture tells us the person who will have intimacy with God is, "He who swears to his own hurt and does not change" (Ps. 15:4). Do you give your word, only not to keep it? Do you habitually sin with your mouth and then wonder why your faith is weak? I could go on and on with the questions.

The point is that we live our lives seeking to be fully obedient to the Word of God! For we are in no uncertain terms told:

> My dear children, I write this to you *so that you will not sin.*
> (1 John 2:1 NIV, *author's emphasis*)

Many have looked at sin in either a loose or legalistic way. Those who see it casually believe they can violate God's Word because we have grace and mercy, and it's all been covered on the cross. Yes, it has been dealt with on the cross, but we must remember what Paul says to believers, "Do you not know that if you continually surrender yourselves to anyone to do his will, you are the slaves of him whom you obey, whether that be to sin, which leads to death, or to obedience which leads to righteousness" (Rom. 6:16 AMP). Again Jesus Himself will say to those who called Him Lord, yet habitually sinned, "Depart from Me, you who practice lawlessness" (Matt. 7:23).

The legalists see the violation of sin as removing a person from their "holiness club." That is not what should motivate us to stay away from any form of disobedience; in fact that motivation can't keep us from sin. However, when we see sin as damaging to our faith, which in turn will hinder our intimacy with God, we will flee from it! Why? Because we desire, more than anything else, closeness to Him.

Now we understand why James tells us just prior to and after giving the invitation to draw near to God:

> Therefore *submit to God*. Resist the devil and he will flee from you. Draw near to God and He will draw near to you. *Cleanse your hands, you sinners.* (James 4:7–8, *author's emphasis*)

It all centers around obedience! Why? So we can draw near with full assurance. Again let's look at the Scripture from the beginning of this chapter:

> Therefore, brethren, having *boldness* to enter the Holiest by the blood of Jesus, by a new and living . . . let us *draw near* with a true heart in *full assurance of faith*, having our hearts sprinkled from an evil conscience and our bodies washed with pure water. Let us *hold fast the confession of our hope* without wavering, for He who promised is faithful. (Heb. 10:19–23, *author's emphasis*)

Our confidence or full assurance stems from faith, which comes by hearing God's Word, which in turn increases by our continued obedience. If we sin, we have an Advocate with the Father, and if we are quick to repent, then our conscience will be free from condemnation because His blood cleanses us whiter than snow. However, if we willfully continue in sin, then our conscience will condemn us, and God is greater than our conscience. We in turn are hindered from approaching the living God with assurance.

HOPE

Now we turn to the second statement made in the above Scripture: "Let us hold fast the confession of our hope." Hope is often misunderstood; it is not a "maybe so" word. Rather it means "a confident expectation."

When God first appeared to Abraham He promised, "I am your shield, your exceedingly great reward" (Gen. 15:1). Abraham had no *natural hope* of having children with a barren wife so his answer was a bit despondent:

> O Sovereign Lord, what good are all your blessings when I don't even have a son? Since I don't have a son, Eliezer of Damascus, a servant in my household, will inherit all my wealth. You have given me no children, so one of my servants will have to be my heir. (Gen 15:2–3 NLT)

It was clear, this man had little or no hope, and God knew Abraham couldn't receive His promises unless he did. So the Lord took him outside that evening and told him to count the stars. I believed this is how it happened. Abraham eventually fell asleep while counting the innumerable stars. The next morning the Lord woke him with a question, "Did you count them all?"

Abraham said, "No, there are too many!"

God had the answer He was looking for and followed it with, "Your descendants will be like that—too many to count!" (Gen. 15:5 NLT). God had placed within him divine hope—a clear picture of His promise to Abraham—multitudes of children. Whenever he looked at the stars he was reminded of God's promise and heard countless offspring cry, "Father Abraham, Father Abraham!" In reference to this the New Testament says Abraham:

Who against hope believed in hope, that he might become the father of many nations, according to that which was spoken. (Rom. 4:18 KJV)

What was spoken? "Your descendants will be like that—too many to count!" Without natural hope, the divine stepped in to overshadow the seen with the promise. Divine hope looked beyond the evident into God's realm of confident expectation. Abraham chose to override the obvious with the divine. In fact, Scripture tells he was "fully convinced that what He had promised He was also able to perform" (Rom. 4:21). He received the promise by faith empowered by hope. We are told,

Now faith is the substance of things hoped for. (Heb. 11:1)

Our faith gives substance to the hope or promises of God. As we've seen in Abraham, divine hope is the vision or blueprint of God's will that we are yet unable to see with our natural eye. Divine hope is extremely important, for without hope, faith has nothing to give substance to. The Word of God not only places faith within our hearts, it also gives us hope, or vision, to the faith.

It could be compared to a collection of building materials, such as tile, windows, shingles, wood, cement, bricks, and so forth. We could have all the resources, yet without a blueprint, the building process would be a disaster! You may think, *I could build without a blueprint*. Perhaps if there were a blueprint in your mind, but there would still need to be some sort of plan.

ENTERING THE PRESENCE BEHIND THE VEIL

Regarding intimacy, let's look again at our flagship Scripture:

Therefore, brethren, having *boldness* to enter the Holiest by the blood of Jesus, by a new and living . . . let us *draw near* with a true heart in *full assurance of faith*, having our hearts sprinkled from an evil conscience and our bodies washed with pure water.

> Let us *hold fast the confession of our hope* without wavering, for He who promised is faithful. (Heb. 10:19–23, *author's emphasis*)

The writer is clearly speaking of drawing near to the Lord. Again look at the words, "Let us hold fast the confession of our hope." Remember hope is a blueprint—a vision—a divine picture of what we cannot see with our natural eye. With this in mind carefully read the following:

> For men indeed swear by the greater, and an oath for confirmation is for them an end of all dispute. Thus God, determining to show more abundantly to the heirs of promise the immutability of His counsel, confirmed it by an oath, that by two immutable things, in which it is impossible for God to lie, we might have strong consolation, who have fled for refuge to lay hold of the hope set before us. This hope we have as an anchor of the soul, both sure and steadfast, and *which enters the Presence behind the veil.* (Heb. 6:16–19, *author's emphasis*)

Do you see this? Put these verses together and you have:

> Let us *draw near* with a true heart in full assurance of faith . . . *[holding] fast the confession of our hope* without wavering, for He who promised is faithful. . . . This hope we have as an anchor of the soul, both sure and steadfast, and *which enters the Presence behind the veil.* (Heb. 10:22–23; 6:19, *author's emphasis*)

The New Living Translation says it like this: "It leads us through the curtain of heaven into God's inner sanctuary." It was God who gave Abraham the clear vision of divine hope. When it comes to intimacy, the Holy Spirit gives the divine vision of what our earthly eyes cannot see, the Lord Himself, who dwells in the throne room of heaven.

When we draw near we turn to the Spirit of God within, and pass through the veil of our flesh and limited natural thinking, and enter His presence. Once there we have passed through into the inner sanctuary of heaven where we encounter Jesus and the Father. In this inner sanctuary we experience intimacy with the Lord of Glory!

Believers often try to imagine themselves walking into a throne room as they pray. Yet without the help of the Holy Spirit this could be likened to Abraham's inability to grasp the promise of God without the vision. Only after the Lord Himself painted a clear picture for him did Abraham lay hold of what God had promised.

We cannot experience true and close intimacy in the inner sanctuary without the Holy Spirit. He gives us the hope, or clear vision, of what our natural eye cannot see. With this vision, we draw near with the full assurance of faith and with all boldness to enjoy what Jesus paid so great a price for us to live in. Oh, thank you, Jesus, for shedding your royal blood for us so that we may come with confidence into the very presence of God, both now and forever!

STUDY QUESTIONS

1. The biblical word hope—confident expectation—is contrasted with the "maybe so" hope which has evolved in the English language. Have you found yourself speaking words into the air with a "maybe so" attitude, lacking a confident expectation? If so, what might this tell you about the condition of your faith?

2. Two questions have been asked by believers since the time of the apostles. The questions are much the same in their wording, but profoundly different in what they are asking:
   • How do we get faith?
   • How do we increase our faith?
   From what you have learned in this chapter, how would you answer these questions?

3. As you compare the nature of Saul's obedience with that of David, what differences do you see? How did their obedience influence their intimacy with God?

4. How does obedience affect one's ability to approach God with boldness?

CHAPTER FOURTEEN

DRAWING
NEAR

✠

You can dare to come near Him, because
He has given you His timeless invitation.

In this final chapter I'll address a more practical side of drawing near
to the One who loves us so richly. Yet, to do this could be compared
to giving detailed instruction to one who is about to be married of how
to engage in intimacy in the bedchamber. You can only teach so much,
as the rest flows from the heart. And in this lies the beauty of intimacy:
it flourishes from our hearts; it's not taught from our minds.

In approaching the Lord we must remember that we are created in
His image. Just as our emotions differ, so do His. Just as we need to be
sensitive to a close friend's moods, even so we should be sensitive to the
Lord's. For example, there are times to come into His presence with

singing, other times to come broken; times to come boldly and times to come in with trembling. We will experience times of laughter, and times of weeping, times of warring with His aid against the forces of darkness, and times of peace and tranquility in His wonderful presence.

An example of this latter contrast would be a home under the threat of bandits. Suppose criminals are in process of breaking down the back door. Imagine at that moment one of the sons approaching his father, who is looking for a weapon, and saying, "Dad, I just think you are the greatest. You provide well for us, you're fun, and smart . . ."

The father would interrupt his son by sternly saying, "This is not the time to tell me your feelings, go get your baseball bat and let's go together to the rear of the house!"

You must remember we, the church of Jesus Christ, are God's house. There are real enemies. So there are times I've gone into prayer and the urgency of the Holy Spirit was to battle, and the manner in which He's led me to battle has varied as well. It could be through speaking the Word, praying strong in the Spirit, or even through strong praise (Jehoshaphat and the armies of Israel, see 2 Chron. 20:20–24). Not only are we to be sensitive to the atmosphere, but sensitive to how to accomplish His desire as well.

Back to our example; let's look at the flip side. Imagine the same household: all is well, and the father is resting by the fireplace. This time the son comes in with his helmet on and his baseball bat shouting, "Let's get them, Dad!"

The father would look at him and say, "Son, there is nothing wrong at the moment; why don't you just sit down and let's enjoy each other."

I'm sure by now you can think of many different scenarios we encounter with those we're close to. Even so there are various times and seasons of prayer. Scriptures reference each of those I've listed above and more. The key is to know what is on the heart of God at the moment.

GOD'S INTERESTS

How do you feel if a friend always comes to you with his own interests in mind? How does a father feel if all his son ever comes to him for is requests? Will you open your heart to those who are selfish, or to those who you know have no compassion? If we are to touch the Lord's heart we must seek to know what He desires and needs. Oh yes, needs! Even though He is omnipotent, all-powerful, and lacks nothing, He has still given mankind a free will, and certain freedoms on this earth. In doing so He made Himself vulnerable. Because of the fall of man along with the forces of darkness to misguide, trap, and torment, there are many in need and hurting. He longs to move on their behalf and waits for those who will cry out for them. For this reason you will find the Lord is very near to those who intercede and bring aid by God's grace to hurting people. Jesus says at the judgment seat:

> I was hungry and you gave Me food; I was thirsty and you gave Me drink; I was a stranger and you took Me in; I was naked and you clothed Me; I was sick and you visited Me; I was in prison and you came to Me. (Matt. 25:35–36)

Here you see the Lord of glory, the One who possesses all authority and power in the universe saying He was in need. His need is ours, those whom He loves. For He says, "Inasmuch as you did it to one of the least of these My brethren, you did it to Me." (v. 40). Those who intercede, give physical aid, preach the liberating Word of God, heal hurts through the power of God, and so forth, will find His heart quicker than anyone else.

God's people at one point were coming to Him diligently, and He even said of them, "They seek Me daily, and delight to know My ways" (Isa. 58:2). However, the Lord was not responding. The people began to question why God didn't draw near to them. They couldn't figure out why He did not respond to their prayers. He then said,

> I will tell you why! It's because you are living for yourselves even while you are fasting. You keep right on oppressing your workers. What good is fasting when you keep on fighting and quarreling? (Isa. 58:3–4 NLT)

Notice that they were fighting and quarreling. Let's return to our flagship Scripture of this book: "Draw near to God and He will draw near to you." You will find James starts out the chapter by saying,

> What causes fights and quarrels among you? Don't they come from your desires that battle within you? You want something but don't get it. You kill and covet, but you cannot have what you want. You quarrel and fight. You do not have, because you do not ask God. When you ask, you do not receive, because you ask with wrong motives, that you may spend what you get on your pleasures. You adulterous people . . . Submit yourselves, then, to God. Resist the devil, and he will flee from you. Come near to God and he will come near to you. (James 4:1–8 NIV)

So there you have it. Here is practical step number one: We must lose our lives for His sake and the gospel. We must live for His desires. We must love what He loves and hate what He hates. What is important to Him must become important to us, and what is not so important to Him must not be so important to us. We must have His heart!

Does this mean our lives will not have any times of personal refreshment? Does God deny his people recreation and rest? Absolutely not! The Scripture tells us that God "gives us richly all things to enjoy" (1 Tim. 6:17). It's when we seek our own desires to the neglect of His, that we lose touch with His heart.

There are those who believe that we are not fulfilling God's desires unless we are physically helping the poor. Yet if this is true, then why when widows needed to be fed did Peter say, "It is not desirable that we should leave the word of God and serve tables. Therefore, brethren, seek out from among you seven men of good reputation, full of the Holy Spirit and wisdom, whom we may appoint over this business; but we will give ourselves continually to prayer and to the ministry of the word." (Acts 6:2–4). Peter realized that there were some who would meet the needs of the poor (needy people) by feeding them the Word of God, and others who would meet their physical needs. Yet they all have one thing in common; they are meeting the need of Jesus, "When I was hungry you gave Me . . ."

Those who have the Lord's interest at heart are those who will more easily come near Him. Moses was such a man, because he shepherded God's people with the Lord's interests in mind, he was sensitive to God's heart, and had rich communion with Him.

God spoke of Josiah, who was a good leader, and said of him, "'He made sure that justice and help were given to the poor and needy, and everything went well for him. Isn't that what it means *to know me?*' asks the Lord'" (Jer. 22:16 NLT, author's emphasis).

Those who fulfill their ministries well, whether it is helps, government, teaching, administrations, giving, and so forth, will more easily draw near than those who have their own agendas fueling their lives and even ministries. Because as the Lord Himself said, "Isn't that what it means to know Me?"

COME NEAR TO LISTEN

The next practical counsel that can be given to those who desire to come near the Master is found in the following Scriptures:

> Guard your steps when you go to the house of God. Go near [Draw near] to listen rather than to offer the sacrifice of fools, who do not know that they do wrong. Do not be quick with your mouth, do not be hasty in your heart to utter anything before God. God is in heaven and you are on earth, so let your words be few. As a dream comes when there are many cares, so the speech of a fool when there are many words. (Eccl. 5:1–3 NIV)

Let's isolate the first part of these verses. We read in the NKJV, "Draw near to hear rather than to give the sacrifice of fools." I find there are so many who every time they approach God come with speaking or singing. This is certainly valid. However, I have found great success in approaching Him silently and listening before I speak a word, or sing a song of praise.

Recently I was with a pastor of a very large and powerful church. At lunch he said to me, "John, I came to the place that I said to the Lord, 'I'm tired of coming into this room every morning and hearing myself talk with no response. So until You speak to me, I'm going to just come in here each morning and listen.' "

It took several mornings because the Lord was testing the sincerity of his heart, but one morning he walked into his room and all of a sudden the Holy Spirit began to speak to him. It was in this time period that God gave him the most powerful revelations he had ever been given, and he proclaimed them to his people for several weeks. His prayer life had been revolutionized.

I've learned that a very powerful way to come into God's presence is by taking the Bible and reading a Scripture (especially from Psalms or the New Testament); not many Scriptures but one, and sometimes even half of one, and chew on it through meditation, then read slowly another and eventually the presence of the Lord will manifest. Then I'll stop reading and focus on Him and allow Him to teach me or show me things to come.

In any case it's usually very effective to come into His presence to hear before speaking. I've walked into praise services before and stilled my mind and looked within to the Spirit of God to sense His desire or mood. Then I'll begin to sing with the ministers of praise. This is not always true, as there are other times I've immediately approached Him with thanksgiving, praise, or rejoicing flowing from my heart. It was as if the Spirit of God was saying, "Let's go!" For Scripture also tells us,

> Let us come before His presence with thanksgiving;
> Let us shout joyfully to Him with psalms.
> (Ps. 95:2)

And again,

> Serve the Lord with gladness;
> Come before His presence with singing.
> (Ps. 100:2)

So hear we find Scripture exhorting us to come into the Lord's presence with singing and thanksgiving, while previous Scripture compels us to draw near to hear. It all comes down to being sensitive to Him! Just as you cannot tell a man a step-by-step process to make love to his wife, even so with our coming near to our Lord for intimacy.

Can you imagine a man coming in with his point-by-point card to have intimacy with his new bride? He reads from the card, step one: tell her she is beautiful. Step two: run your hand through her hair. Step three: turn down the lights. Step four: (woops, can't read that one, we'll have to use a flashlight). How ridiculous! Yet, that is about how ridiculous some have made prayer. They have taken away their ability to touch and feel His heart. Oh, don't get me wrong, there are certain guidelines we're to follow from the Scriptures, but we are to come with the aid of the Spirit of God, for the Scripture clearly tells us, "the letter kills, but the Spirit gives life" (2 Cor. 3:6). So the Spirit of God may lead us to intercede, sing, shout, cry out, be silent, and so forth.

The other thing we are exhorted to do is not to be hasty with our requests or words. Even natural relationships show us this. When someone rambles too much, we tend not to listen as closely. However, when a person wisely chooses their words, we listen carefully, even if they speak frequently. For this reason I find much of my time in prayer will either be silent, speaking in tongues, or speaking the Word of God.

I know that when I'm speaking in tongues, I'm praying the perfect will of God. The Holy Spirit is giving me words to utter to my Father in Jesus' name. I cannot pray incorrectly or utter vain words when I'm in the Spirit! When I'm speaking His written Word I also find my entire being edified, which of course includes my mind. This is why praying in the understanding is also so important.

However, when I know I'm in His presence and I'm listening, that is when revelation, understanding, and wisdom comes. It is so important that we give the Lord time to speak to us. Can you imagine a person who every time they approached you spoke nonstop and didn't give you a chance to get in a single word? I think that is how the Holy Spirit sometimes feels with us. We need to listen, as well as speak. Remember, prayer is a dialogue, not a monologue!

MANIFOLD WAYS OF IMPARTATION

When God draws near to us He reveals Himself as well as His ways. He shows us great and mighty things, which we know not (Jer. 33:3). The key to understanding this is that we must realize there are different ways He will impart to us when He comes. Sometimes we will hear Him speak. It can be a strong voice in our hearts, which can sometimes be mistaken as an audible voice we hear with our physical ears; or it can be a still quiet voice we hear deep in our hearts, which, as with all other ways, is always accompanied by His inner peace and lines up with Scripture. Sometimes He'll communicate through another believer or leader; as they speak, or we read their writings, an explosion sets off in our hearts. He may choose to speak to us through a vision or a dream. Other times, and I find this way to be quite frequent, we will just know things we didn't previously know. There are also frequent times He deposits His Word and it is not unveiled until we speak. As we open our mouths and speak, the illumination comes.

This is the way it happened with Peter on the day of Pentecost. Prior to the presence of God coming upon Him he really only had a mental knowledge of the Word of God, with the exception of the revelation God gave him of Jesus being the Christ (Matt. 16). Other than that revelation, he had more or less stuck his foot in his mouth just about any time he opened it to talk about spiritual things. While in the Upper Room he attempted some spiritual administration by choosing a replacement for Judas. It was obvious by the fruit that he was premature, as the man chosen was not heard of again; and later Paul said of himself that he was "one born out of due time" (1 Cor. 15:8). Paul seemed to be God's choice to replace Judas, not Peter's out-of-step attempt to pick God's man by casting lots.

In essence, spiritually Peter seemed to be consistently out of step. However, once God drew near to him, within moments he was speaking a profound and powerful message out of Joel and the Psalms explaining what had just transpired to the 120. He couldn't have studied such an insightful message in just the few moments before the crowds gathered. He now, almost instantaneously, had knowledge he never had before. Not only Peter but all the others as well, for moments after the presence of God came on them they all began to speak "the wonderful works of God" (Acts 2:11).

So in essence, there are diverse manners He imparts to us when He comes near; but one thing is for sure, we are never the same again after each and every time He draws near.

A FINAL WORD

As stated in the first chapter of this book, this message is not intended to be a "how to" message, for intimacy can never become a step-by-step process. It is meant to be a treasure map, leading to the heart of God. I believe it is a prophetic message, a call from His heart, to all of us, the ones He so affectionately and passionately desires. If we will exert the energy and time to follow the map of the Word of God laid out in this book, we will surely find the presence and heart of God. For remember, His promise to draw near to us individually, if we first draw near to Him, is not a hit-and-miss scenario; rather it is His Word of promise which He will always honor and never turn from.

Allow me to end this book with a few more Scriptures that will inspire your coming near Him:

> For the crooked man is an abomination to the LORD; but He is intimate with the upright. (Prov. 3:32 NASB)

> But it is good for me to draw near to God. (Ps. 73:28)

> The Lord is close to all who call on him, yes, to all who call on him sincerely. He fulfills the desires of those who fear him; he hears their cries for help and rescues them. The Lord protects all those who love him. (Ps. 145:18–20 NLT)

I will bring him near and he will come close to me, for who is he who will devote himself to be close to me? declares the Lord. (Jer. 30:21 NIV)

You can dare to come near Him, because He has given you His time-less invitation. So devote yourself to being one of those who dwell in His presence. He's waiting for you—what are you waiting for? Draw near!

Now to Him who is able to keep you from stumbling,
And to present you faultless
Before the presence of His glory with exceeding joy,
To God our Savior,
Who alone is wise,
Be glory and majesty,
Dominion and power,
Both now and forever.
Amen.
(Jude 24–25)

STUDY QUESTIONS

1. Before reading this chapter, had you ever considered that God has "needs"? In what ways do we minister to those needs?

2. How important is it for you to listen the for Holy Spirit to speak? Even though you may have a wealth of praise and worship songs and/or Spirit-filled writings available to you, have you tried approaching God in silence? Consider trying this exercise in inti-macy and write down or share with others what you learn.

3. In the first chapter, the author describes this book as a treasure map leading to the heart of God rather than a step-by-step "how to" message on drawing near. As you meditate on what you have learned, what treasures have you discovered? What treasures do you have yet to uncover?

OUR NEED FOR
A SAVIOR

There are two standards for living; one set by society and one set by God. Our culture may deem you "good" according to its parameters, but what does God think? Scripture tells us every person has fallen short of God's standard of right: "As the Scriptures say: 'There is no one who always does what is right, not even one.'" (Rom. 3:10 NCV) and again, "For all have sinned; all fall short of God's glorious standard." (Rom. 3:23 NLT)

To sin means to miss the mark of God's standard. Man was not created to be a sinner; rather Adam chose this course of his own free will. God placed the first man, Adam, in a beautiful world without sickness, disease, poverty, or natural disasters. There was no fear, hatred, strife, jealousy, and so forth. God called this place Eden, the very garden of God.

Adam chose to disobey God's command and experienced an immediate spiritual death, even though he did not die physically until hundreds of years later. Darkness entered his heart, and this spiritual death differs from physical death because in physical death the body ceases to exist; however, spiritual death is best described as separation from God, the very giver and source of all life.

Sin had entered Adam's makeup, and he fathered children after this nature: "And Adam lived one hundred and thirty years, and begot a son in his own likeness, after his image" (Gen. 5:3).

As a father his offspring were born after his nature and from this point forward each and every human is born into the image of his sin through their parents. Adam gave himself and his descendants over to a new lord, Satan, and with this captivity the natural world followed suit. A cruel lord now had legal claim to God's beloved creation. This is made clear in the following verses: "Then the devil, taking Him [Jesus] up on a high mountain, showed Him all the kingdoms of the world in a moment of time. And the devil said to Him, 'All this authority I will give You, and their glory; for this *has been delivered to me,* and I give it to whomever I wish'" (Luke 4:5–6, *author's emphasis*).

Notice it was delivered to him. When? The answer is in the garden, for God originally gave the dominion of earth to man (see Gen. 1:26–28), Adam lost it all . . . this included himself and his seed for all generations. Again we read, "The whole world lies under the sway of the wicked one" (1 John 5:19).

Before God sent Adam from the garden, He made a promise. A deliverer would arise and destroy the bondage and captivity mankind had been subjected to.

This deliverer was born four thousand years later to a virgin named Mary. She had to be virgin, as the father of Jesus was the Holy Spirit who impregnated her. If Jesus had been born to natural parents He would have been born into the captivity of Adam.

He was Fathered by God and His mother was human. This made Him completely God and completely man. It had to be a son of man, who would purchase our freedom. For this reason Jesus constantly referred to Himself as the "Son of man." Though He was with the Father from the beginning, He stripped Himself of His divine privileges and became a man in order to give Himself as an offering for sin.

When He went to the cross, He took the judgment of our sin on Himself to free us from our bondage. Scripture declares, "He personally carried away our sins in his own body on the cross so we can be dead to sin and live for what is right." (1 Peter 2:24, NLT)

It's amazing: man sinned against God, and yet God (manifest in the flesh) paid the price for man's grave err. We read again, "For God made Christ, who never sinned, to be the offering for our sin, so that we could be made right with God through Christ." (2 Cor. 5:20-21, NLT)

Notice it says that we could be made right. We do not receive the freedom which He paid so great a price for until we believe in our hearts that He died for us and was raised from the dead, and receive Him as our Lord; that is when He becomes our personal Savior. As Scripture states, "But to all who believed him and accepted him, he gave the right to become children of God. They are reborn! This is not a physical birth resulting from human passion or plan — this rebirth comes from God." (John 1:12-13, NLT)

When we receive Jesus Christ as our personal Lord and Savior, we die and are spiritually reborn. We die as slaves in the kingdom of Satan and are born as brand new children of God in His kingdom. How does this happen? Simple, when we believe this in our heart all we have to do is confess with our mouth Jesus as our Lord, and we are born again. Scripture affirms this: "For if you confess with your mouth that Jesus is Lord and believe in your heart that God raised him from the dead, you will be saved. For it is by believing in your heart that you are made right with God, and it is by confessing with your mouth that you are saved." (Rom. 10:9-10, NLT)

It's that simple! We are not saved by our good deeds. Our good deeds could never earn us a place in His Kingdom. For if that was true, Christ died in vain. We are saved by His grace. It is a free gift that we cannot earn. All we have to do to receive it is to renounce living for ourselves and commit our life to Him as Lord, which means Supreme Master. "He died for all, that those who live should live no longer for themselves, but for Him who died for them and rose again." (2 Cor. 5:15)

So if you believe Christ died for you and you are willing to give Him your life and no longer live for yourself; then we can pray this prayer together and you will become a child of God:

God in Heaven, I acknowledge that I am a sinner and have fallen short of Your righteous standard. I deserve to be judged for eternity for my sin. Thank You for not leaving me in this state, for I believe You sent Jesus Christ, Your only begotten Son, who was born of the virgin Mary, to die for me and carry my judgment on the Cross. I believed He was raised again on the third day and is now seated at Your right hand as my Lord and Savior. So on this day of _____, 20__, I give my life entirely to the Lordship of Jesus.

Jesus, I confess you as my Lord and Savior. Come into my life through Your Spirit and change me into a child of God. I renounce the things of darkness which I once held on to, and from this day forward I will no longer live for myself, but for You who gave Yourself for me that I may live forever.

Thank You Lord; my life is now completely in Your hand and heart, and according to Your Word I shall never be ashamed.

Now, you are saved; you are a child of God. All heaven is rejoicing with you at this very moment! Welcome to the family!

APPENDIX B

HOW TO BE FILLED WITH THE HOLY SPIRIT

Receiving the fullness of the Holy Spirit is as easy as receiving Jesus as your Lord and Savior. Some struggle, become discouraged, and can't receive most often due to the neglect of receiving basic scriptural instructions before asking. I've learned it is always best to show seekers what God says before praying, as this develops their faith to receive. So before I lead you in a prayer to receive, allow me first to instruct. (Note: It is important that you have completed Chapter 11 before proceeding any further.)

First and foremost, you must have already received Jesus Christ as your personal Lord and Savior (see John 14:17).

There can be no pattern of disobedience in your life. We are told that God gives His Spirit "to those who obey Him" (Acts 5:32). I've learned from experience this especially includes the area of unforgiveness. In our meetings I've seen many times hundreds receive the Holy Spirit and immediately speak in other tongues, yet a dozen or two of the hundreds stand and look bewildered. In almost every case in going to those few dozen I would find the Lord leading me to deal with harbored offense. Once the seekers forgave they immediately received and spoke in tongues. So before we go any further let's pray together.

> Father, I ask that You would search me and show me if there is any disobedience in my heart. Please show me if there is any person I have withheld forgiveness from. I purpose to obey and forgive no matter what You reveal to me. I ask this in the name of Jesus and thank You so very much.

To receive the Holy Spirit all you have to do is ask! Jesus simply says, "If a son asks for bread from any father among you, will he give him a stone? Or if he asks for a fish, will he give him a serpent instead of a fish? Or if he asks for an egg, will he offer him a scorpion? If you then, being evil, know how to give good gifts to your children, how much more will your heavenly Father give the Holy Spirit to those who ask Him!" (Luke 11:11–13). He is simply saying that if our children ask us for something which is our will to give them, we won't give them something evil and different. In the same way, if you ask the Father for His Spirit, He won't give you an evil spirit. All you have to do is ask the Father in Jesus' name, and you will receive His Holy Spirit.

You must ask in faith. The New Testament tells us it is impossible to receive from God without faith. James 1:6–7 states: "But let him ask in faith, with no doubting, for he who doubts is like a wave of the sea driven and tossed by the wind. For let not that man suppose that he will receive anything from the Lord. So ask yourself at this moment, "When will I receive? Will it be when I speak in other tongues, or will it be the moment I ask?" Your answer should be— the moment you ask! For in the Kingdom, we believe then receive. Those who do not have faith say, "Show me and I will believe" but Jesus says, "I say to you, whatever things you ask when you pray, believe that you receive them, and you will have them" (Mark 11:24). Notice you believe first, and then you will have what you've asked for.

Acts 2:4 says, "And they were all filled with the Holy Spirit and began to speak with other tongues, as the Spirit gave them utterance." Notice they spoke with tongues; it was not the Holy Spirit who spoke in tongues. They had to do it, as the Spirit gave them the words. So there is a yielding! I can be in a swift moving river, but if I don't pick up my feet and yield to the river, I won't flow with it. So there are three areas we must yield: First, our lips. If I don't move my lips, words, whether English, a Foreign language, or a heavenly tongue, cannot come forth. Second, our tongue. If I don't move my tongue, I cannot speak. Third, our vocal cords. If I don't yield my vocal cords to my lungs, then I cannot speak.

You may at this point think I'm being sarcastic, but I'm not. After years of seeing people struggle, I've learned many subconsciously think the Holy Spirit is going to grab ahold of their lips, tongues, and vocal cords and make them speak. No, we speak, or yield, as He gives the utterance.

Jesus says, "'He who believes in Me, as the Scripture has said, out of his heart will flow rivers of living water.' But this He spoke concerning the Spirit, whom those believing in Him would receive; for the Holy Spirit was not yet given, because Jesus was not yet glorified" (John 7:38–39). When you ask for the Holy Spirit, you may have a syllable bubbling up, or rolling around in your head. If you will speak it in faith, it will be as if you open a dam, and the language will come forth. I like to see it as a spool of thread in your gut and the tip, or beginning of the thread, is glimpsed at your tongue, but as you begin to pull (speak), out comes the rest of the thread. Some think they are going to have the entire language in their mind then they will speak. No, we are to speak in faith.

I remember when my wife prayed to receive the Holy Spirit she didn't speak in tongues for a time, then she and a few friends were praying a few weeks later and she began to speak in tongues. She then said, "I had that syllable running through my head the past few weeks while praying, but didn't yield to it till tonight." I believe this is the case for so many—they ask, receive, but don't yield.

Scripture states, "The spirits of the prophets [spokespersons] are subject to the prophets" (1 Cor 14:32). This simply tells us that we are the ones who speak, and that the Holy Spirit will not force Himself on us. I recall the day after I was filled with the Holy Spirit I didn't know how to speak again. I went to another brother at the gym and asked, "How can I do it again?" He said, "John, just do it!" I went out for a run and began to speak in tongues again while running. I was overcome with joy. We must remember the Holy Spirit is always ready to go; we are the ones who must yield. It is like a water fountain. The water is always there; all you have to do is turn the knob and out comes the water. So pray in tongues frequently!

Now that you have received basic instructions from the Scripture, if you believe you will receive we can pray together. One last thing: you cannot speak English and Spanish at the same time. Even so you can't speak in English and tongues at the same time. So remember, just believe and yield! Let's pray:

> *Father, in the name of Jesus, I come to you as Your child. You said if I asked You for the Holy Spirit You would give Him to me. With joy I now ask in faith; please baptize and fill me at this very moment with Your Holy Spirit. I receive all You have for me including the ability to speak in tongues. So now in faith I will speak in new tongues! Amen!*

Please contact us today to receive your free copy of John Bevere Ministries' *Messenger* newsletter and our 24 page color catalog of ministry resources!

FREE NEWSLETTER & CATALOG

The vision of JBM is to strengthen believers, awaken the lost and captive in the church and proclaim the knowledge of His glory to the nations. John and Lisa are reaching millions of people each year through television and by ministering at churches, bible schools and conferences around the world. We long to see God's Word in the hands of leaders and hungry believers in every part of the earth.

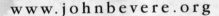

JOHN BEVERE MINISTRIES

www.johnbevere.org

UNITED STATES
PO Box 888
Palmer Lake, CO 80133-0888
800-648-1477 (US & Canada)
Tel: 719-487-3000
Fax: 719-487-3300
E-mail: jbm@johnbevere.org

EUROPE
PO Box 622
Newport, NP20 4WR
UNITED KINGDOM
Tel: 44 (0) 870-745-5790
Fax: 44 (0) 870-745-5791
E-mail: jbmeurope@johnbevere.org

AUSTRALIA
PO Box 6200
Dural, D.C. NSW 2158
Australia
In AUS 1-300-650-577
Tel: +61 2 8850 1725
Fax +61 2 8850 1735
Email: jbmaustralia@johnbevere.org

The *Messenger* television program broadcasts in 214 countries on The God Digital Network in Europe, the Australian Christian Channel and on the New Life Channel in Russia. Please check your local listings for day and time.

Other Books by John

A Heart Ablaze

The Bait of Satan

Breaking Intimidation

The Devil's Door

The Fear of the Lord - softback

Thus Saith the Lord?

Under Cover

Victory in the Wilderness

The Voice of One Crying

Books by Lisa

Be Angry, but Don't Blow It!

Kissed the Girls and Made Them Cry

Out of Control and Loving It

The True Measure of a Woman

You Are Not What You Weigh

ADDITIONAL MINISTRY RESOURCES

BOOKS • AUDIO CDs • DVDs • AUDIO CASSETTES • VHS • CURRICULUMS

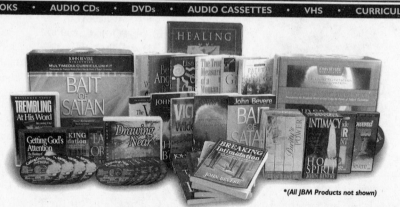

*(All JBM Products not shown)

Call us today and ask about our **Value Packs!** 1-800-648-1477 (US & Canada)
Australia: +61 2 8850 1725 • *Europe:* 44 (0) 870-745-5790

OTHER RELATED RESOURCES
TO DRAWING NEAR

Intimacy with the Holy Spirit
2 Videos or 2 DVDs

Paul writes, "The communion (intimate fellowship) of the Holy Spirit be with you" (2 Cor. 13:14). Yet so many do not enjoy this…why? As with all things in the Kingdom, we enter into this communion by faith. This faith is quickened by hearing His Word on how He communicates with us. In this important two-part series John addresses: Is the infilling of the Holy Spirit for all? Is the gift of tongues only for a select few? Why even speak in tongues? The benefits of praying in the Spirit. How God reveals His secrets. How to communicate with God on His level and much more!

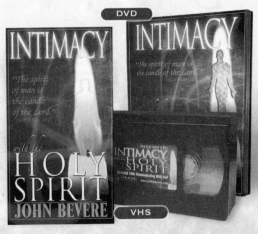

These messages will ignite a passion and bring understanding of how to have intimacy with the Holy Spirit. It is a must for you and those you love.

Our Special Edition "Intimacy with the Holy Spirit" DVD packaging comes with an attractive custom shaped die cut package and holographic gold foil image on the case.

The Hidden Power of Humility - 2 Cassettes, 2 Cd's, 2 DVD's or 2 Videos
The Key to your High Calling

Humility strengthens and protects you from the enemy. It keeps you sensitive to the heart of God so He can reveal His ways… and it empowers us to complete the race. In Psalms 25:9 we learn God leads the humble in what is right, teaching them His way. Humility is a characteristic of His nature we are to excel in. Yet too many do not know what true humility is. They mistake it for a weakness or lack of courage. Without it we lead a fruitless Christian life. Now more than ever before we need to acquire a good understanding of humility and the skills to walk in it.